The Commonwealth of Massachusetts

HISTORICAL DATA

RELATING TO

Counties, Cities and Towns in Massachusetts

PREPARED BY
WILLIAM FRANCIS GALVIN
SECRETARY OF THE COMMONWEALTH

PUBLISHED BY
THE NEW ENGLAND HISTORIC GENEALOGICAL SOCIETY

1997

© 1997 THE SECRETARY OF THE COMMONWEALTH OF MASSACHUSETTS

ISBN 0-88082-066-7

PUBLISHED AND DISTRIBUTED WITH PERMISSION FROM THE
SECRETARY OF THE COMMONWEALTH OF MASSACHUSETTS BY:

The New England Historic Genealogical Society
101 Newbury Street
Boston, MA 02116

Printed by Thomson-Shore, Inc., Dexter, Michigan

PREFACE, 1997 EDITION

It is with great pleasure that this fifth edition of *Historical Data Relating to Counties, Cities and Towns* is presented to the public.

It is a matter of real signicance to know the date when each separate town was legislated into existence. Historians need this information, to help them interpret the past. Genealogists need this information, to help them trace the lines of descent through the vital records that Massachusetts towns have kept since the 1630's. Surveyors need to know about the legislation that set up towns and cities and define their boundaries. The people in general, want to know how their communities have evolved over time, how the present is linked to the past.

This new edition of *Historical Data* includes county and town maps and a comprehensive index. Information about towns is now summarized: dates of incorporating legislation, archaic and section/village names are included under one entry. Information on sources for *Historical Data is* also provided as well as reference to survey maps held by the Massachusetts Archives.

Martha Clark and Richard White of the Massachusetts Archives have contributed greatly to the publication of this edition.

William Francis Galvin
Secretary of the Commonwealth

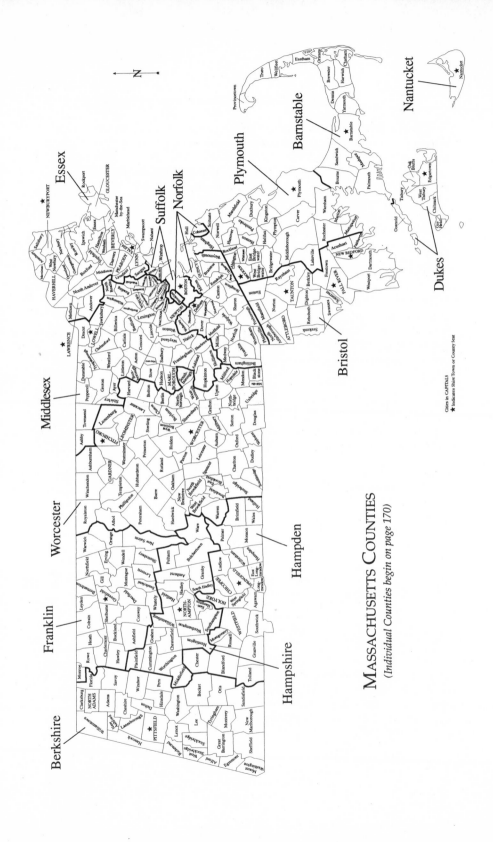

MASSACHUSETTS COUNTIES
(Individual Counties begin on page 170)

INTRODUCTION

The fifth edition of *Historical Data Relating to Counties, Cities and Towns in Massachusetts*, like its predecessors, provides summary information relating to counties and municipalities in Massachusetts. In this edition, however, the format has been restructured and additional information relating to town charters, archaic names and section/village names added.

Part I of this publication contains a list of counties and provides the date of their incorporation or the date when the name of the county first appeared in the records.

Part II provides an alphabetical listing of Massachusetts municipalities as they exist in 1997. Cities are identified with bold upper case letters; plain bold type indicates that the entry pertains to a town. Those towns that have adopted a charter with a city form of government are italicized. All information relating to the specific community is grouped under the current name of the municipality, regardless of any earlier names that were used. The only exceptions to this practice are the annexed towns of Boston, which are listed separately in the alphabetical sequence.

If the town was incorporated by an act of the General Court, the citation for that act is included. This information is followed by the date and any data regarding the town as it first appeared in the colonial or provincial records, and a concise summary of subsequent legislation considered pertinent to changes in territorial limits, and the later incorporation of the town as a city. It is also noted if a town adopted a town charter under the provisions of the Home Rule Act of 1966.

Sections in each entry provide whatever archaic names of the municipality appeared in legislation or other formal documentation. A list of section or village names within the community is also included. Those section or village names that are no longer used are marked as "extinct." All current names of municipalities, archaic names, and section and village names are listed in a comprehensive index following Part II.

The asterisk (*) used with a date means Old Style or according to the Julian calendar. The present calendar, the Gregorian or New Style, was adopted by an act of Parliament of Great Britain which ordered that September 8, 1752 should become September 14, and that the legal year should commence with the first of January instead of March 25, beginning January 1, 1752.

A NOTE ON SOURCES

The information found in *Historical Data* is taken from several series of records held by the Massachusetts Archives. These include legislative records, town charters filed with the State Secretary's office, maps and plans, and the collection of colonial, provincial and revolutionary era documents known as "The Massachusetts Archives." We have relied on various indices of archaic place names drawn up by Archives staff over the past one hundred years; earlier editions of *Historical Data*; comments and information from local officials; and several publications relating to place names. These include *A Geographic Dictionary of Massachusetts*, by Henry Gannett, originally published in 1894 and reprinted by the Genealogical Publishing Company in 1978; *Massachusetts Localities: A Finding List*, reprinted in 1966 in the Massachusetts Department of Public Works; and the *Directory of Massachusetts Place Names*, compiled by Charlotte Pease Davis in 1987 for the Massachusetts Daughters of the American Revolution and published by Bay State News.

General Acts Passed Relative to the Incorporation of Towns
Several towns in Massachusetts share the same act of incorporation. Originally designated as districts or townships, these municipalities started as groups of individuals within clearly defined areas that were not ready to function fully as towns. Districts lacked certain town privileges, most notably the power to choose a representative to the legislature. Gradually the General Court incorporated the districts as towns, either through specific acts of incorporation or the general acts noted below.

Acts 1775, Chapter 3, Section 3, passed August 23, 1775
"...every corporate Body in this Colony; which in the Act for the incorporation thereof is said, & declared to be made a *district*; and has by such Act granted to it, or is declared to be vested with the rights, powers, priviledges, or immunities of a Town with the exception above mentioned, or chusing, and sending a Representative to the great, and general Court, or Assembly [shall hence f]orth be, and shall be holden, taken, and intended to be a Town to all intents [and purposes] whatsoever." (Prov. Laws, Vol. V, p.420.)

Acts 1785, Chapter 75, passed March 23, 1786
"...the inhabitants of every Town within this Government, are hereby declared to be a body politic and corporate..."

Revised Statutes, Chapter 15, Section 9, passed November 4, 1835
"All places now incorporated by the name of districts, except the district of Marshpee in the County of Barnstable, shall have all the powers and privileges, and be subject to all the duties to which towns are entitled or subject by the provisions of this chapter."

Maps on File in the Massachusetts Archives

Maps are a critical resource for the study of local history and legal documentation of town boundaries. The Massachusetts Archives holds three series of maps which researchers may wish to consult. Pursuant to Resolves 1794, Chapter 101, passed June 26, 1794, accurate plans of the towns and districts in Massachusetts and the District of Maine were ordered to be filed in the Secretary's office. The plans were to be made on a scale of 200 rods to an inch, and to show rivers, bridges, county roads, court houses and meeting houses. The only Massachusetts town of the appropriate age not included in the plans is Chelsea. These plans were bound into sixteen volumes; the Archives series number for them is SC1-47X.

Another set of town plans were made pursuant to Resolves 1829, Chapter 50, passed March 1, 1830. These were made on a scale of 100 rods to an inch, and included rivers, roads, public buildings, mills, and manufactures. Carver, Chelsea, Littleton, New Bedford, and Plympton are not included in this set of plans, which was also bound into sixteen volumes and designated as SC1-48X.

Many other plans have been deposited in the Secretary's office or directly in the Massachusetts Archives. These range from early plans showing land grants from the General Court, to boundary changes, land ceded to the United States government, and plans mentioned in specific legislation. These plans, many of which were bound into volumes, are given the series number SC1-50.

Martha Clark
Massachusetts Archives
February 7, 1997

ABBREVIATIONS

Court Rec.	Legislative Records of the Governor's Council (Massachusetts Archives, Series 327)
Mass. Archives	Massachusetts Archives Collection (Massachusetts Archives, Series 45X)
Mass. Bay Rec.	Records of the Governor and Company of the Massachusetts Bay
Mass. Reports	Massachusetts Reports (published reported decisions of the Massachusetts Supreme Judicial Court)
Ply. Col. Rec.	Records of the Colony of New Plymouth
Prov. Laws	Acts and Resolves of the Province of the Massachusetts Bay

HISTORICAL DATA RELATING TO COUNTIES
PART I

Names of Counties	Date Of Incorporation Or First Mention In The Records		Reference to Act
Barnstable	June	2, 1685	Ply. Col. Rec. Vol. VI, p. 169.
Berkshire	April	21, 1761[1]	Prov. Laws, Vol. IV, p. 432.
Bristol	June	2, 1685	Ply. Col. Rec. Vol. VI, p. 169.
Dukes County	June	22, 1695[2]	Prov. Laws, Vol. I, p. 216.
Essex	May	10, 1643	Mass. Bay Rec., Vol. II, p. 38.
Franklin	June	24, 1811[3]	Chapter 61, Acts of 1811.
Hampden	February 25, 1812[4]		Chapter 137, Acts of 1811.
Hampshire	May	7, 1662	Mass. Bay Rec., Vol. IV, Part 2, p. 52.
Middlesex	May	10, 1643	Mass. Bay Rec., Vol. II, p. 38.
Nantucket	June	22, 1695	Prov. Laws, Vol. I, p. 216.
Norfolk (Extinct)	May	10, 1643[5]	Mass. Bay Rec., Vol. II, p. 38.
Norfolk	March	26, 1793[6]	Chapter 72, Acts of 1792.
Plymouth	June	2, 1685	Ply. Col. Rec., Vol. VI, p. 169.
Suffolk	May	10, 1643	Mass. Bay Rec., Vol. II, p. 38.
Worcester	April	2, 1731[7]	Prov. Laws, Vol. II, p. 584.

[1] Act took effect June 30, 1761.
[2] By an act passed by the legislature of New York, November 1, 1683, entitled, "An act to divide this province and dependence into shires and Countyes," the County of Dukes County was established as follows: Dukes County so contayns the Island and nomans Land." By the Province Charter in 1692 (Prov. Laws, Vol. I, p. 9) the "Isles of Cappawock and Nantucket near Cape Cod" were granted to the Province of Massachusetts Bay. June 13, 1693 (Prov. Laws, Vol. I, p. 117), the "Islands of Capawock, alias Martha's Vinyard," are referred to. June 22, 1695 (Prov. Laws, Vol. I, p. 216), it was ordered that "The Islands of Martha's Vineyard, Elisabeth Islands, the islands called Noman's land and all the dependencies formerly belonging to Dukes County (the Islands of Nantucket only excepted) shall be and remain, and continue to be one county to all intents and purposes, by the name of Duke's County."
[3] Act took effect December 2, 1811.
[4] Act took effect August 1, 1812.
[5] February 4, 1680, the towns remaining in Norfolk County were re-annexed to Essex county (Mass. Bay Rec., Vol. V, p. 264).
[6] Act took effect June 20, 1793.
[7] Act took effect July 10, 1731.

HISTORICAL DATA RELATING TO CITIES AND TOWNS
PART II

Abington, Plymouth County.
Established as a town by St 1712, c 24.

1712.	June	10.*	Established as a town, from part of Bridgewater and certain lands adjoining. (Prov. Laws, Vol. XXI, p. 605.)
1727.	June	14.*	Part included in the new town of Hanover.
1847.	Mar.	31.	Bounds between Abington and Weymouth established.
1861.	Mar.	21.	Bounds between Abington and Randolph established.
1861.	Mar.	21.	Bounds between Abington and Hingham established.
1874.	Mar.	9.	Part established as Rockland.
1875.	Mar.	4.	Part included in the new town of South Abington.
1970.	Mar.	7.	Town charter adopted.

Archaic Names of the Municipality:
Manamooskeagin.

Section/Village Names:
Center Abington, Musterfield, North Abington, Thicket, West Abington.

Acton, Middlesex County.
Established as a town by St 1735, c 10.

1735.	July	3.*	Established as a town, from part of Concord called "The Village" or New Grant " together with "Willard's Farm". (Prov. Laws, Vol. II, p. 763.)
1747.	Dec.	11.*	Bounds between Acton and Concord established.
1780.	Apr.	28.	Part included in the district of Carlisle.

Archaic Names of the Municipality:
Iron Work Farm, New Grant, Concord Village, Willard's Farms.

Section/Village Names:
Acton Center, East Acton, Ellsworth (extinct), North Acton, South Acton, West Acton.

Acushnet, Bristol County.
Incorporated as a town by St 1860, c 24.

1860.	Feb.	13.	Incorporated as a town, from part of Fairhaven.
1875.	Apr.	9.	Part annexed to New Bedford.

Section/Village Names:
Ball's Corner, Coulomb Manor, Long Plain, Parting Ways, Perry Hill, Slocum, Taber Hill.

Adams, Berkshire County.
Established as a town by St 1778, c 20.

1778.	Oct.	15.	Established as a town, formerly the plantation called "East Hoosuck". (Prov. Laws, Vol. V, p. 909.)
1780.	Apr.	10.	The plantation called "New Providence" annexed.
1793.	Mar.	14.	Part included in the new town of Cheshire.
1878.	Apr.	16.	Part established as North Adams.

Archaic Names of the Municipality:
East Hoosuck Plantation, Fort Massachusetts, New Providence Plantation, Plantation Number One.

Section/Village Names:
Bowen's Corner, Cheshire Harbor, Maple Grove, Arnoldsville Renfrew, Siggsville, Zylonite (formerly Howlands).

Agawam, Hampden County.
Incorporated as a town by St 1855, c 365.

1855.	May	17.	Incorporated as a town, from part of West Springfield.
1960.	May	2.	Bounds between Agawam and West Springfield re-established.
1971.	Nov.	16.	Town charter adopted which established city form of government.

Archaic Names of the Municipality:
Feeding Hills.

Section/Village Names:
Agawam Center, Feeding Hills, Hubbard Corners.

Alford, Berkshire County.
Made a town by St 1775-1776, c 3.

1773.	Feb.	16.	Established as the district of Alford from part of Great Barrington and certain common lands. (Prov. Laws, Vol. V, p. 236.)
1775.	Aug	23.	Made a town, by general act under which districts became towns.
1779.	Feb.	11.	Part of Great Barrington annexed.
1790.	Feb.	6.	Bounds between Alford and Egremont established.
1819.	Feb.	18.	Part of Great Barrington annexed.
1847.	Mar.	17.	Part of West Stockbridge annexed.

Archaic Names of the Municipality:
Podunke, Podunkville, Shawanon Purchase.

Section/Village Names:
Alford Center, East Alford, West Alford.

Amesbury, Essex County.

1666.	May	23.*	**Salisbury-new-town** established as a town, from part of Salisbury - "...this Court doeth grant them liberty of a township ...." (Mass. Bay Rec., Vol IV, Part 2, p. 300.)
1667.	May	15.*	Bounds between Salisbury-new-towne and Haverhill established.
1668.	May	27.*	Name of the town of Salisbury-new-towne changed. "Salisbury new toune...may be named Emesbury." The spelling in the margin of the records is "Amsbury". (Mass. Bay. Rec., Vol. IV, Part 2, p. 376.)
1675.	May	12.*	Just and full bounds allowed to "**Amesbury**". (Mass. Bay Rec., Vol. V, p. 40.)
1844.	Mar.	15.	Part of Salisbury called "Little Salisbury" annexed.
1876.	Apr.	11.	Part established as Merrimac.
1886.	June	16.	Part of Salisbury annexed.
1886.	July	1.	Act of June 16, 1886, took effect.
1981.	Apr.	13.	Town charter adopted.
1996.	Apr.	9.	New town charter adopted which established city form of government.

Archaic Names of the Municipality:
Emesbury, Little Salisbury, New Salisbury, Salisbury-new-toune.

Section/Village Names:
Allen's Corner, Amesbury Ferry, Attitash, Meadow Brook, Pleasant Valley, Pond District, Rings Corner, Rocky Hill, Salisbury Point.

Amherst, Hampshire County.
Made a town by St 1775-1776, c 3.

1759.	Feb.	13.	Part of Hadley established as the district of Amherst. (Prov. Laws, Vol. IV, p. 173.)
1775.	Aug.	23.	Made a town, by general act under which districts became towns.
1789.	Jan.	15.	Part of Hadley annexed.
1811.	Feb.	28.	Part of Hadley annexed.
1812.	Feb.	18.	Part of Hadley annexed.
1814.	Feb.	17.	Part of Hadley annexed.
1815.	Mar.	1.	Bounds between Amherst and Hadley established and parts of each town annexed to the other town.

Archaic Names of the Municipality:
Hadley Third Precinct.

Section/Village Names:
Amherst City (extinct), Amherst Fields, Amherst Woods, Blackbird Island (extinct), Broad Gutter (extinct), Centre Village (extinct), Clark's Mill (extinct), Crow Hill (extinct), Cushman, Depot (extinct), East Amherst, Amherst East Parish (extinct), East Village (extinct), Echo Hill, Factory Hollow, Fairgrounds (extinct), Flat Hill, Hampshire Village, Irish Hill (extinct), Kelloggville (extinct), Mill Valley, North Amherst, North Amherst City (extinct), Amherst North Parish (extinct), Nuttingville (extinct), Orchard Valley, The City (extinct), The Curragh (aka Curry no longer used), The Patch (extinct), Slab City (extinct), South Amherst, Struthersville (extinct), West Amherst (extinct), Westville (extinct).

Andover, Essex County.

1646.	May	6.*	A purchase of land by the "...inhabitants of Cochichawick, now called Andiver...ye towne,...." (Mass. Bay Rec., Vol. II, p. 159.)
1658.	May	26.*	Bounds between Andover and "Billirikey" established.
1678.	May	9.*	Bounds between Andover and "Wills Hill" established.
1728.	June	20.*	Part included in the new town of Middleton.
1847.	Apr.	17.	Part included in the new town of Lawrence.
1855.	Apr.	7.	Part established as North Andover.
1879.	Feb.	4.	Part annexed to Lawrence.
1903.	May	21.	Bounds between Andover and Tewksbury established.
1904.	Apr.	22.	Bounds between Andover and North Reading established.

Archaic Names of the Municipality:
Cochickawick, Cochituit, Quichickichick.

Section/Village Names:
Abbott Village, Andover North Parish, Andover South Parish, Andover West Parish, Bailey, Centre, Chandler, Frye Village, Andover Village, Ballardvale, Haggetts Station, Holt, Lowell Junction Station, Phillips, Poor, Osgood, Marland Village, Scotland, Shawsheen Village, West Andover.

Arlington, Middlesex County.
West Cambridge incorporated as a town by St 1807, c 95.

1807.	Feb.	27.	**West Cambridge** incorporated as a town, from a part of Cambridge.
1842.	Feb.	25.	Part of Charlestown annexed to West Cambridge.
1850.	Apr.	30.	Part of West Cambridge included in the new town of Winchester.
1859.	Mar.	18.	Part of West Cambridge included in the new town of Belmont.

1861.	Jan.	31.	Bounds between West Cambridge and Belmont established.
1862.	Feb.	25.	Bounds between West Cambridge and Cambridge established and part of each place annexed to the other place.
1867.	Apr.	13.	Name of the town of West Cambridge changed to **Arlington**.
1867.	Apr.	30.	Act of Apr. 13, 1867, took effect.
1910.	Mar.	16.	Bounds between Arlington and Somerville established.
1911.	May	5.	Bounds between Arlington and Cambridge established if accepted by the selectmen and city council.
1911.	May	22.	Act of May 5, 1911, accepted by selectmen of Arlington.
1911.	May	31.	Act of May 5, 1911, accepted by city council of Cambridge.
1938.	May	26.	Bounds between Arlington and Belmont established.
1938.	Oct.	3.	Act of May 26, 1938, took effect.
1975.	Dec.	16.	Bounds between Arlington and Belmont changed and established.

Archaic Names of the Municipality:
Menotomy, West Cambridge.

Section/Village Names:
Arlington Heights, Brattle Station, East Arlington, Turkey Hill.

Ashburnham, Worcester County.
Incorporated as a town by St 1764-1765, c 22.

1765.	Feb.	22.	Incorporated as a town, formerly the plantation of "Dorchester-Canada". (Prov. Laws, Vol. IV, p. 739.)
1767.	Mar.	6.	Part included in the new town of Ashby.
1785.	June	27.	Part included in the new town of Gardner.
1792.	Nov.	16.	Part annexed to Ashby.
1815.	Feb.	16.	Part of Gardner annexed.
1824.	Jan.	28.	Part of Westminster annexed.

Archaic Names of the Municipality:
Dorchester-Canada Plantation, Watatick Hill.

Section/Village Names:
Blackburn Village, Burrageville, Factory Village, Lane Village, Naukeag, North Ashburnham, South Ashburnham, South Hill.

Ashby, Middlesex County.
Established as a town by St 1765-1766, c 15.

1767.	Mar.	6.	Established as a town, from parts of Ashburnham, Fitchburg and Townsend. (Prov. Laws, Vol. IV, p. 908.)
1792.	Nov.	16.	Part of Ashburnham annexed.
1829.	Mar.	3.	Part of Fitchburg annexed.

Section/Village Names:
Ashby Center, Mill Village, South Village.

Ashfield, Franklin County.
Established as a town by St 1765-1766, c 13.

1736.	Jan.	19.*	The grant of a township to Capt. Ephraim Hunt's company confirmed. (Prov. Laws, Vol. XII, p. 332.)
1764.	June	15.	Bounds between Huntstown and Deerfield established.
1765.	June	18.	Plan for the township of Huntstown confirmed.
1765.	June	21.	Plantation of "Huntstown" established as a town by the name of Ashfield. (Prov. Laws, Vol. IV, p. 815.)

Archaic Names of the Municipality:
Huntstown Plantation, Weymouth Canada.

Section/Village Names:
Apple Valley, Ashfield Plain, Baptist Corner, Brier Hill, Howesville, Peter Hill, South Ashfield, Spruce Corner, Wardville, Watson.

Ashland, Middlesex County.
Incorporated as a town by St 1846, c 100.

1846.	Mar.	16.	Incorporated as a town, from parts of Framingham, Holliston and Hopkinton.
1853.	Apr.	28.	Part to be annexed to Hopkinton when a certain sum of money is paid by Hopkinton.
1853.	May	2.	Act of Apr. 28, 1853, took effect.
1988.	May	2.	Town charter adopted.

Section/Village Names:
Chattanooga, Oregon.

Athol, Worcester County.
Established as a town by St 1761-1762, c 46.

1762.	Mar.	6.	Established as a town, formerly the plantation of "Payquage". (Prov. Laws, Vol. IV, p. 534.)
1783.	Oct.	15.	Part included in the district of Orange.
1786.	Oct.	20.	Part included in the new town of Gerry.
1799.	Feb.	26.	Part annexed to Royalston.
1803.	Mar.	7.	Part annexed to Royalston.
1806.	Feb.	28.	Part of Gerry annexed.
1816.	Feb.	7.	Part of Orange annexed.
1829.	June	11.	Certain tract of land annexed.
1830.	Feb.	5.	Part of New Salem annexed.
1837.	Mar.	16.	Part of New Salem annexed.

Archaic Names of the Municipality:
Payquage Plantation, Provincetown on Millis River, Poguaige.

Section/Village Names:
Athol Center, Eagleville, Fairview, Fryeville, Hillside, Intervale Lake Park, Partridgeville, Pinedale, Pleasant Valley, Proctorville, Riceville, South Athol, South Park, Sunnyside.

ATTLEBORO, Bristol County.
Established as a town by St 1694-1695, c 17.
Incorporated as a city by St 1914, c 680.

1694.	Oct.	19.*	Established as a town, from part of Rehoboth known as "The North Purchase", to be called **Attleborough**. (Prov. Laws, Vol. I, p. 184.)
1697.	Sept.	10.*	Bounds between Attleborough and Rehoboth established.
1710.	June	26.*	Part of Rehoboth called "Mile & Half of Land" annexed to Attleborough.
1830.	Feb.	18.	Bounds between Attleborough and Rehoboth established and part annexed to Wrentham.
1887.	June	14.	Part established as North Attleborough.
1887.	July	30.	Act of June 14, 1887, accepted by the town.
1888.	Mar.	6.	Acceptance of the act of June 14, 1887, ratified and confirmed.
1914.	June	17.	Incorporated as a city, under the name of **Attleboro**, formerly the town of Attleborough.
1914.	Nov.	3.	Act of June 17, 1914, accepted by the town.
1973.	Nov.	3.	City charter adopted.

Archaic Names of the Municipality:
Attleborough, Mile & Half of Land, North Purchase.

Section/Village Names:
Attleborough Gore (set off to R.I. in 1747), Bearcroft (former R.R. station), Briggs Corner, Deantown, Dodgeville, East Junction, Farmer's, Fisherville, Hebronville, Lonicut, Mechanics, Robinsonville, Sibleyville, South Attleboro.

Auburn, Worcester County.
Ward incorporated as a town by St 1778, c 28.

1778.	Apr.	10.	**Ward** incorporated as a town, from a "parish lately set off from the towns of Worcester, Sutton, Oxford and Leicester" (Prov. Laws, Vol. V, p. 796.)
1837.	Feb.	17.	Name of the town of Ward changed to **Auburn.**
1851.	May	24.	Part annexed to Millbury.
1908.	Mar.	27.	Bounds between Auburn and Oxford established.
1969.	Mar.	10.	Town charter adopted.

Archaic Names of the Municipality:
Ward.

Section/Village Names:
Auburn Center, Auburn Station, City Line, Drury Square, Lamedville, Maywood (former R.R. station), Packachoag Hill, Patch, Pondville, Stone's Crossing (former R.R. station), Stoneville, Oxford Heights, West Auburn.

Avon, Norfolk County.
Incorporated as a town by St 1888, c 47.

1888.	Feb.	21.	Incorporated as a town, from part of Stoughton.
1889.	Apr.	16.	Parts of Holbrook and Randolph annexed.

Section/Village Names:
Highland Park.

Ayer, Middlesex County.
Incorporated as a town by St 1871, c 23.

1871.	Feb.	14.	Incorporated as a town, from parts of Groton and Shirley.

Section/Village Names:
Gibson Corner, Mitchellville, Pingreyville, Sandy Pond, Shaker Village, Willows (former R.R. station).

Barecove - see Hingham.

Barnstable, Barnstable County.

1638.	Mar.	5.*	Mentioned in a list of those "allowed to exercise men in Armes",...."ffor Barnestable...Mr. Thom Dimmack...."

(Ply. Col. Rec., Vol. XI, p. 30.)

1641.	June	17.*	Bounds between Barnstable and Yarmouth established.
1652.	Mar.	2.*	Bounds between Barnstable and Sandwich to be established.
1658.	Mar.	11.*	Barnstable and Yarmouth agreed upon bounds.
1662.	June	3.*	Additional lands granted to Barnstable.
1662.	June	10.*	Bounds between Barnstable and Sandwich to be established.
1672.	Oct.	29.*	Bounds between Barnstable and Sandwich established.
1795.	Jan.	22.	Bounds between Barnstable and the district of Mashpee established.
1894.	Mar.	28.	Bounds between Barnstable and Mashpee established.
1916.	Apr.	24.	Bounds between Barnstable and Mashpee established and part of Sandwich annexed.
1989.	Apr.	11.	Town charter adopted which established city form of government.

Archaic Names of the Municipality:
Chequocket, Chuckomug, Coa or Cotuit, Cokachoise, Cotachesett, Cummaquid, Kokachoise, Mattakeeset, Mistic, Moskeehtucketqut, Peymechit, Santuite, Satuite, Sepoese, Sepuit, Sipnesset, Skonkonet, Skunkamug, Tamahappaseeacon, Waskotussoo, Wequaquet, Yanno's Land.

Sections/Village Names:
Centerville, Cotuit, Craigville, Cummaquid, Grand Island, Hyannis, Hyannis Port, Marston's Mills, Newtown (extinct), Osterville, Oyster Harbors, Pondsville (extinct), Sandy Neck, Santuit, South Hyannis (extinct), West Barnstable, West Hyannisport, Wianno.

Barre, Worcester County.
Hutchinson incorporated as a town by St 1774, c 3.

1753.	Apr.	12.	District of Rutland established from part of Rutland. (Prov. Laws, Vol. III, p. 654.)
1774.	June	17.	**Hutchinson** incorporated as a town, formerly incorporated as the District of Rutland. (Prov. Laws, Vol. V, p. 389.)
1776.	Nov.	7.	Name of the town of Hutchinson changed to **Barre**. (Prov, Laws, Vol. V, p. 592.)

Archaic Names of the Municipality:
Hutchinson, Rutland District.

Section/Village Names:
Barre Center, Barre Falls, Barre Four Corners, Barre Plains, Bogue, Christian Hill, Coldbrook, Dennyville, East Barre, Harwoods Crossing, Heald Village, High Plains, Powder Mill, Rice Village, Ryder Village, South Barre, West Barre, White Valley (previously called Smithville).

Barrington - see Rehoboth and Swansea. (Ceded to Rhode Island in 1747.)

Becket, Berkshire County.
Established as a town by St 1765-1766, c 17.

1765.	June	21.	Established as a town, formerly the plantation called "Number Four". (Prov. Laws, Vol. IV, p. 817.)
1783.	Mar.	12.	Part included in the new town of Middlefield.
1798.	Feb.	3.	Certain lands lying between Becket, Blandford, Chester and Loudon annexed.
1810.	Mar.	1.	Part of Loudon annexed.

Archaic Names of the Municipality:
Houssatonic Township Number Four, Plantation Number Four.

Section/Village Names:
Bancroft, Becket Center, Benton Hill, Bonny Rig, Bowlder Grange, Charcoal City, East Becket, Four Corners, Greenwater Pond, Horn Pond, North Becket, Quarry, Reservoir, Rose Hill, South Becket, West Becket, Yokum Pond.

Bedford, Middlesex County.
Established as a town by St 1729, c 1.

1729.	Sept.	23.*	Established as a town, from parts of Billerica and Concord. (Prov. Laws, Vol. II, p. 527.)
1767.	Feb.	26.	Part of Billerica annexed.
1768.	June	9.	Part of Lexington annexed.
1974.	Mar.	2.	Town charter adopted.

Section/Village Names:
Bedford Springs, Shady Hill (former R.R. station), West Bedford.

Belchertown, Hampshire County.
Established as a town by St 1761-1762, c 7.

1761.	June	30.	Established as a town, by the name of "Belcher's Town" formerly the plantation called "Cold Spring". (Prov. Laws, Vol. IV, p. 464.)

1765.   Feb.   27.   Part annexed to Greenwich.
1771.   June   22.   Part annexed to Greenwich.
1787.   June   21.   Part annexed to Greenwich.
1788.   June   16.   Part annexed to Pelham.
1816.   Feb.   15.   Part included in the new town of Enfield.
1927.   Apr.   26.   Part of Enfield annexed.
1938.   Apr.   26.   Act of Apr. 26, 1927, amended.
1938.   Apr.   28.   Act of Apr. 26, 1927, as amended, took effect.

Archaic Names of the Municipality:
Belcher's Town, Cold Spring Plantation.

Section/Village Names:
Bardwell, Barrett's Junction, Belchertown Center, Blue Meadow, Chestnut Hill, Cold Spring, Dwight, East Hill, Federal, Franklin, Holyoke, Lakeville, Laurel, Liberty, Mill Valley, Pansy Park (former R.R. station), Slab City, South Belchertown, Turkey Hill, Tylerville, Washington, West Hill.

Bellingham, Norfolk County.
Established as a town by St 1719-1720, c 96.
1719.   Nov.   27.* Established as a town, from parts of Dedham, Mendon and
                      Wrentham. (Prov. Laws, Vol. IX, p. 688.)
1735.   Apr.   11.* Bounds between Bellingham and Wrentham established.
1832.   Feb.   23.   Bounds between Bellingham and Franklin established.
1872.   Mar.   7.   Bounds between Bellingham and Mendon established.
1941.   Oct.   9.   Bounds between Bellingham and Franklin established.
1941.   Dec.   9.   Act of Oct. 9, 1941, took effect.

Section/Village Names:
Bellingham Center, Bellingham Four Corners, Bellingham Junction, Caryville, Crimpville, Crook's Corner, North Bellingham, Rakeville, Scott Hill, South Bellingham.

Belmont, Middlesex County.
Incorporated as a town by St 1859, c 109.
1859.   Mar.   18.   Incorporated as a town, from parts of Waltham, Watertown,
                      and West Cambridge.
1861.   Jan.   31.   Bounds between Belmont and West Cambridge established.
1862.   Feb.   25.   Bounds between Belmont and Cambridge established and
                      part of each place annexed to the other place.
1880.   Apr.   19.   Part annexed to Cambridge.
1891.   Apr.   28.   Bounds between Belmont and Cambridge established and
                      part of each place annexed to the other place.
1903.   May   23.   Bounds between Belmont and Watertown established.
1906.   Feb.   16.   Bounds between Belmont and Cambridge changed and
                      established.
1911.   Apr.   29.   Bounds between Belmont and Watertown established.
1922.   Mar.   24.   Bounds between Belmont and Watertown established.
1938.   May   26.   Bounds between Belmont and Arlington established.
1938.   Oct.   3.   Act of May 26, 1938, took effect.
1939.   Mar.   22.   Bounds between Belmont and Waltham established.
1955.   Aug.   18.   Bounds between Belmont and Cambridge established.
1975.   Dec.   16.   Bounds between Belmont and Arlington changed and
                      established.

Section/Village Names:
Harvard Lawn, Hill Crossing (former R.R. station), Payson Park, Waverley.

Berkley, Bristol County.
Established as a town by St 1735, c 18.

1735.	Apr.	18.*	Established as a town, from parts of Dighton and Taunton. (Prov. Laws, Vol. II, p. 741.)
1799.	Feb.	26.	Part of Dighton annexed.
1810.	Feb.	6.	Certain lands in Berkley belonging to Taunton annexed.
1842.	Mar.	3.	Certain lands in Berkley belonging to Taunton annexed.
1879.	Apr.	1.	Part of Taunton annexed.
1879.	Apr.	12.	Act of Apr. 1, 1879, accepted by the town and took effect.

Section/Village Names:
Assonet Neck, Berkley Bridge, Berkley Common, Burt's Corner, Myricks.

Berlin, Worcester County.
Incorporated as a town by St 1812, c 95.

1784.	Mar.	16.	Established as the district of Berlin from parts of Bolton and Marlborough.
1791.	Feb.	8.	Part of Lancaster annexed.
1806.	Feb.	15.	Bounds between the district of Berlin and Northborough established and part of each place annexed to the other place.
1812.	Feb.	6.	Incorporated as a town, formerly the district of Berlin.
1905.	May	1.	Bounds between Berlin and Marlborough; Berlin and Hudson; and Berlin and Clinton established.

Section/Village Names:
Berlin Station, Carters (former R.R. station), East Berlin, South Berlin, West Berlin, Wheeler's Hill.

Bernardston, Franklin County.
Established as a town by St 1761-1762, c 42.

1762.	Mar.	6.	Established as a town, formerly the new plantation called "Falltown". (Prov. Laws, Vol. IV, p. 530.)
1779.	Dec.	2.	Part annexed to Colrain.
1784.	Mar.	12.	Part established as the district of Leyden.
1838.	Apr.	14.	Part of Greenfield annexed.
1886.	May	7.	Part of Leyden annexed upon acceptance by the town.
1886.	June	7.	Act of May 7, 1886, accepted.

Archaic Names of the Municipality:
Falls Fight, Falltown Plantation.

Section/Village Names:
Bald Mountain, Burke Flat, East Bernardston, Fox Hill, Huckle Hill, North Bernardston, West Mountain.

Bethlehem, District - see Otis.

BEVERLY, Essex County.

1668.	Nov.	7.*	Established as a town, formerly part of Salem called "Basse Riuer". (Mass. Bay Rec., Vol. IV, Part 2, p. 407.)
1679.	May	28.*	Bounds between Beverly and "the village" and Wenham established.
1753.	Sept.	11.	Part of Salem annexed.
1857.	Apr.	27.	Part annexed to Danvers.
1894.	Mar.	23.	Incorporated as a city.
1894.	May	1.	Act of Mar. 23, 1894, accepted by the town.

Archaic Names of the Municipality:
Basse River.

Section/Village Names:
Beverly Cove, Beverly Farms, Centreville, Montserrat, North Beverly, Pride's
Crossing, Ryal Side, West Beach, West Farms, West Park.

Billerica, Middlesex County.

1655.	May	29.*	Mentioned as a tract of land granted to "seuerall proprietors & inhabitants of Shawshin,...by the side of Concord Riuer,...plantacon to be called Billirikeyca." (Mass. Bay Rec., Vol. IV, Part 1, p. 237.)
1656.	May	14.*	"...this Court doth graunt the toune of Billirrikey eight thousand acres of lands...." (Mass. Bay. Rec., Vol. IV, Part I, p. 268.)
1657.	May	15.*	Lands of the Grant of May 14, 1656, laid out.
1658.	May	26.*	Bounds between "Billirikey" and Andover established.
1661.	May	22.*	Four thousand acres of land granted to Billerica.
1666.	Oct.	10.*	Bounds between Billerica and Woburn established.
1669.	Oct.	12.*	Bounds between Billerica and Woburn "shall stand as it doeth."
1701.	June	27.*	Bounds between Billerica, Chelmsford and Concord established.
1729.	Sept.	23.*	Part included in the new town of Bedford.
1733.	June	13.*	Part annexed to Wilmington.
1734.	Dec.	17.*	Part established as Tewksbury.
1737.	Dec.	23.*	Bounds between Billerica and Wilmington established.
1741.	July	28.*	Bounds between Billerica and Woburn established.
1767.	Feb.	26.	Part annexed to Bedford.
1780.	Apr.	28.	Part included in the district of Carlisle.
1979.	Mar.	3.	Town charter adopted.

Archaic Names of the Municipality:
A "Praying Indian" (Christian) town, Billirikey, Shawshin, Shawshinnock.

Section/Village Names:
Billerica Center, Bennett Hall (former R.R. station), East Billerica, North Billerica,
Nutting Lake, Pattenville, Pinehurst, South Billerica, Turnpike, West Billerica.

Blackstone, Worcester County.
Incorporated as a town by St 1845, c 201.

1845.	Mar.	25.	Incorporated as a town, from part of Mendon.
1916.	May	1.	Part established as Millville.
1972.	Mar.	6.	Town charter adopted.

Section/Village Names:
Blackstone Village, Central Village, Chestnut Hill, East Blackstone, Farnum's Gate,
Five Corners, High Rocks, Millerville, Millville, New City, Privilege, Rural District,
Waterford, Wheelockville, Woonsocket Junction.

Blandford, Hampden County.
Established as a town by St 1740-1741, c 25.

1741.	Apr.	10.*	Established as a town, formerly "Suffield Equivalent Lands" "...commonly called Glasgow...." (Prov. Laws, Vol. II, p. 1058.)
1809.	Feb.	22.	Bounds between Blandford and Russell, and Blandford and Chester established.
1810.	June	13.	Bounds between Blandford and Chester established.
1853.	May	25.	Part annexed to Norwich.

Archaic Names of the Municipality:
Glasgow, New Glasgow, Suffield Equivalent Lands.

Section/Village Names:
Beech Hill, Blandford Center, Gore, North Blanford, Phelps District, Taggart.

Bolton, Worcester County.
Established as a town by St 1738-1739, c 7.

1738.	June	24.*	Established as a town, from part of Lancaster. (Prov. Laws, Vol. II, p. 942.)
1784.	Mar.	16.	Part included in the new district of Berlin.
1829.	Feb.	11.	Part of Marlborough annexed.
1838.	Mar.	16.	Bounds between Bolton and Marlborough established.
1868.	Mar.	20.	Part annexed to Hudson.

Section/Village Names:
Bolton Center, Bolton Station, East End, Fiddler's Green, Forbush Hill, Fryeville, Long Hill, Pan, South Bolton, Still River, Vaughn's Hill, Wattoquotoc Hill, West End.

BOSTON, Suffolk County.
(The sections of Brighton, Charlestown, Dorchester, Hyde Park, Roxbury and West Roxbury were annexed to Boston. See individual listing for history.)
Incorporated as a city by St 1822, c 10.

1630.	Sept.	7.*	First mentioned, "It is ordered, that Trimountaine shalbe called Boston...." (Mass. Bay Rec., Vol. I, p. 75.)
1632.	Nov.	7.*	"...ordered, that the necke of land betwixte Powder Horne Hill & Pullen Poynte shall belonge to Boston, ..." (Mass. Bay Rec., Vol. I, p. 101.)
1633.	Mar.	4.*	Bounds between Boston and Roxbury established.
1634.	May	14.*	"...Boston shall haue convenient inlargemt att Mount Wooliston, ... & prsent it to the nexte Genall Court...." (Mass. Bay Rec., Vol. I, p. 125.)
1634.	Sept.	3.*	"...ordered, that Wunetsemt shall belonge to Boston,...as pte of that towne." (Mass. Bay Rec., Vol. I, p. 125.)
1634.	Sept.	25.*	"...ordered, that Boston shall haue inlargemt att Mount Wooliston & Rumney Marsh." (Mass. Bay Rec., Vol. I, p. 139.)
1635.	Mar.	4.*	Bounds between Boston and Dorchester, at Mount Wooliston and Wessaguscus to be determined.
1635.	Mar.	4.*	"Deere Iland, Hogg Iland, Longe Ieland, & Spectakle Ieland are graunted...to Boston...." (Mass. Bay Rec., Vol. I, p. 139.)
1635.	July	8.*	Bounds between Boston and Charlestown established.
1635.	July	8.*	Bounds to be set out between Boston and Saugus about Rumney Marsh.
1636.	Mar.	28.*	Bounds between Boston and Charlestown, and Boston and Dorchester established.
1637.	Mar.	9.*	"Nodles Iland" annexed.
1639.	June	6.*	Bounds to be settled between Boston, Charlestown and Lynn.
1640.	May	13.*	Part known as "Mount Woolaston" established as Braintree.
1641.	Oct.	7.*	Bounds between Boston and Roxbury, at Muddy River established.
1641.	Oct.	7.*	Bounds between Boston and Cambridge established.
1705.	Nov.	13.*	Part called Muddy River established as Brookline.
1739.	Jan.	10.*	Part called "Winnissimet", "Rumney Marsh", and "Pullin Point" (excepting Noddle's Island and Hog Island) established as Chelsea.

1804.	Mar.	6.	Part of Dorchester annexed.
1822.	Feb.	23.	Incorporated as a city.
1822.	Mar.	4.	Act of Feb. 23, 1822, accepted by the town.
1825.	Feb.	22.	Bounds between Boston and Brookline established.
1834.	Mar.	25.	Thompson's Island set off from Dorchester and annexed to Boston as long as it is used for charitable purposes.
1836.	Mar.	16.	Bounds between Boston and Roxbury established.
1837.	Apr.	19.	Bounds between Boston and Roxbury established.
1850.	May	3.	Part of Roxbury annexed and bounds established.
1855.	May	21.	Part of Dorchester annexed.
1860.	Apr.	3.	Part of Roxbury annexed and bounds established.
1860.	Apr.	16.	Act of April 3, 1860, accepted by Roxbury.
1860.	May	8.	Act of April 3, 1860, accepted by Boston.
1867.	June	1.	City of **Roxbury** annexed to Boston.
1867.	Sept.	9.	Act of June 1, 1867, accepted by Boston and Roxbury.
1868.	Jan.	5.	Act of June 1, 1867 took effect.
1869.	June	4.	Town of **Dorchester** annexed to Boston.
1869.	June	22.	Act of June 4, 1869, accepted by Boston and Dorchester.
1870.	Jan.	3.	Act of June 4, 1869, took effect.
1870.	Apr.	2.	Bounds between Boston and West Roxbury established.
1870.	June	18.	Part of Brookline annexed.
1870.	Nov.	4.	Act of June 18, 1870, accepted by Boston and took effect.
1872.	Apr.	12.	Part of West Roxbury, known as Mount Hope Cemetery annexed.
1872.	Apr.	27.	Bounds between Boston and Brookline established.
1873.	May	14.	City of **Charlestown** annexed to Boston.
1873.	May	21.	The town of **Brighton** annexed to Boston.
1873.	May	29.	The town of **West Roxbury** annexed to Boston.
1873.	Oct.	7.	Acts of May 14, 21 and 29, 1873, accepted by Boston and Charlestown, Boston and Brighton, Boston and West Roxbury.
1874.	Jan.	5.	Acts of May 14, 21 and 29, 1873, took effect.
1874.	May	8.	Part of Brookline annexed.
1874.	May	29.	Bounds between Boston and Newton established.
1875.	May	5.	Part annexed to Newton.
1875.	June	23.	Act of May 5, 1875, accepted by Newton.
1875.	July	1.	Act of May 5, 1875, took effect.
1890.	May	27.	Bounds between Boston and Brookline established.
1891.	May	4.	Bounds between Boston and Somerville established.
1894.	Apr.	13.	Bounds between Boston and Brookline established.
1898.	Mar.	29.	Bounds between Boston and Newton established.
1898.	Mar.	29.	Bounds between Boston and Cambridge established.
1898.	Apr.	1.	Bounds between Boston and Hyde Park established.
1898.	May	13.	Bounds between Boston and Newton established.
1910.	Mar.	29.	Bounds between Boston and Cambridge established.
1911.	May	24.	The town of **Hyde Park** annexed to Boston.
1911.	June	22.	Act of May 24, 1911, amended.
1911.	Nov.	7.	Act of May 24, 1911, as amended, accepted by Boston and Hyde Park.
1912.	Jan.	1.	Act of May 24, 1911, as amended, took effect.

Archaic Names of the Municipality:
Nodles Iland, Shawmut, Tremont, Trimountaine.

Section/Village Names:
Aberdeen, Academy Hill, Allston, Allston Heights, Andrew Square, Ashmont, Bay Village, Back Bay, Barry's Corner, Bay View, Beacon Hill, Belle Isle, Bellevue, Boylston, Brighton, Canterbury, Castle Island, Cedar Grove, Central District, China Town, City Point, Charlestown, Clarendon Hills, Commercial Point, Deer Island, Dorchester, Dorchester Center, Dorchester Heights, Dorchester Lower Mills, East Boston, Egleston Square, Fairmount, Faneuil, Fenway, Fields Corner, Financial District, Forest Hills, Four Corners, Franklin Park, Germantown, Glover's Corner, Granite Bridge, Grove Hall, Harbor View, Harrison Square, Hazelwood Highland, Hog Island, Hommfield, Hyde Park, Jamaica Plain, Jeffries Point, Leather District, Long Island, Lovel's Island, Mattapan, Meeting House Hill, Mission Hill, Mount Bowdoin, Mount Hope, Mount Pleasant, Neponset, Nonantum Hill, North End, Oak Square, Old Harbor Village, Orient Heights, Parker Hill, Parley Vale, Pope's Hill, Readville, Roslindale, Roxbury, Roxbury Crossing, Rugby, Savin Hill (previously called Rocky Hill), Shawmut, South Boston, South Cove, South End, Spectacle Island, Sunnyside, Theatre District, Thompson's Island, Union Square, Upham's Corner, Washington Village, Wellington Hill, West End, West Roxbury, Wood Island.

Boston Corner, District of, Berkshire County
1838. Apr. 14. A tract of unincorporated land called Boston Corner incorporated into a district by the name of Boston Corner.
1847. Mar. 12. Bounds between the district of Boston Corner and Mount Washington established.
1853. May. 14. Ceded to the State of New York.

Bourne, Barnstable County.
Incorporated as a town by St 1884, c 127.
1884. Apr. 2. Incorporated as a town, from part of Sandwich.
1897. Apr. 14. Bounds between Bourne and Wareham established.

Archaic Names of the Municipality:
Cataumet, Monument Village, North Sandwich, West Sandwich.

Section/Village Names:
Bournedale, Buzzards Bay, Cataumet, Gray Gables, Head of the Bay, Mashnee Island, Monument Beach, North Pocasset, Pocasset, Sacconeesett, Sagamore, Sagamore Beach, Sagamore Highlands, South Pocasset, Wenammet Neck (also called Wing's Neck).

Boxborough, Middlesex County.
Made a town by Revised Statutes c 15, Sect. 9.
1783. Feb. 25. Incorporated as the district of Boxborough from parts of Harvard, Littleton and Stow.
1794. Feb. 20. Bounds between the district of Boxborough and Littleton established.
1835. Nov. 4. Made a town, formerly the district of Boxborough.
1836. May 1. Act of Nov. 4, 1835, took effect.
1890. Apr. 30. Bounds between Boxborough and Littleton established.
1906. June 14. Bounds between Boxborough and Harvard established.
1906. June 15. Bounds between Boxborough and Littleton established.

Boxford, Essex County.
1685. Aug. 12.* Part of Rowley established as township of Rowley Village and bounds established
1694. Sept. 14.* **Boxford** is mentioned in the tax act. (Prov. Laws, Vol. I, p. 178.)
1701. Feb. 25.* Bounds between Boxford and Topsfield established.

1707.	Nov.	28.*	Bounds between Boxford and Topsfield established.
1728.	June	20.*	Part included in the new town of Middleton.
1808.	June	10.	Part of Rowley annexed.
1810.	June	13.	Part of Rowley annexed.
1825.	June	18.	Bounds between Boxford and Rowley established.
1846.	Mar.	7.	Part of Ipswich annexed.
1856.	Mar.	21.	Part annexed to Groveland.
1897.	Apr.	15.	Part annexed to Georgetown.
1904.	Mar.	12.	Bounds between Boxford and North Andover established.
1904.	Mar.	12.	Bounds between Boxford and Rowley established.
1904.	Apr.	22.	Bounds between Boxford and Middleton established.
1904.	Apr.	22.	Bounds between Boxford and Georgetown established.

Archaic Names of the Municipality:
Rowley Village.

Section/Village Names:
Boxford Village, East Boxford, Boxford First Parish, Howe Village, Boxford Second Parish, West Boxford.

Boylston, Worcester County.
Incorporated as a town by St 1785, c 55.

1786.	Mar.	1.	Incorporated as a town, from part of Shrewsbury.
1808.	Jan.	30.	Part included in the new town of West Boylston.
1820.	Feb.	10.	Part annexed to West Boylston.
1820.	June	17.	Part annexed to West Boylston.
1905.	May	2.	Bounds between Boylston and West Boylston established.

Section/Village Names:
Boylston Center, East Section, Morningdale, South Boylston, Straw Hollow, Windsor Park.

Bradford - see Haverhill.

Braintree, Norfolk County.

1640.	May	13.*	Established as a town, from part of Boston known as "Mount Woollaston". (Mass. Bay Rec., Vol. I, p. 291.)
1712.	May	30.*	Blue Hill lands divided between Braintree and Milton.
1792.	Feb.	22.	Part included in the new town of Quincy.
1793.	Mar.	9.	Part incorporated as the town of Randolph, with a proviso that certain estates of the remonstrants be allowed to remain in Braintree.
1811.	June	22.	The estates of Samuel Cheesman and Levi Thayer, remonstrants, under the act of Mar. 9, 1793, re-annexed to Randolph.
1856.	Apr.	24.	Part annexed to Quincy.
1903.	Mar.	11.	Bounds between Braintree and Holbrook established.

Archaic Names of the Municipality:
Blue Hill Lands, Merry Mount, Monatiquot, Mount Dagan, Mount Wollaston.

Section/Village Names:
Braintree Highlands (formerly Monatiquot Heights), East Braintree Five Corners, Mayflower Park, South Braintree, South Braintree Heights.

Brewster, Barnstable County.
Incorporated as a town by St 1802, c 76.

| 1803. | Feb. | 19. | Incorporated as a town, from part of Harwich, with a proviso that certain estates of the remonstrants be allowed to remain in Harwich. |

1811.	June	21.	The Daniel Rogers estate in Harwich annexed to Brewster.
1848.	Apr.	25.	Part annexed to Harwich.
1861.	Feb.	20.	Bounds between Brewster and Orleans established.
1935.	June	20.	Bounds between Brewster and Orleans re-established.
1945.	July	12.	Bounds between Brewster and Dennis established.

Archaic Names of the Municipality:
Satucket, Sawkatucket.

Section/Village Names:
Brewster Station, East Brewster, North Brewster, South Brewster, West Brewster.

Bridgewater, Plymouth County.

1656.	June	3.*	Established as a town, "Ordered, that henceforth Duxborrow New Plantation bee allowed to bee a townshipe of yt selfe, destinct from Duxburrow, and to bee called by the name of Bridgewater,...." (Ply. Col. Rec., Vol. III, p. 101.)
1662.	June	3.*	Certain land granted Bridgewater.
1675.	June	1.*	Boundary line established, Court ordered "... to Run the line between Bridgwater and Middlebury". (Ply. Col. Rec., Vol. XI, p. 241.)
1691.	Feb.	11.*	Lands between Bridgewater and Weymouth, called "Foords Farms", and parts adjacent annexed.
1712.	June	10.*	Part included in the new town of Abington.
1770.	Nov.	20.	Part of Stoughton annexed.
1798.	Feb.	8.	Part of Stoughton annexed.
1821.	June	15.	Part established as North Bridgewater.
1822.	Feb.	16.	Part established as West Bridgewater.
1823.	June	14.	Part established as East Bridgewater.
1824.	Feb.	20.	Part annexed to Halifax.
1838.	Feb.	23.	Bounds between Bridgewater and East Bridgewater established.
1846.	Mar.	20.	Bounds between Bridgewater and East Bridgewater established and part of each town annexed to the other town.
1931.	Apr.	21.	Bounds between Bridgewater and East Bridgewater established.

Archaic Names of the Municipality:
Duxburrow Plantation, Foords Farm, Hockomock, Ketiticut, Nunketest, Titicut.

Section/Village Names:
Bridgewater Iron Works, Bridgewater Junction, Dublin, Japan, Nippenicket Park, Paper Mill Village, Pratt Town, Scotland, Sprague's Hill, Stanley (former R.R. station), State Farm, Titicut.

Brighton - see Boston.
Incorporated as a town by St 1806, c 65.

1807.	Feb.	24.	Incorporated as a town, from part of Cambridge.
1816.	Jan.	27.	Part of Cambridge annexed.
1873.	May	21.	Annexed to Boston.
1873.	Oct.	27.	Act of May 21, 1873, accepted by Brighton and Boston.
1874.	Jan.	5.	Act of May 21, 1873, took effect.

Archaic Names of the Municipality:
Little Cambridge, Cambridge South Parish.

Brimfield, Hampden County.

| 1714. | June | 10.* | Mentioned in petition to General Court, "...for the Township of Brinfield...." (Prov. Laws, Vol. XXI, p. 846.) |
| 1722. | Aug. | 16.* | Mentioned in a list of frontier towns. (Prov. Laws, Vol. II, p. 260.) |

1731.	Dec.	24.*	Established as a town. The act of establishment has been lost. The bill was enacted by the House of Representatives, Dec. 23,* 1731 (House Journal 1730/31, p. 34) by the Council, Dec. 24,* 1731 (Court Rec., Vol. 15, p. 201.)
1742.	Jan.	16.*	Part included in the new town of Western.
1760.	Apr.	23.	Part annexed to Palmer.
1760.	Apr.	28.	Part established as the district of Monson.
1762.	Sept.	18.	Part established as the district of South Brimfield.
1763.	Feb.	7.	Bounds definitely established.

Section/Village Names:
Brimfield Center, East Brimfield, Fentonville, Foskett's Mills, Little Rest, Parksville, Powers Corner, West Brimfield.

Bristol, Bristol County.

1679.	June	3.*	Mount Hope mentioned and certain bounds established.(Ply. Col. Rec., Vol. VI, p. 16.)
1679.	Nov.	1.*	Bounds between Mount Hope and Swansea established.
1681.	Oct.	28.*	Mount Hope established as a town by the name of Bristol.(Ply. Col. Rec., Vol. VI, p 77.)
1747.	———.		Massachusetts/Rhode Island boundary settled, Bristol ceded to the State of Rhode Island.

BROCKTON, Plymouth County.
North Bridgewater established as a town by St 1812, c 12.
Brockton incorporated as a city by St 1881, c 192.

1821.	June	15.	**North Bridgewater** established as a town, from part of Bridgewater.
1825.	Jan.	26.	Bounds between North Bridgewater and West Bridgwater established.
1874.	Mar.	28.	Act to authorize the town of North Bridgewater to change its name.
1874.	May	5.	Name of **Brockton** adopted by North Bridgewater, under Act of Mar. 28, 1874.
1875.	Apr.	24.	Part annexed to South Abington and parts of East Bridgewater and South Abington annexed.
1881.	Apr.	9.	Incorporated as a city.
1881.	May	23.	Act of Apr. 9, 1881, accepted by the town.
1893.	May	8.	Part of West Bridgewater annexed, if the act is accepted by Brockton.
1893.	Nov.	7.	Act of May 8, 1893, accepted.
1894.	Mar.	1.	Act of May 8, 1893, took effect.

Archaic Names of the Municipality:
North Bridgewater.

Section/Village Names:
Belleview Park, Brockton Heights, Bumpus Corner, Bush, Campello, Cary Hill, Centreville, Clifton Heights, Douglas Park, Ellis Park, Elmhurst, Factory Village, Happy Hollow, Highland Terrace, Hovenden Park, Intervale Park, Leyden Park, Marshall's Corner, Menlo Park, Montello, Morse's Corner, Oak Hill, Pleasant Park, Pleasantville, Prospect Hill, Prospect Park, Porter's Pass, Rangeley Park, Ridge Hill, Salisbury Heights, Sawtelleville, Shaw's Corner, Sunnyside, Sylvester Corner, Thomaston Park, Tower Hill, Walnut Bottom, Wheeler Park, Winchester Park, Winter's Corner.

Brookfield, Worcester County.
Established as a town by St 1718-1719, c 87.

1673.	Oct.	15.*	In answer to the petition of the inhabitants of "Quobauge" the Court granted "... the liberty & priuiledge of a touneship, and that the name thereof be Brookfeild,....." when forty or fifty families shall have settled there. (Mass. Bay Rec., Vol. V, Part 2, p. 568.)
1718.	Nov.	12.*	Established as a town. (Prov. Laws, Vol. IX, p. 620.)
1730.	Sept.	11.*	Bounds between Brookfield and Leicester established.
1742.	Jan.	16.*	Part included in the new town of Western.
1751.	Jan.	31.*	Part included in the district of New Braintree.
1791.	June	10.	Bounds between Brookfield and New Braintree established and part of each town annexed to the other town.
1792.	Mar.	8.	Bounds between Brookfield and New Braintree established and part of each town annexed to the other town.
1812.	Feb.	28.	Part established as North Brookfield.
1823.	Feb.	8.	Part annexed to Ware.
1848.	Mar.	3.	Part established as West Brookfield.
1854.	Apr.	15.	Part of North Brookfield annexed.
1910.	Mar.	18.	Bounds between Brookfield and North Brookfield established.
1910.	May	13.	Bounds between Brookfield and West Brookfield established.
1920.	Mar.	24.	Part incorporated as East Brookfield.

Archaic Names of the Municipality:
Quabaug Territory, Quobauge, Quaboag.

Section/Village Names:
Over the River District, Potopoag, Rice Corner District.

Brookline, Norfolk County.
Established as a town by St 1705, c 73.

1705.	Nov.	13.*	Established as a town, formerly part of Boston called "Muddy River". (Prov. Laws, Vol. XXI, p. 737.)
1825.	Feb.	22.	Bounds between Brookline and Boston established.
1844.	Feb.	24.	Part of Roxbury annexed.
1870.	June	18.	Part annexed to Boston.
1870.	Nov.	4.	Act of June 18, 1870, accepted by Boston and took effect.
1872.	Apr.	27.	Bounds between Brookline and Boston established.
1874.	May	8.	Part annexed to Boston.
1890.	May	27.	Bounds between Brookline and Boston established.
1894.	Apr.	13.	Bounds between Brookline and Boston established.
1907.	Mar.	28.	Bounds between Brookline and Newton established.

Archaic Names of the Municipality:
Muddy River.

Section/Village Names:
Aspinwall Hill, Brookline Hills, Brookline Village, Chestnut Hill, Coolidge Corner, Corey Hill, Cottage Farm, Fisher Hill, Longwood, Pill Hill, Reservoir, The Point, Town Green, Washington Square.

Buckland, Franklin County.
Incorporated as a town by St 1779, c 40.

1779.	Apr.	14.	Incorporated as a town, from the plantation called "Notown" and part of Charlemont. (Prov. Laws, Vol. V. p. 957.)
1838.	Apr.	14.	Part of Conway annexed.

Archaic Names of the Municipality:
No Town Plantation.

Section/Village Names:
Buckland Center, Buckland Four Corners, East Buckland, Shelburne Falls.

Burlington, Middlesex County.
Incorporated as a town by St 1798, c 74.

1799.	Feb.	28.	Incorporated as a town, from part of Woburn.
1800.	Jan.	20.	Part annexed to Lexington.
1970.	Aug.	14.	Bounds between Burlington and Wilmington changed and established.

Section/Village Names:
Cumston Village, Garden Acres (extinct), Havenville (extinct), Winnmere.

CAMBRIDGE, Middlesex County.
Incorporated as a city by St 1846, c 109.

1631.	July	26.*	**Newe Towne** mentioned in a training act— "... Charlton, Misticke & the newe towne ...." (Mass. Bay Rec., Vol. I, p. 90.)
1632.	Mar.	6.*	Bounds between "Charles-Towne" and Newe Towne established.
1635.	Apr.	7.*	Bounds between Newe Towne and "Waterton" established.
1635.	Apr.	7.*	Bounds between Newe Towne and Roxbury established.
1636.	Sept.	8.*	"...Newe Towne, now called Cambridge." (Mass. Bay Rec., Vol. I, p. 180.)
1638.	May	2.*	"...ordered, that Newe Towne shall henceforward be called **Cambridge.**" (Mass. Bay Rec., Vol. I, p. 228.)
1639.	Mar.	13.*	Bounds between Cambridge and Watertown established.
1641.	Oct.	7.*	Bounds between Cambridge and Boston established.
1659.	Nov.	12.*	One thousand acres of land granted to Cambridge.
1664.	Oct.	19.*	The grant made on Nov. 12, 1659, renewed.
1713.	Mar.	20.*	Part called "The Northern Precinct" established as Lexington.
1754.	Apr.	19.	Part of Watertown annexed and bounds established.
1755.	June	4.	Part annexed to Waltham.
1761.	Apr.	18.	Part annexed to Charlestown.
1802.	Mar.	6.	Part of Charlestown annexed.
1807.	Feb.	24.	Part incorporated as Brighton.
1807.	Feb.	27.	Part incorporated as West Cambridge.
1816.	Jan.	27.	Part annexed to Brighton.
1818.	Feb.	12.	Part of Charlestown annexed.
1820.	June	17.	Part of Charlestown annexed.
1846.	Mar.	17.	Incorporated as a city.
1846.	Mar.	30.	Act of Mar. 17, 1846, accepted by the town.
1855.	Apr.	27.	Part of Watertown annexed.
1856.	Apr.	30.	Bounds between Cambridge and Somerville established and part of each place annexed to the other place.
1862.	Feb.	25.	Parts of Belmont and West Cambridge annexed. Parts annexed to Belmont and West Cambridge and bounds established.
1862.	Apr.	29.	Bounds between Cambridge and Somerville established and part of each place annexed to the other place.
1880.	Apr.	19.	Part of Belmont annexed.
1885.	Mar.	10.	Part of Watertown annexed.
1891.	Apr.	28.	Bounds between Cambridge and Belmont established and part of each place annexed to the other place.
1898.	Mar.	9.	Bounds between Cambridge and Watertown established and part of each place annexed to the other place.
1898.	Mar.	29.	Bounds between Cambridge and Boston established.
1906.	Feb.	16.	Bounds between Cambridge and Belmont changed and established.

1910.	Mar.	29.	Bounds between Cambridge and Boston established.
1911.	May	5.	Bounds between Cambridge and Arlington established if accepted by the city council and selectmen.
1911.	May	22.	Act of May 5, 1911, accepted by selectmen of Arlington.
1911.	May	31.	Act of May 5, 1911, accepted by city council of Cambridge.
1922.	Mar.	24.	Bounds between Cambridge and Watertown established.
1955.	Aug.	18.	Bounds between Cambridge and Belmont established.

Archaic Names of the Municipality:
Newe Towne, Newtown.

Section/Village Names:
Avon Hill, Agassiz, Cambridge Highlands, Cambridgeport, East Cambridge, Central Square, Coolidge Hill, Harvard Square, Inman Square, Kendall Square, Larchwood, Lechmere Point, Lechmere Square, Lower Port, Mid Cambridge, Mount Auburn Station, North Cambridge, Old Cambridge, Porter Square, Porter's Station, Riverside, Reservoir Hill, Strawberry Hill, West Cambridge.

Canton, Norfolk County.
Incorporated as a town by St 1796, c 54.

1797.	Feb.	23.	Incorporated as a town, from part of Stoughton.
1847.	Mar.	31.	Part annexed to Stoughton.
1899.	Mar.	24.	Bounds between Canton and Sharon established.

Archaic Names of the Municipality:
Dorchester Village, Punkapoag.

Section/Village Names:
Canton Center, Canton Corner, Canton Farms, Canton Junction, Dedham Road Station, Ponkapoag, Springdale, Stone Factory, York.

Cape Ann - see Gloucester.

Carlisle, Middlesex County.
Incorporated as a town by St 1779-1780, c 42.

1780.	Apr.	28.	Incorporated as the district of Carlisle from parts of Acton, Billerica, Chelmsford and Concord. (Prov. Laws, Vol. V, p. 1189.)
1780.	Sept.	12.	Part of the district of Carlisle annexed to Concord.
1783.	Mar.	1.	Part of the district of Carlisle annexed to Chelmsford.
1805.	Feb.	18.	Incorporated as a town, formerly the district of Carlisle.
1865.	Feb.	17.	Part of Chelmsford annexed and bounds established.
1903.	May	23.	Bounds between Carlisle and Concord established.

Section/Village Names:
Carlisle Station.

Carver, Plymouth County.
Incorporated as a town by St 1790, c 2.

1790.	June	9.	Incorporated as a town, from part of Plympton.
1793.	Feb.	8.	Bounds between Carver and Plympton established.
1827.	Jan.	20.	Part annexed to Wareham.
1849.	Mar.	24.	Bounds between Carver and Middleborough established.
1901.	May	16.	Bounds between Carver and Wareham established.
1921.	Mar.	7.	Bounds between Carver and Middleborough established.

Archaic Names of the Municipality:
Mohootset.

Section/Village Names:
Annasnappet, Bate's Pond, East Carver, Ellis Furnace, John's Pond, North Carver, Popes Point, Quitticus, Shoestring District, South Carver, Wenham.

Charlemont, Franklin County.
Established as a town by St 1765-1766, c 15.

1765.	June	21.	Established as a town, formerly the plantation called Charlemont. (Prov. Laws, Vol. IV, p. 816.)
1774.	Feb.	4.	Three thousand acres of land annexed.
1779.	Apr.	14.	Part included in the new town of Buckland.
1785.	Feb.	14.	Part included in the new town of Heath.
1793.	Mar.	19.	Certain tract of land between Charlemont and "North River" annexed.
1838.	Apr.	2.	Part of a tract of land called "Zoar" annexed.

Archaic Names of the Municipality:
Boston Township Number One, Charley Mount, Plantation Chickleystown, Zoar.

Section/Village Names:
East Charlemont, Gilead, Zoar.

CHARLESTOWN - see Boston.
Incorporated as a city by St 1847, c 29.

1630.	Aug.	23.*	"The first Court of Assistants, holden att Charlton...." (Mass. Bay Rec., Vol. I, p. 73.)
1632.	Mar.	6.*	Bounds between Charlestown and Newetowne established.
1633.	July	2.*	Granted the land betwixte North River and the Creeke.
1635.	July	8.*	Bounds between Charlestown and Boston established.
1636.	Mar.	3.*	Bounds established, "...eight myles into the country from their meeteing-howse...."
1636.	Mar.	28.*	Bounds between Charlestown and Boston established.
1636.	Oct.	28.*	"Lovels Iland is graunted to Charlestowne pvided they imploy it for fishing by their owne townesmen, or hinder not others."
1639.	June	6.*	Bounds to be settled between Charlestown, Boston and Lynn.
1640.	May	13.*	Certain land granted "...two miles at their head line,...."
1640.	Oct.	7.*	Certain land granted "...4 mile square,...to make a village...."
1641.	June	2.*	"The bounds for Charlstowne village are to bee set out...the contents of a 4 mile square."
1642.	Sept.	27.*	"Charlestowne village is called Wooborne."
1648.	Oct.	27.*	"The iland called Lovels Iland" granted to Charlestown "pvided, that halfe of the timber and firewood shall belong to the garrison at the Castle,...."
1649.	May	2.*	"Upon the petition of Mistick side men, they are granted to be a district towne, ... called Mauldon."
1659.	Nov.	12.*	One thousand acres of land granted.
1663.	Oct.	21.*	Five hundred acres of land granted.
1664.	Oct.	19.*	Grant of Nov. 12,* 1659, renewed.
1666.	Oct.	10.*	Grant of Oct. 21,* 1663, confirmed.
1725.	Dec.	17.*	Part established as Stoneham.
1726.	June	7.*	Part annexed to Malden.
1754.	Apr.	18.	Part annexed to Medford.
1754.	Apr.	20.	Part annexed to Medford.
1761.	Apr.	18.	Part of Cambridge annexed.
1802.	Mar.	6.	Part annexed to Cambridge.
1811.	June	21.	Part of Medford annexed.
1818.	Feb.	12.	Part annexed to Cambridge.
1820.	June	17.	Part annexed to Cambridge.
1842.	Feb.	25.	Part annexed to West Cambridge.
1842.	Mar.	3.	Part incorporated as the town of Somerville.

1847.	Feb.	22.	Incorporated as a city.
1847.	Mar.	10.	Act of Feb. 22, 1847, accepted by the town.
1873.	May	14.	Annexed to Boston.
1873.	Oct.	7.	Act of May 14, 1873, accepted by Charlestown and Boston.
1874.	Jan.	5.	Act of May 14, 1873, took effect.

Archaic Names of the Municipality:
Charlton, Mishawum.

Charlton, Worcester County.
Made a town by St 1775-1776, c 3.

| 1754. | Nov. | 21. | "An Engross'd Bill,... setting off the Inhabitants as also the Estates of the Westerly part of Oxford, as also the Westerly part of the Country Gore, into a separate Town by the name _____...." (Court Rec., Vol. 20, p. 327.) |

The above engrossed bill is printed, as an act, in Prov. Laws,
Vol. III, p. 781, in which appears the name of Charlton.
However, on Jan. 6, 1755, the Secretary informed the House that his Excellency, the
Governor, had not signed the bill, "erecting the Westerly Part
of Oxford into a Town...." (House Journal, Jan. 6, 1755.)

1755.	Jan.	10.	"An Engrossed Bill...setting off the Inhabitants as also the Estates of the Westerly part of Oxford into a separate District by the Name of _____...." (Court Rec., Vol. 20, p. 379.)
1757.	June	3.	Lands called "The Gore" annexed to the district of Charlton.
1775.	Aug	23.	Made a town by general act, under which districts became towns.
1789.	Jan.	5.	Part annexed to Oxford.
1792.	June	26.	Part annexed to Sturbridge.
1809.	Feb.	23.	Part annexed to Oxford.
1816.	Feb.	15.	Part included in the new town of Southbridge.
1907.	Feb.	11.	Bounds between Charlton and Oxford established.
1907.	Feb.	11.	Bounds between Charlton and Southbridge established.

Section/Village Names:
Albee Corners, Baylies Corner, Bearfoot District, Berry's Corner, Brookside,
Buffum's, Charlton Center, Charlton City, Charlton Depot, Coppville, Dodge,
Dresser Hill, Glenmere, Hamerock, Lelandsville, Millward, Morseville, Morton
Station, Muggett, North Charlton, North Side, Olney Corners, Parker School House,
Partridge Hill, Phillipdale, Putnam's Village, Richardson's Corner, Snake Hill,
South Charlton, Thompson Corners.

Chatham, Barnstable County.
Established as a town by St 1712, c 34.

| 1712. | June | 11.* | Established as a town, formerly a village or district of |

"Manamoit". (Prov. Laws, Vol. XXI, p. 806.)

| 1862. | Apr. | 14. | Bounds between Chatham and Orleans, and Chatham and Harwich established. |
| 1995. | May | 11. | Town charter adopted. |

Archaic Names of the Municipality:
Manamoit Village, Monamoiet, Monomoy, Weguasset.

Section/Village Names:
Chatham Port, Mill Pond Bluff, Monomoy Island, Neck, North Chatham, Old
Harbor, South Chatham, West Chatham.

Chelmsford, Middlesex County.

1655.	May	29.*	A new plantation "the name thereof to be called Chelmsford." (Mass. Bay Rec., Vol. IV, Part 1, p. 237.)
1656.	May	14.*	Certain lands granted to Chelmsford.
1660.	May	31.*	Bounds between Chelmsford and the Indian plantation at "Patucket" established and part of each place annexed to the other place.
1701.	June	27.*	Bounds between Chelmsford and Billerica established.
1725.	Nov.	23.*	Part annexed to Littleton.
1726.	June	13.*	"Wameset" annexed.
1729.	Sept.	23.*	Part established as Westford.
1755.	Apr.	24.	Part annexed to Dunstable.
1780.	Apr.	28.	Part included in the district of Carlisle.
1783.	Mar.	1.	Part of the district of Carlisle annexed.
1826.	Mar.	1.	Part established as Lowell.
1865.	Feb.	17.	Part annexed to Carlisle and bounds established.
1874.	May	18.	Part annexed to Lowell.
1874.	June	23.	Act of May 18, 1874, accepted by Lowell.
1874.	Aug.	1.	Act of May 18, 1874, took effect.
1955.	Mar.	14.	Bounds between Chelmsford and Lowell established and part annexed to Lowell.
1955.	Aug.	4.	Bounds as established by act of Mar. 14, 1955, struck out and bounds between Chelmsford and Lowell established and part annexed to Lowell.
1975.	May	19.	Bounds between Chelmsford and Westford altered, revised and relocated.

Archaic Names of the Municipality:
Pawtucket, Wameset.

Section/Village Names:
Chelmsford Center, East Chelmsford, Golden Cove, Homestead, North Chelmsford, South Chelmsford, West Chelmsford, Westlands.

CHELSEA, Suffolk County.
Established as a town by St 1738-1739, c 17,
Incorporated as a city by St 1857, c 18.

1739.	Jan.	10.*	Established as a town, from part of Boston, "called Winnissimet, Rumney Marsh and Pullin Point, or otherwise called number Thirteen (excepting only the said islands called Noddle's Island and Hog Island)...." (Prov. Laws,

Vol. II, p. 969.)

1841.	Feb.	22.	Part annexed to Saugus.
1846.	Mar.	19.	Part established as North Chelsea.
1857.	Mar.	13.	Incorporated as a city.
1857.	Mar.	23.	Act of Mar. 13, 1857, accepted by the town.
1967.	Nov.	7.	City charter adopted.
1994.	Aug.	26.	City charter approved establishing a council manager form of government.

Archaic Names of the Municipality:
Number Thirteen, Pullen Poynte, Pullin Point, Rumney Marsh, Winnissimet.

Section/Village Names:
Bellingham, Forbes, Powder Horn Hill, Prattville.

Cheshire, Berkshire County.
Incorporated as a town by St 1792, c 56.

1793.	Mar.	14.	Incorporated as a town, from parts of the towns of Adams, Lanesborough, Windsor and part of the district of New Ashford.
1794.	Feb.	26.	Part re-annexed to Windsor.
1798.	Feb.	6.	Part of district of New Ashford annexed.
1912.	May	28.	Bounds between Cheshire and New Ashford established.

Archaic Names of the Municipality:
New Providence, New Providence Purchase, New Providence Hill.

Section/Village Names:
Cheshire Corner, Cheshire Harbor, Cheshire Village, East Cheshire, Farnams, Furnace Hill, Hell's Kitchen, Hut Meadow, Jones' Nose, Muddy Brook, New Dublin, North Cheshire, Pork Lane, Pumpkin Hook, Reynolds' Rock, Scrabbletown, Stafford's Hill, The Cobbles, The Kitchen, Thunder, West Mountain.

Chester, Hampden County.
Murrayfield established as a town by St 1765-1766, c 23.

1765.	Oct.	31.	**Murrayfield** established as a town, formerly the plantation called Murrayfield. (Prov. Laws, Vol. IV, p. 837.)
1773.	June	29.	Part of Murrayfield established as the district of Norwich.
1781.	May	8.	Part of Murrayfield annexed to Norwich.
1783.	Feb.	21.	Name of the town of Murrayfield changed to **Chester**.
1783.	Mar.	12.	Part included in the new town of Middlefield.
1799.	June	21.	Part annexed to Worthington.
1809.	Feb.	22.	Bounds between Chester and Blandford established.
1810.	June	13.	Bounds between Chester and Blandford established.
1853.	May	25.	Part annexed to Norwich.

Archaic Names of the Municipality:
Murrayfield, Plantation Number Nine (1762 Township).

Section/Village Names:
Bonney Ridge, Four Corners, Chester Center, Chester Village, Dayville, Littleville, Mica Mill, North Chester.

Chesterfield, Hampshire County.
Incorporated as a town by St 1762-1763, c 4.

1762.	June	11.	Incorporated as a town, formerly the new plantation called "New Hingham." (Prov. Laws, Vol. IV, p. 573.)
1763.	Jan.	31.	Certain tract of land annexed.
1781.	May	14.	Part included in the new town of Goshen.
1789.	June	8.	Part of Goshen annexed.
1794.	Feb.	22.	Part of Norwich annexed.
1795.	June	24.	Bounds between Chesterfield and Goshen and Williamsburg established.
1797.	Feb.	7.	Bounds between Chesterfield and Goshen and Williamsburg established.
1810.	Feb.	16.	Bounds between Chesterfield and Goshen and Williamsburg established.

Archaic Names of the Municipality:
Andrewstown, New Hingham Plantation, Plantation Number One (Western Township of 1762).

Section/Village Names:
Bisbees, Bofat Hill, Chesterfield Center, Ireland Street, Sugar Hill, Taylor's Bridge, West Chesterfield.

CHICOPEE, Hampden County.
Incorporated as a town by St 1848, c 233.
Incorporated as a city by St 1890, c 189.

1848.	Apr.	29.	Incorporated as a town, from part of Springfield.
1890.	Apr.	18.	Incorporated as a city.
1890.	May	6.	Act of April 18, 1890, accepted by the town.
1945.	May	7.	Bounds between Chicopee and Springfield established.
1946.	Oct.	15.	Act of May 7, 1945, took effect.

Archaic Names of the Municipality:
Cabotville.

Section/Village Names:
Aldenville, Chicopee Center, Chicopee Falls, Chicopee Junction, Crowleyville,
Fairview, North Chicopee, Sandy Hill, Westover Air Base (U.S.A.F.), Willimansett.

Chilmark, Dukes County.

1694.	Sept.	14.*	Mentioned in the tax act. (Prov. Laws, Vol. I, p. 179.)
1696.	June	17.*	Mentioned as "the town of Chilmark". (Prov. Laws, Vol. VII, p. 118.)
1697.	Oct.	29.*	Tax act mentions Chilmark "alias the manner [sic] ofTisbury...." (Prov. Laws, Vol. I, p. 303.)
1714.	Oct.	30.*	"... all the Powers of a Town given & granted ...." formerly "the Mannor of Tisbury commonly called Chilmark....with an island called No Mans Land." (Prov. Laws, Vol. XXI, p. 854.)
1716.	Nov.	30.*	Certain lands annexed - "... all the Lands upon Martha's Vineyard lying to the Westward of the said Town...together with an Island call'd No Mans Land...Providing that it extend not to or take in any Part of the Gay Head Neck...." (Prov. Laws, Vol. IX, p. 508.)
1736.	Dec.	30.*	Ordered that the residents of Chekamo be set off from Chilmark to Tisbury.
1855.	Mar.	9.	Bounds between Chilmark and the lands of the Indians of Gay Head to be established.
1856.	May	28.	Bounds between Chilmark and the lands of the Indians of Gay Head, as laid out under a resolve of Mar. 9, 1855, confirmed.
1864.	Mar.	17.	Part of Chilmark known as "Elizabeth Islands" established as Gosnold.
1882.	Feb.	27.	Bounds between Chilmark and Tisbury established.
1896.	Mar.	25.	Bounds between Chilmark and Gay Head to be determined.
1897.	Apr.	29.	Bounds between Chilmark and Gay Head re-established.

Archaic Names of the Municipality:
Manor of Tysbury, Nashowakemmuck, Noman's Land.

Section/Village Names:
Abel's Hill, Chickemoo, Elizabeth Island, Keephikkon, Menemsha-Indian
Wawaytick, Nashaquitsa, Noman's Land, Prospect Hill, Peaked Hill, Quansoo,
Quenames, Squibnocket, Stonewall.

Clarksburg, Berkshire County.
Incorporated as a town by St 1797, c 76.

1798.	Mar.	2.	Incorporated as a town, formerly a tract of land lying north of Adams.
1848.	May	2.	Part annexed to Florida.
1852.	May	20.	Part of Florida annexed.

1913.   Apr.   10.   Bounds between Clarksburg and Florida established.

Archaic Names of the Municipality:
Bullocks Grant.

Section/Village Names:
Briggsville, Four Corners, Hall's Ground, Houghtonville, Red Mills.

Clinton, Worcester County.
Incorporated as a town by St 1850, c 72.
1850.   Mar.   14.   Incorporated as a town, from part of Lancaster.
1905.   May   1.   Bounds between Clinton and Berlin established.

Section/Village Names:
Acre, Burditt Hill, California, Duck Harbor, Germantown, Woodruff Heights.

Cohasset, Norfolk County.
Made a town by St 1775-1776, c 3.
1770.   Apr.   26.   Incorporated as a district by the name of Cohasset from part
                        of Hingham. (Prov. Laws, Vol. V, p. 49.)
1775.   Aug.   23.   Made a town, by general act under which districts became
                        towns.
1823.   June   14.   Part of Scituate annexed.
1840.   Mar.   20.   Bounds between Cohasset and Scituate established and part
                        of each town annexed to the other town.
1897.   Apr.   30.   Bounds between Cohasset and Scituate established.
1897.   Apr.   30.   Bounds between Cohasset and Hingham established.
1928.   Mar.   23.   Bounds between Cohasset and Hingham re-established.

Archaic Names of the Municipality:
Conahasset.

Section/Village Names:
Beechwood, Black Rock, Cohasset Cove, Lincoln Hill, North Cohasset.

Colechester - see Salisbury.

Colrain, Franklin County.
Established as a town by St 1761-1762, c 10.
1761.   June   30.   Established as a town, formerly the new plantation called
                        Colrain. (Prov. Laws, Vol. IV, p. 466.)
1772.   Apr.   22.   Gore of Province Land granted to Colrain.
1779.   Dec.   2.   Part of Bernardston annexed.
1911.   Apr.   24.   Bounds between Colrain and Leyden established.

Archaic Names of the Municipality:
Boston Township Number Two.

Section/Village Names:
Adamsville, Bliss Corner, Catamount Hill, Chandler Hill, Christian Hill, Colrain
Center, East Colrain, Elm Grove, Foundry Village, Griswoldville, Line, Lyonsville,
North River, Shattuckville, South Colrain, Willis Place, Wilson Hill.

Concord, Middlesex County.
1635.   Sept.   3.*   "...shalbe a plantacon att Musketequid, ... & the name of the
                        place is changed, & hereafter to be called Concord." (Mass.
                        Bay Rec., Vol. I, p. 157.)
1638.   June   8.*   Bounds between Concord, Dedham, and Watertown
                        established.
1651.   May   13.*   Bounds between Concord and Watertown established.
1701.   June   27.*   Bounds between Concord and Billerica established.

1717.	Apr.	12.*	Bounds between Concord and Stow established.
1725.	Nov.	23.*	Part annexed to Littleton.
1729.	Sept.	23.*	Part included in the new town of Bedford.
1735.	July	3.*	Part included in the new town of Acton.
1747.	Dec.	11.*	Bounds between Concord and Acton established.
1754.	Apr.	19.	Part included in the new town of Lincoln.
1754.	Apr.	19.	District of Carlisle established from part of Concord. (Prov. Laws, Vol. III, p. 729.)
1756.	Oct.	6.	The District of Carlisle annexed to Concord.
1780.	Apr.	28.	Part included in the district of Carlisle.
1780.	Sept.	12.	Part of the district of Carlisle annexed.
1903.	May	23.	Bounds between Concord and Carlisle established.

Archaic Names of the Municipality:
Musketequid.

Section/Village Names:
Concord Junction, East Quarter, Harness Shop Hill, Lake Walden, Nine Acre Corner, North Quarter, Reformatory Station, Riverside Park, West Concord, Westvale.

Conway, Franklin County.
Made a town by St 1775-1776, c 3.

1767.	June	17.	Established as the district of Conway from part of Deerfield. (Prov. Laws, Vol. IV, p. 955.)
1775.	Aug.	23.	Made a town, by general act under which districts became towns.
1781.	Feb.	19.	Part of Shelburne annexed.
1785.	Feb.	9.	Part annexed to Goshen.
1791.	June	17.	Part of Deerfield annexed.
1811.	June	21.	Part of Deerfield annexed and bounds between Conway and Whately established.
1838.	Apr.	14.	Part annexed to Buckland.

Section/Village Names:
Baptist Hill, Boyden (extinct), Broomshire, Burkville, Chapel Falls (extinct), Church Green (extinct), Crickett Hill, Franklin (extinct), Guinea (extinct), Hardscrabble (extinct), Harding (extinct), Hoosac (extinct), Poland, Pumpkin Hollow, Shirkshire, South Part, South West (extinct).

Cottage City - see Oak Bluffs.

Cummington, Hampshire County.
Established as a town by St 1779-1780, c 6.

1779.	June	23.	Established as a town, from part of the plantation called "Number Five." (Prov. Laws, Vol. V, p. 1072.)
1785.	Mar.	16.	Part established as the district of Plainfield.
1788.	Mar.	21.	Certain gore of land, of two thousand two hundred acres, and grants known as "Murrayfield Grant" and "Minot's Grant" annexed.

Archaic Names of the Municipality:
Minot's Grant, Murrayfield Grant, Plantation Number Five (1762 Township).

Section/Village Names:
Lightning Bug, Swift River, West Cummington.

Dalton, Berkshire County.
Incorporated as a town by St 1783, c 64.

1784.	Mar.	20.	Incorporated as a town, formerly "Ashuelot Equivalent."
1795.	Feb.	28.	Part of Windsor annexed.
1796.	Feb.	23.	Part of Windsor annexed.
1804.	June	21.	Part included in the new town of Hinsdale.
1962.	July	25.	Bounds between Dalton and Pittsfield altered, revised and relocated.
1972.	June	8.	Bounds between Dalton and Pittsfield changed and established.

Archaic Names of the Municipality:
Ashuelot Equivalent.

Section/Village Names:
Bartonville, Craneville, Carsonville, Glennonville, Jericho, Kittredgeville, Renfrew.

Dana, (A Drowned Town) - see Petersham.
Incorporated as a town by St 1800, c 50.

1801.	Feb.	18.	Incorporated as a town, from parts of Greenwich, Hardwickand Petersham.
1803.	Feb.	12.	Bounds between Dana and Petersham established.
1811.	June	19.	Bounds between Dana and Greenwich established.
1842.	Feb.	4.	Parts of Hardwick and Petersham annexed.
1882.	Apr.	10.	Bounds between Dana and Petersham established.
1911.	May	4.	Bounds between Dana and Greenwich established.
1927.	Apr.	26.	All of Dana annexed to Petersham.
1938.	Apr.	26.	Act of Apr. 26, 1927, amended.
1938.	Apr.	28.	Act of Apr. 26, 1927, as amended took effect.

Section/Village Names:
Dana Center (extinct), Doubleday (extinct), Millington (extinct), North Dana (extinct), Storesville (extinct).

Danvers, Essex County.
Made a town by St 1775-1776, c 3.

1752.	Jan.	28.*	Established as a separate district, by the name of Danvers, from part of Salem known as the "Village and Middle parishes". (Prov. Laws, Vol. III, p. 598.)
1757.	June	16.	"...said district...erected into a township...." (Prov. Laws, Vol. IV, p. 5.)
1759.	Aug.	10.	Act of June 16, 1757, disallowed by the privy council. (Side note, Prov. Laws, Vol. IV, p. 5.) (A footnote shows this record taken from Public-Record Office, England.) Danvers was annually represented in the House of Representatives from and after the year 1758. (Journals of House of Representatives.).
1772.	July	14.	Danvers is called a town. (Prov. Laws, Vol. V, p. 213.)
1775.	Aug.	23.	Made a town, by general act under which districts became towns.
1840.	Mar.	17.	Bounds between Danvers and Salem established.
1855.	May	18.	Part established as South Danvers.
1856.	May	31.	Bounds between Danvers and South Danvers established.
1857.	Apr.	27.	Part of Beverly annexed.

Archaic Names of the Municipality:
Salem Farms, Salem Middle Parish, Salem Village Parish.

Section/Village Names:
Beaver Brook (extinct), Danvers Centre (also known as Salem Village), Danvers Highlands, Danvers Plains, Danversport (also known as Newmills and Neck of Land), East Danvers (also known as Ryal Side), Ferncroft, Hathorne, Putnamville, Tapleyville.

Dartmouth, Bristol County.

1652.	Oct.	5.*	"The Rates of the seuerall Townes within this Jurisdiction...Dartmouth is to pay...." (Ply. Col. Rec., Vol. III, p. 19.)
1664.	June	8.*	Established as a town. "... all that tracte of land comonly called and knowne by then named of Acushena, Ponagansett and Coaksett...knowne by the name of Dartmouth." (Ply. Col. Rec., Vol. IV, p. 65.)
1668.	June	3.*	Bounds of Dartmouth established.
1682.	June	6.*	**Little Compton** established as a town, from lands formerly called "Saconett". (Ply. Col. Rec., Vol. VI, p.88.)
1693.	Mar.	13.*	Dartmouth bounds re-established.
1694.	June	14.*	**Tiverton** established as a town by St 1694-1695, c 8, from a certain land lying between Little Compton, Freetown and Dartmouth. (Prov. Laws, Vol. I, p. 174.)
1701.	June	13.*	Boundary line between town of Dartmouth, and the towns of Little Compton and Tiverton established.
1747.	Feb.	5.*	"The Remainder of Tiverton & the whole of Little Compton in this Province,....." annexed to Dartmouth after settlement of Rhode Island boundry. (Prov. Laws, Vol. XIII, p. 685.)
1787.	Feb.	23.	Part established as New Bedford.
1787.	July	2.	Part established as Westport.
1793.	Feb.	25.	Part annexed to Westport.
1795.	Feb.	25.	Part annexed to Westport.
1805.	Mar.	4.	Part annexed to Westport.
1828.	Feb.	20.	Bounds between Dartmouth and Westport established.
1831.	Feb.	19.	Bounds between Dartmouth and New Bedford established.
1845.	Mar.	20.	Part annexed to New Bedford.
1888.	May	3.	Part annexed to New Bedford.

Archaic Names of the Municipality:
Acushena, Agawam, Apponegansett, Coaksett, Coaxit, Cookset, Coquit, Fort Phoenix, Little Compton, Ponagansett, Saconett, Tiverton.

Section/Village Names:
Apponegansett, Bakerville, Bay View, Bliss Corner, Cove Village, Faunce Corner, Hicksville, Kempton Park, Mishamet Point, Nonquitt, North Dartmouth, Padanaram, Potenska Point, Round Hill Point, Russell Mills, Salter's Point, Smith's Mills, Smith's Neck, South Dartmouth, Summit Grove, Westport Factory, Westport Mills.

Dedham, Norfolk County.

1636.	Sept.	8.*	"...the plantation to bee setled above the falls of Charles Ryver, ... to bee Deddam, ..." (Mass. Bay Rec., Vol. I, p. 179.)
1638.	May	16.*	Bounds between Dedham and Roxbury established.
1638.	May	17.*	Bounds between Dedham and Dorchester established.
1638.	June	8.*	Bounds between Dedham, Concord and Watertown established.
1639.	May	22.*	Bounds between Dedham and Watertown established.
1649.	Oct.	17.*	Land granted to Dedham for a village.
1650.	May	22.*	Part established as Medfield.
1651.	Oct.	30.*	Certain bounds challenged as allowed by act of May 22,* 1639.
1675.	May	12.*	Bounds between Dedham and Roxbury established.
1701.	Oct.	18.*	Bounds between Dedham and Natick established.
1711.	Nov.	6.*	Part established as Needham.
1712.	Aug.	22.*	Bounds between Dedham and Needham established.
1714.	Nov.	3.*	Bounds between Dedham and Needham established.

1719.	Nov.	27.*	Part included in the new town of Bellingham.
1724.	Dec.	10.*	Part established as Walpole.
1733.	Apr.	25.*	Part of Stoughton annexed.
1737.	Dec.	10.*	Part of Stoughton annexed.
1738.	Dec.	11.*	Bounds between Dedham and Stoughton established.
1739.	June	7.*	Part annexed to Dorchester.
1780.	June	17.	Part of Stoughton annexed.
1784.	Feb.	12.	Part of Walpole annexed.
1784.	July	7.	Part established as the district of Dover.
1791.	Mar.	7.	Bounds between Dedham and Dover established.
1811.	June	21.	Part re-annexed to Walpole.
1831.	June	17.	Part annexed to Dorchester.
1852.	Apr.	21.	Part annexed to West Roxbury.
1852.	Apr.	30.	Act of Apr. 21, 1852, accepted by West Roxbury.
1852.	Apr.	30.	Part annexed to Walpole.
1853.	July	4.	Act of Apr. 21, 1852, took effect.
1868.	Apr.	22.	Part included in the new town of Hyde Park.
1868.	May	1.	Act of Apr. 22, 1868, amended and bounds established.
1872.	Feb.	23.	Part included in the new town of Norwood.
1897.	Apr.	2.	Part established as the town of Westwood.
1974.	Feb.	23.	Town charter adopted.
1995.	Mar.	18.	Revised town charter adopted.

Archaic Names of the Municipality:
Contentment.

Section/Village Names:
Ashcroft, Charles River Heights, Connecticut Corner, Dedham Island, East
Dedham, Ellis Station, Elmwood, Endicott, Fairbank's Park, Federal Hill, Four
Corners, Germantown, Greenlodge, Jerusalem, Mill Village, Oakdale, Pine Heights,
Pine Ridge, Readville Manor, Riverdale, Riverside Heights, Riverview Heights,
Sandy Valley, South Dedham, Stone Haven, Stormy Hill, Upper Dedham, West
Dedham, Wilson's Mountain.

Deerfield, Franklin County.

1677.	Oct.	22.*	"...there being twenty persons taken from Hattfield & Deerfield, ..." (Mass. Bay Rec., Vol. V, p. 167.)
1678.	Oct.	—.*	Provisions made for the encouragement of the rebuilding of the plantation of Deerfield. (Mass. Bay Rec., Vol. V, p. 209.)
1712.	June	7.*	Bounds to extend nine miles from the river into the Western Woods.
1717.	Nov.	19.*	Grant of land seven miles square confirmed.
1741.	Aug.	3.*	Bounds of the grants made June 7,* 1712, and Nov. 19,* 1717, established.
1753.	June	9.	Part established as the district of Greenfield.
1764.	June	15.	Bounds between Deerfield and Huntstown established.
1767.	June	17.	Part established as the district of Conway.
1768.	June	21.	Part established as the district of Shelburne.
1791.	June	17.	Part annexed to Conway.
1810.	Mar.	5.	Part annexed to Whately.
1811.	June	21.	Part annexed to Conway and bounds established.
1896.	May	2.	Part annexed to Greenfield.

Archaic Names of the Municipality:
Pocomtuck.

Section/Village Names:
Bardwell's Ferry, Cheapside, Deerfield Center, East Deerfield, Great River, Hillside,
Hoosac, Mill & Barre, Mill River, Mill Village, Old Deerfield, Petty's Plain, Pine
Nook, Riverbank, Stillwater, South Deerfield, The Bars, Wapping, West Deerfield.

Dennis, Barnstable County.
Incorporated as a town by St 1793, c 6.

1793.	June	19.	Incorporated as a town, from part of Yarmouth.
1945.	July	12.	Bounds between Dennis and Brewster and Dennis and Harwich established.
1947.	May	8.	Act of July 12, 1945, amended and bounds between Dennis and Harwich established.

Archaic Names of the Municipality:
Nobscusset, Sesuet.

Section/Village Names:
Dennisport, East Dennis, North Dennis, South Dennis, West Dennis.

Dighton, Bristol County.
Established as a town by St 1712, c 1.
Wellington incorporated as a town by St 1814, c 11.

1712.	May	30.*	Dighton established as a town, from part of Taunton. (Prov. Laws, Vol. XXI, p. 801.)
1735.	Apr.	18.*	Part of Dighton included in the new town of Berkley.
1743.	Mar.	2.*	Dighton bounds reported by a committee.
1745.	Jan.	8.*	Dighton bounds established.
1799.	Feb.	26.	Part of Dighton annexed to Berkley.
1814.	June	9.	**Wellington** incorporated as a town from part of Dighton.
1824.	Feb.	12.	Bounds between Dighton and Wellington established and part annexed to Wellington.
1826.	Feb.	22.	Dighton and Wellington united as the town of Dighton. Act to take effect one year from date of passage.
1827.	June	16.	Town of Welligton revived to exist one year for certain purposes.
1828.	June	16.	Act of June 16, 1827, expired. The towns of Wellington and Dighton united as the town of Dighton.
1854.	Apr.	4.	Part annexed to Somerset.

Archaic Names of the Municipality:
Wellington, Taunton, South Purchase.

Section/Village Names:
Broad Cove, Dighton Rock Park, North Dighton, Segreganset, South Dighton, West Dighton.

Dorchester - see Boston.

1630.	Sept.	7.*	It was ordered that Mattapan be called Dorchester. (Mass. Bay Rec., Vol. I, p. 75.)
1635.	Mar.	4.*	Thompson's Island granted to Dorchester.
1636.	Mar.	28.*	Bounds between Dorchester and Boston established.
1638.	May	17.*	Bounds between Dorchester and Dedham established.
1641.	June	2.*	"Squantums Neck & Mennens Moone" annexed.
1659.	Nov.	12.*	One thousand acres of land granted Dorchester.
1662.	May	7.*	Part established as Milton.
1726.	Dec.	22.*	Part established as Stoughton.
1728.	Aug.	1.*	Land belonging to Dorchester annexed to Lunenburg.
1739.	June	7.*	Part of Dedham annexed.
1792.	Feb.	22.	Part of that part called "Squantum and the farms" annexed to Quincy.
1804.	Mar.	6.	Part annexed to Boston.
1814.	Feb.	10.	Part of that part called "Squantum and the farms" annexed to Quincy.
1819.	Feb.	12.	Part annexed to Quincy.

1820.	Feb.	21.	Bounds between Dorchester and Quincy established and part of that part called "Squantum" annexed.
1831.	June	17.	Part of Dedham annexed.
1834.	Mar.	25.	Thompson's Island set off and annexed to Boston.
1855.	May	2.	Part of that part called "Squantum" annexed to Quincy.
1855.	May	21.	Part annexed to Boston.
1868.	Apr.	22.	Part included in the new town of Hyde Park.
1868.	May	1.	Act of Apr. 22, 1868, amended and bounds established.
1869.	June	4.	Annexed to Boston.
1869.	June	22.	Act of June 4, 1869, accepted by Dorchester and Boston.
1870.	Jan.	3.	Act of June 4, 1869, took effect.

Archaic Names of the Municipality:
Mattapan, Mennens Moone, Squantums Neck.

Douglas, Worcester County.
Made a town by St 1775-1776, c 3.

1742.	June	19.*	New Sherburn mentioned in an order as a "...tract of land called New Sherburn...." (Prov. Laws, Vol. XIII, p. 144.)
1746.	Mar.	14.*	Established as a district or precinct of New Sherburn from lands commonly called New Sherburn and adjoining lands.
1746.	June	4.*	Part of New Sherburn annexed to Uxbridge.
1746.	June	5.*	Mentioned in the records as a "District or Precinct to be called by the name of Douglas", formerly the district of "New Sherburn." (Court Rec., Vol. 17-5, p. 434.)
1749.	Jan.	30.*	Act mentions district of Douglas.
1775.	Aug.	23.	Made a town, by general act under which districts became towns.
1841.	Feb.	27.	Bounds between Douglas and Webster established.
1864.	Apr.	25.	Bounds between Douglas and Uxbridge established.
1907.	May	16.	Bounds between Douglas and Sutton established.

Archaic Names of the Municipality:
New Sherburn.

Section/Village Names:
Centerville, Clear River, Douglas Center, Douglas Station, East Douglas, Gilboa, South Douglas, Tasseltop, Wallum Pond, West Douglas.

Dover, Norfolk County.
Made a town by St 1836, c 106.

1784.	July	7.	Incorporated into a district by the name Dover from part of Dedham.
1791.	Mar.	7.	Bounds between district of Dover and Dedham established.
1836.	Mar.	31.	Made a town.
1836.	May	2.	Act of Mar. 31, 1836, accepted by the district.
1872.	Feb.	27.	Bounds between Dover and Walpole established.
1903.	May	27.	Bounds between the town of Medfield and the towns of Dover, Walpole and Norfolk established.
1904.	Mar.	12.	Bounds between Dover and Walpole established.
1927.	Mar.	28.	Bounds between Dover and Walpole established.

Archaic Names of the Municipality:
Springfield Parish.

Section/Village Names:
Dover Center.

Dracut, Middlesex County.
Established as a town by St 1701-1702, c 89.

1701.	Feb.	26.*	Established as a town, formerly a tract of land called Dracut. (Prov. Laws, Vol. XXI, p. 717.)
1851.	Feb.	28.	Part annexed to Lowell.
1874.	May	18.	Part annexed to Lowell.
1874.	June	23.	Act of May 18, 1874, accepted by Lowell.
1874.	Aug.	1.	Act of May 18, 1874, took effect.
1879.	Apr.	1.	Part annexed to Lowell.

Archaic Names of the Municipality:
Pawtucket.

Section/Village Names:
Belle Grove, Brookside, Collinsville, Dracut Center, East Dracut, Elesmere, Kenwood, Mount Pleasant, Navy Yard, New Boston, Riverdale.

Dudley, Worcester County.
Established as a town by St 1731-1732, c 17.

1732.	Feb.	2.*	Established as a town, from part of Oxford and certain lands. (Prov. Laws, Vol. II, p. 626.)
1794.	June	25.	Part of a gore of land called "Middlesex Gore" annexed.
1816.	Feb.	15.	Part included in the new town of Southbridge.
1822.	Feb.	23.	Part annexed to Southbridge.
1832.	Mar.	6.	Part included in the new town of Webster.
1907.	Feb.	11.	Bounds between Dudley and Southbridge established.

Archaic Names of the Municipality:
Chabakongomum, Chabanagungamug, Manchaug, Middlesex Gore.

Section/Village Names:
Brandon, Chaseville, Dudley Center, Dudley Hill, Garden City, Jericho, Merino Village, Perryville, Quinebaug, Ram's Horn, Steven's Village, Tufts Village, West Dudley.

Dunstable, Middlesex County.
Nottingham established as a town by St 1732-1733, c 10.
Litchfield established as a town by St 1734-1735, c 11.

1673.	Oct.	17.*	Certain men granted the liberty to settle a plantation about Groton. Note in margin calls this tract, as described in the act, Dunstable. (Mass. Bay Rec., Vol. IV, Part 2, p. 570.)
1680.	Oct.	13.*	"That the towne & companjes of... Dunstable, wth the troope... raysed in those tounes...." be another regiment commanded by Major Bulkley. (Mass. Bay Rec., Vol. V, 295.)
1733.	Jan.	4.*	**Nottingham** established as a town, from part of Dunstable. (Prov. Laws, Vol. II, p. 60.)
1734.	July	4.*	**Litchfield** established as a town, from lands at Naticock and parts of Dunstable and Nottingham. (Prov. Laws, Vol. II, p. 720.) In Mass. Archives, Vol. V, pp. 115 to 119 is the King's decision settling the dispute as to the boundary line between the Provinces of Massachusetts Bay and New Hampshire. (Mar. 10, 1740*)
1747.	June	8.*	Part of Groton annexed to Dunstable.
1747.	June	8.*	Part of Nottingham annexed to Dunstable.
1752.	Jan.	6.*	Part of Dunstable annexed to Groton.
1753.	June	7.	Part of Groton annexed to Dunstable.
1754.	June	14.	Part of Nottingham annexed to Dunstable.
1755.	Apr.	24.	Part of Chelmsford annexed to Dunstable.
1789.	June	22.	Part of Dunstable established as the district of Tyngsborough.

1792.	Mar.	3.	Part of Dunstable annexed to the district of Tyngsborough.
1793.	Feb.	25.	Part of Groton annexed to Dunstable.
1796.	Jan.	26.	Part of Groton annexed to Dunstable.
1798.	Jan.	29.	Part of Dunstable annexed to the district of Tyngsborough and bounds established.
1803.	June	18.	Part of Groton annexed to Dunstable.
1814.	June	10.	Bounds between Dunstable and Tyngsborough established.
1820.	Feb.	15.	Bounds between Dunstable and Groton established.

Archaic Names of the Municipality:
Noticock, Nottingham, Litchfield.

Duxbury, Plymouth County.

1637.	June	7.*	"...Ducksburrow shall become a towneship,...and to have the prveledges of a towne...." (Ply. Col. Rec., Vol. I, p. 62.)
1641.	Mar.	2.*	Bounds established.
1656.	June	3.*	Part called the "Duxburrow New Plantation" established as Bridgewater.
1658.	Mar.	2.*	"Namassakeesett" annexed.
1661.	Mar.	5.*	Certain tract of land granted to Duxbury and Marshfield.
1670.	July	5.*	Bounds between Duxbury and the "Major's Purchase" established.
1678.	June	5.*	Bounds established.
1683.	Feb.	23.*	Bounds between Duxbury and Marshfield established.
1712.	Mar.	21.*	Part included in the new town of Pembroke.
1726.	June	16.*	Part included in the new town of Kingston.
1813.	June	14.	Bounds between Duxbury and Marshfield established.
1857.	Apr.	14.	Part annexed to Kingston.

Archaic Names of the Municipality:
Ducksburrow, Green Harbor, Namassakeesett, Mattakeeset.

Section/Village Names:
Ashdod, Captain's Hill, Cedar Crest, Duxbury Beach, Fordsville, Gardnerville, Hall's Corner, Hatchville, Island Creek, Millbrook, North Duxbury, Powder Point, South Duxbury, Tarklin, Tinkertown, West Duxbury.

East Bridgewater, Plymouth County.
Incorporated as a town by St 1823, c 131.

1823.	June	14.	Incorporated as a town, from part of Bridgewater.
1838.	Feb.	23.	Bounds between East Bridgewater and Bridgewater established.
1846.	Mar.	20.	Bounds between East Bridgewater and Bridgewater established and part of each town annexed to the other town.
1857.	Apr.	11.	Part of Halifax annexed and bounds established.
1875.	Mar.	4.	Part included in the new town of South Abington.
1875.	Apr.	24.	Part annexed to Brockton.
1931.	Apr.	21.	Bounds between East Bridgewater and Bridgewater established.

Section/Village Names:
Beaver, Brown's Crossing, Cinder Hill, Curtisville, Eastville, Elmwood, Harmony, Matfield, Northville, Satucket, West Crook, Westdale, Westlake.

East Brookfield, Worcester County.
Incorporated as a town by St 1920, c 178.

| 1920. | Mar. | 24. | Incorporated as a town, from part of Brookfield. |

Archaic Names of the Municipality:
Quabaug Territory.

East Longmeadow, Hampden County.
Incorporated as a town by St 1894, c 418.

1894.	May	19.	Incorporated as a town, from part of Longmeadow.
1894.	July	1.	Act of May 19, 1894, took effect.
1928.	Mar.	1.	Part annexed to Springfield.

Section/Village Names:
Baptist Village.

East Sudbury - see Wayland.

Eastham, Barnstable County.

1643.			——Nawsett mentioned in a list of towns having freemen able to bear arms. (Ply. Col. Rec., Vol. VIII, p. 177.)
1645.	Mar.	3.*	"... those that goe to dwell at Nossett ...." granted land. (Ply. Col. Rec., Vol. II, p. 81.)
1646.	June	2.*	**Nawsett** established as a town. (Ply. Col. Rec., Vol. II, p. 102.)
1651.	June	7.*	"That the Towne of Nawsett be henceforth called and knowne by the name of **Eastham** ...." (Ply. Col. Rec., Vol. XI, p. 59.)
1678.	Mar.	5.*	Eastham and purchasers on both sides to settle the bounds.
1763.	June	16.	Part established as the district of Wellfleet.
1772.	July	14.	Part of Harwich annexed.
1797.	Mar.	3.	Part established as Orleans.
1839.	Mar.	9.	Part annexed to Orleans.
1847.	Apr.	26.	Part annexed to Wellfleet.
1867.	Mar.	23.	Bounds between Eastham and Orleans established and part of each town annexed to the other town.
1887.	May	6.	Bounds between tidewaters of Eastham and Wellfleet established.

Archaic Names of the Municipality:
Nossett, Nawsett.

Section/Village Names:
Eastham Center, Great Pond, Long Pond, Nausett, North Eastham, South Eastham.

Easthampton, Hampshire County.
Incorporated as a town by St 1809, c 102.

1785.	June	17.	Incorporated into a district by the name of Easthampton, from parts of Northampton and Southampton.
1809.	June	16.	Incorporated as a town, formerly the district of Easthampton.
1828.	Feb.	1.	Bounds between Easthampton and Southampton established.
1841.	Mar.	13.	Part of Southampton annexed.
1850.	Apr.	4.	Part of Southampton annexed.
1862.	Feb.	21.	Bounds between Easthampton and Southampton established.
1872.	Mar.	12.	Bounds between Easthampton and Westhampton established.
1914.	Apr.	21.	Bounds between Easthampton and Northampton established.
1986.	Apr.	7.	Town charter adopted.
1996.	Apr.	1.	New home rule charter adopted which established city form of government.

Archaic Names of the Municipality:
Passacomuck.

Section/Village Names:
Crow Hill, Factory Village, Glendale, Hampton Mills, Loudville, Mount Tom, New City, Park Hill, Williston Mills.

Easton, Bristol County.
Established as a town by St 1725-1726, c 13.

1725.	Dec.	21.*	Established as a town, from half of that tract of land of Norton called the "Taunton North Purchase. (Prov. Laws, Vol. II, p. 368.)
1972.	Mar.	27.	Town charter adopted.

Archaic Names of the Municipality:
Hockamock, Taunton North Purchase.

Section/Village Names:
Easton Center, Eastondale, Easton Furnace, Furnace Village, North Easton, Poquanticut, South Easton Green, South Easton Unionville.

Edgartown, Dukes County.

1671.	July	8.*	"Edgar: Towne", formerly known as "great Harbour", mentioned. (New York Original Books of Letters Patent, Vol. IV, p. 80.)
1691.	Oct.	7.*	The Province Charter grants the Isles of Capawock [Martha's Vineyard] and Nantucket to the Province of Massachusetts. (Prov. Laws, Vol. I, pp. 9 and 73.)
1830.	Feb.	5.	Bounds between Edgartown and Tisbury established.
1862.	Apr.	23.	Bounds between Edgartown and Tisbury established.
1880.	Feb.	17.	Part established as Cottage City.
1937.	May	5.	Bounds between Edgartown and Oak Bluffs re-established.

Archaic Names of the Municipality:
Chappequiddick, Edgar Towne, Great Harbour, Nunnepog, Waqua, Washqua.

Section/Village Names:
Cape Poge, Chappaquiddic Island, Clevelandtown, Felix Neck, Great Plains, Katama, Little Pond, Long Hill, Mill Hill, Ocean Heights, Plains, Pohoganut, Quampacha, South Beach, Vineyard Grove, Wintucket.

Egremont, Berkshire County.
Made a town by St 1775-1776, c 3.

1760.	Feb.	13.	Established as the district of Egremont, from certain lands lying west of Sheffield. (Prov. Laws, Vol. IV, p. 286.)
1775.	Aug.	23.	Made a town, by general act under which districts became towns.
1790.	Feb.	6.	Bounds between Egremont and Alford established.
1790.	Feb.	22.	Part of Sheffield annexed.
1817.	June	17.	Bounds between Egremont and Mount Washington established and part of each town annexed to the other town.
1824.	Feb.	16.	Part of Sheffield annexed.
1869.	June	4.	Bounds between Egremont and Sheffield established.

Archaic Names of the Municipality:
Shawanon, York.

Section/Village Names:
Baldwin Hill, Egremont Plain, Little York (extinct), North Egremont, South Egremont, West Egremont.

Enfield, (A Drowned Town) see Belchertown, New Salem, Pelham and Ware.
Incorporated as a town by St 1815, c 128.

1816.	Feb.	15.	Incorporated as a town, from parts of Belchertown and Greenwich.
1818.	June	12.	Bounds between Enfield and Greenwich established and part of each town annexed to the other town.
1910.	May	26.	Bounds between Enfield and Greenwich established.

1927.	Apr.	26.	All of Enfield annexed in parts to Belchertown, New Salem, Pelham and Ware.
1938.	Apr.	26.	Act of Apr. 26, 1927, amended.
1938.	Apr.	28.	Act of Apr. 26, 1927, as amended, took effect.

Archaic Names of the Municipality:
Greenwich (extinct), South Parish (extinct).
Section/Village Names:
Smiths Station, Thomsonville.

Erving, Franklin County.
Incorporated as a town by St 1838, c 139.

1838.	Apr.	17.	Incorporated as a town, formerly the tract of land called "Erving's Grant."
1841.	Feb.	27.	Bounds between Erving and Orange established.
1860.	Feb.	10.	Part of Northfield called "Hack's Grant" annexed.

Archaic Names of the Municipality:
Erving's Grant, Hack's Grant.

Section/Village Names:
Farley Village, Miller's Falls.

Essex, Essex County.
Incorporated as a town by St 1818, c 85.

1819.	Feb.	15.	Incorporated as a town, from part of Ipswich.
1892.	Apr.	19.	Boundary lines in tidewater between Essex and Gloucester, and Essex and Ipswich established.
1904.	Mar.	12.	Bounds between Essex and Hamilton established.

Archaic Names of the Municipality:
Chebacco, Ipswich Eighth Parish.

Section/Village Names:
Chebacco Pond, Conomo Point, Essex Falls, Lakeville, North End, South Essex.

EVERETT, Middlesex County.
Incorporated as a town by St 1870, c 66.
Incorporated as a city by St 1892, c 355.

1870.	Mar.	9.	Incorporated as a town, from part of Malden.
1875.	Apr.	20.	Part annexed to Medford.
1892.	June	11.	Incorporated as a city.
1892.	July	19.	Act of June 11, 1892, took effect.

Archaic Names of the Municipality:
South Malden.

Section/Village Names:
East Everett, Glendale, Mount Washington, South Everett, Washington Park, West Everett, Woodlawn.

Fairhaven, Bristol County.
Incorporated as a town by St 1811, c 130.

1812.	Feb.	22.	Incorporated as a town, from part of New Bedford.
1815.	June	15.	Part of Freetown annexed.
1836.	Apr.	9.	Part of Rochester annexed and bounds established.
1860.	Feb.	13.	Part established as Acushnet.

Archaic Names of the Municipality:
Fair Haven Village, Sconticut.

Section/Village Names:
East Fairhaven, Harbor View, Nasketucket, New Boston, Oxford, Sconticut Neck, Wilbur's Point.

FALL RIVER, Bristol County.
Incorporated as a town by St 1802, c 89.
Incorporated as a city by St 1854, c 257.

1803.	Feb.	26.	Fall River incorporated as a town, from part of Freetown.
1804.	June	18.	Name of the town of Fall River changed to **Troy**.
1834.	Feb.	12.	Name of the town of Troy changed to Fall River.
1854.	Apr.	12.	Incorporated as a city.
1854.	Apr.	22.	Act of April 12, 1854, accepted by the town.
1861.	Apr.	10.	Certain lands on the east side of Mount Hope Bay annexed by the change of the bounds of Massachusetts and Rhode Island.
1894.	June	14.	Bounds between Fall River and Westport located and defined.

Archaic Names of the Municipality:
Freeman's Purchase, Quequechan Region, Troy.

Section/Village Names:
Border City, Bowenville, Brookville, Copecut, Flint Village, Globe Village, Highlands, Indian Town, Interlachen, Maplewood, Mechanicsville, New Boston, Oak Grove Village, Renaud Heights, Sagamore City, Somerset Junction, Steep Brook, Watuppa.

Falmouth, Barnstable County.

1670.	June	7.*	Suckanesset bounds mentioned. (Ply. Col. Rec., Vol. V, p. 41.)
1681.	July	7.*	Bounds between Suckanesset and Sandwich established.
1686.	June	4.*	**Suckanesset** established as a town, "... to become a township, and have the previledges of a town ...." (Ply. Col. Rec., Vol. VI, p. 189.)
1694.	Sept.	14.*	**Falmouth** mentioned in the tax act. (Prov. Laws, Vol. I, p. 178.)
1735.	Nov.	28.*	Bounds between Falmouth and lands of the proprietors of Mashpee confirmed.
1841.	Mar.	17.	A tract of land formerly in the plantation of Mashpee annexed.
1880.	Mar.	19.	Bounds between Falmouth and Sandwich established.
1885.	June	18.	Bounds between Falmouth and Mashpee established.
1990.	May	15.	Town charter adopted.

Archaic Names of the Municipality:
Sacconeesett, Scipuiszet, Seipuiszet, Suckanesset.

Section/Village Names:
Acapesket, Ashumet Pond, Chapaquoit, Davisville, East End (extinct), East Falmouth, Falmouth Heights, Falmouth Village, Hatchville, Maravista, Megansett, Menauhant, North Falmouth (previously called Neyville), Otis Air Force Base, Quissett, Saconnesset, Silver Beach, Sippiwessett, Teaticket, Waquoit, West Falmouth, Woods Hole.

FITCHBURG, Worcester County.
Established as a town by St 1763-1764, c 30.
Incorporated as a city by St 1872, c 81.

1764.	Feb.	3.	Established as a town, from part of Lunenburg. (Prov. Laws, Vol. IV, p. 685.)
1767.	Mar.	6.	Part included in the new town of Ashby.
1783.	Feb.	26.	Certain land, formerly assessed by Westminster, annexed.
1796.	Feb.	27.	Part annexed to Westminster.
1813.	Feb.	16.	Part annexed to Westminster.
1829.	Mar.	3.	Part annexed to Ashby.

1872.	Mar.	8.	Incorporated as a city.
1872.	Apr.	8.	Act of Mar. 8, 1872, accepted by the town.
1925.	Feb.	24.	Bounds between Fitchburg and Leominster established and part of each place annexed to the other place.
1941.	Feb.	27.	Bounds between Fitchburg and Leominster established and part of each place annexed to the other place.
1941.	Oct.	27.	Act of Feb. 27, 1941, amended.
1941.	Dec.	27.	Act of Feb. 27, 1941, as amended, took effect.
1943.	June	3.	Bounds as established by Act of Feb. 27, 1941, struck out and bounds established between Fitchburg and Leominster and part of each place annexed to the other place.
1943.	June	16.	Act of June 3, 1943, took effect.

Archaic Names of the Municipality:
Turkey Hills.

Section/Village Names:
Cleghorn, Crockerville, East Fitchburg, Jacksonville, Notown, Rollstone Hill, South Fitchburg, Tar Hill, Traskville, Wachusett, Waite's Corner, West Fitchburg.

Florida, Berkshire County.
Incorporated as a town by St 1805, c 15.

1805.	June	15	Incorporated as a town, from "Barnardstone's Grant" and part of "Bullock's Grant."
1848.	May	2.	Part of Clarksburg annexed.
1852.	May	20.	Part annexed to Clarksburg.
1913.	Apr.	10.	Bounds between Florida and Clarksburg established.

Archaic Names of the Municipality:
Barnardstone's Grant, Berkshire Equivalent, Bullock's Grant.

Section/Village Names:
Drury, Hoosac Tunnel Village.

Foxborough, Norfolk County.
Incorporated as a town by St 1778, c 1.

1778.	June	10.	Incorporated as a town, from parts of Stoughton, Stoughtonham, Walpole and Wrentham. (Prov. Laws, Vol. V, p. 875.)
1793.	Mar.	12.	Parts of Sharon and Stoughton annexed and bounds established.
1819.	Feb.	3.	Bounds between Foxborough and Wrentham established.
1831.	Feb.	7. ,	Part of Wrentham annexed.
1833.	Jan.	30.	Bounds between Foxborough and Sharon established and part of each town annexed to the other town.
1833.	Mar.	27.	Part annexed to Walpole.
1834.	Mar.	28.	Part annexed to Walpole.
1850.	Feb.	28.	Part of Sharon annexed.
1903.	May	23.	Bounds between Foxborough and Norfolk and Foxborough and Walpole established.
1937.	Mar.	29.	Bounds between Foxborough and Walpole established.

Section/Village Names:
Davis Corner, Donkeyville, East Foxborough, Foxborough Center, Foxvale, Lakeview, New Maine, New State, North Foxborough, Paineburg, Quaker Hill, South Foxborough, West Foxborough.

Framingham, Middlesex County.
Established as a town by St 1700, c 32.

1675.	Oct.	13.*	Mentioned in the tax act as "Framingham." (Mass. Bay Rec., Vol. V, p. 56.)

1700.	June	24.*	Established as a town - "That the said Plantation called Framingham be from henceforth a Township...." (Prov. Laws, Vol. XXI, p. 701.)
1700.	July	5.*	Certain lands annexed.
1700.	July	11.*	Part of Sherborn annexed.
1701.	July	13.*	Bounds between Framingham and Sudbury established.
1710.	June	16.*	Bounds between Framingham and Sherborn established.
1786.	Mar.	7.	Part annexed to Southborough.
1791.	Feb.	23.	Part annexed to Marlborough.
1833.	Feb.	11.	Part of Holliston annexed.
1846.	Mar.	16.	Part included in the new town of Ashland.
1871.	Apr.	22.	Part of Natick annexed.
1924.	Apr.	12.	Part of Sherborn annexed, if the act is accepted by the town of Sherborn.
1925.	Jan.	1.	Act of April 12, 1924, took effect.

Archaic Names of the Municipality:
Danforth's Farms.

Section/Village Names:
Coburnville, Framingham Center, Hastingsville, Lockerville, Millwood, Montwayte, Nobscot, North Framingham, Park's Corner, Saxonville, South Framingham.

Franklin, Norfolk County.
Incorporated as a town by St 1777-1778, c 21.

1778.	Mar.	2.	Incorporated as a town, from part of Wrentham. (Prov. Laws, Vol. V, p. 775.)
1792.	June	25.	Part of Medway annexed.
1792.	Nov.	13.	Bounds between Franklin and Medway established.
1832.	Feb.	23.	Bounds between Franklin and Bellingham, and Franklin and Medway established.
1839.	Mar.	13.	Bounds between Franklin and Medway established and part annexed to Medway.
1870.	Feb.	23.	Part included in the new town of Norfolk.
1941.	Oct.	9.	Bounds between Franklin and Bellingham established.
1941.	Dec.	9.	Act of October 9, 1941, took effect.
1978.	Apr.	4.	Town charter adopted which established city form of government.

Section/Village Names:
Alpine Place, Martin Park, Mount Section, North Franklin, South Franklin, Unionville, Wadsworth.

Freetown, Bristol County.

1683.	July	—.*	Established as a town, "...the inhabitants of the freemens land att the Fall Riuer, shalbe a townshipp, ... and be henceforth called by the name of Freetowne." (Ply. Col. Rec., Vol. VI, p. 113.)
1694.	June	14.*	**Tiverton** established as a town by St 1694-1695, c 8 from a certain land lying between Little Compton, Freetown and Dartmouth. (Prov. Laws, Vol. I, p. 174.)
1700.	June	17.*	Bounds between Freetown and Tiverton established.
1713.	June	3.*	Bounds between Freetown and Tiverton established.
1747.	Feb.	5.*	Certain parts of Tiverton remaining in this province annexed to Freetown, after settlement of Rhode Island boundry.

1803.   Feb.   26.   Part established as Fall River.
1815.   June   15.   Part annexed to Fairhaven.

Archaic Names of the Municipality:
Assonet, Freemens Land, Tiverton, Wattuppa.

Section/Village Names:
Assonet, Braley's (former R.R. station), Chaoe's, Chase's, Clifford, Crystal Springs Station, East Freetown, Furnace Village, Pleasantville, Terry's.

Gageborough - see Windsor.

GARDNER, Worcester County.
Established as a town by St 1785, c 9.
Incorporated as a city by St 1921, c 119.
1785.   June   27.   Established as a town, from parts of Ashburnham, Templeton, Westminster and Winchendon.
1787.   Mar.   2.   Part annexed to Winchendon.
1794.   Feb.   22.   Part of Wichchendon annexed.
1815.   Feb.   16.   Part annexed to Ashburnham.
1851.   May   24.   Part of Wichchendon annexed.
1908.   Apr.   17.   Bounds between Gardner and Winchendon established.
1908.   Apr.   17.   Bounds between Gardner and Westminster established.
1921.   Mar.   15.   Incorporated as a city.
1922.   Mar.   6.   Act of Mar. 15, 1921, accepted by the town.

Section/Village Names:
Crystal Lake, East Gardner, Gardner Center, Heywoods, South Gardner, Union Square, West Gardner.

Gay Head, Dukes County.
Incorporated as a town by St 1870, c 213.
1855.   Mar.   9.   Bounds between the lands of the Indians of Gay Head and Chilmark to be established.
1856.   May   28.   Bounds between Chilmark and the land of the Indians of Gay Head, as laid out under the resolve of Mar. 9, 1855, confirmed.
1863.   Mar.   30.   Mentioned in this resolve - "... the Indian district of Gay Head...."
1870.   Apr.   30.   Incorporated as a town, formerly the district of Gay Head.
1896.   Mar.   25.   Bounds between Gay Head and Chilmark to be determined.
1897.   Apr.   29.   Bounds between Gay Head and Chilmark established.

Archaic Names of the Municipality:
Gay Head Indian District.

Section/Village Names:
Gay Head Neck.

Georgetown, Essex County.
Incorporated as a town by St 1838, c 160.
1838.   Apr.   21.   Incorporated as a town, from part of Rowley.
1897.   Apr.   15.   Part of Boxford annexed.
1904.   Apr.   22.   Bounds between Georgetown and Boxford established.

Archaic Names of the Municipality:
New Rowley.

Section/Village Names:
Baldpate (station), Byfield Parish, Marlborough, South Georgetown.

Gerry - see Phillipston.

Gill, Franklin County.
Incorporated as a town by St 1793, c 22.

1793.	Sept.	28.	Incorporated as a town, from part of Greenfield.
1795.	Feb.	28.	Part of Northfield annexed.
1805.	Mar.	14.	"Great Island" annexed.
1806.	Apr.	1.	Act of March 14, 1805, took effect.

Section/Village Names:
French King, Great Island, Mount Hermon, Riverside.

GLOUCESTER, Essex County.
Incorporated as a city by St 1873, c 246.

1639.	Mar.	13.*	"Mr. Endecott was willed to send 3 to viewe **Cape Ann**...." (Mass. Bay Rec., Vol. I, p. 253.)
1642.	May	3.*	Bounds between Cape Ann, Ipswich and Jeffries Creek, established.
1642.	May	18.*	"Cape Ann is to bee, called **Gloscester**...." (Mass. Bay Rec., Vol. II, p. 2.)
1672.	May	15.*	Bounds between Gloucester and Manchester established.
1840.	Feb.	27.	Part established as Rockport.
1873.	Apr.	28.	Incorporated as a city.
1873.	May	15.	Act of April 28, 1873, accepted by the town.
1892.	Apr.	19.	Boundary lines in tide water between Gloucester and Essex and Ipswich established.
1902.	May	6.	Bounds between Gloucester and Manchester to be established.
1903.	Aug.	25.	Bounds, as established under act of May 6, 1902, confirmed by the Supreme Judicial Court.
1974.	Nov.	4.	City charter adopted.

Archaic Names of the Municipality:
Cape Ann, Five Pound Island, Gloscester, Tragabigzanda, Vinson's Cove, Wyngaersheek.

Section/Village Names:
Agamenticus Heights, Annisquam, Annisquam (or Riverdale) Willows, Banner Hill, Bass Rocks, Bay View, Biskie (Biskey) Island, Boynton's Island, Brace's Cove, Brier Neck, Clam Alley, Cole's Island, Cranberry Hill, Davis's Neck, Diamond Cove, Dogtown Commons, Dunfudgin, Eastern Point, East Gloucester, Fernwood, Five Points,Folly Cove Village, Fox Hill, Fresh Water Cove Village, Good Harbor, Goose Cove Harbor Village, Head of the Harbor, Heartbreak Hill, Hodgkins' Cove, Joppa, Juniper Point, Kettle Cove, Lanesville, Lobster Cove, Long Beach (part in Rockport), Magnolia, Maplewood Park, Milk Island, Millett's Island, Meetinghouse Hill, Niles Pond, Norman's Woe, Norwood Heights, Pilgrim Hill, Pilot's Hill, Planter's Neck, Plum Cove, Portuguese Hill, Rafe's Chasm, Riverdale, Riverdale Mills, Riverdale Park, Rockholm, Rocky Neck, Rust Island, Samp Porridge Hill, Stacy Boulevard (aka The Boulevard), Stage Fort Park (Fisherman's Field), Starknaught Heights, The Cut, The Fort, Ten Pound Island, Trynall (Trenal) Cove, Twopenny Loaf, Union Hill, Walker's Creek, West Gloucester, Wheeler's Point, Window on the Marsh, Wingaersheek, Winniahdin.

Goshen, Hampshire County.
Incorporated as a town by St 1780, c 38.

1781.	May	14.	Incorporated as a town, from part of Chesterfield and the plantation called "Chesterfield Gore."
1785.	Feb.	9.	Part of Conway annexed.

1789.	June	8.	Part annexed to Chesterfield.
1795.	June	24.	Bounds between Goshen and Chesterfield and Williamsburg established.
1797.	Feb.	7.	Bounds between Goshen and Chesterfield and Williamsburg established.
1810.	Feb.	16.	Bounds between Goshen and Chesterfield and Williamsburg established.

Archaic Names of the Municipality:
Chesterfield, Gore Plantation, Narraganset Township Number Four West.

Section/Village Names:
Batesville, Lithia.

Gosnold, Dukes County.
Incorporated as a town by St 1864, c 97.

1864.	Mar.	17.	Incorporated as a town, from part of Chilmark known as "Elizabeth Islands."

Archaic Names of the Municipality:
Elizabeth Islands.

Section/Village Names:
Bull Island, Cuttyhunk Island, Monohansett Island, Nashawena Island, Naushon Island, Nockset, Nonamesset Island, Pasque Island, Penikese Island, Uncatena Island, Vekatimest Island, Wepecket Island.

Grafton, Worcester County.
Established as a town by St 1734-1735, c 20.

1735.	Apr.	18.*	Established as a town, formerly the plantation at "Hassanamisco". (Prov. Laws, Vol. II, p. 743.)
1737.	June	10.*	Part of Sutton annexed.
1742.	Jan.	9.*	Part of Sutton and Shrewsbury annexed.
1823.	June	14.	Gore of land annexed.
1826.	Mar.	3.	Part of Shrewsbury annexed.
1842.	Mar.	3.	Part of Sutton annexed.
1907.	Feb.	11.	Bounds between Grafton and Worcester established.
1907.	Feb.	11.	Bounds between Grafton and Shrewsbury established.
1907.	Feb.	11.	Bounds between Grafton and Westborough established.
1987.	May	4.	Town charter adopted.

Archaic Names of the Municipality:
A "Praying Indian" (Christian) town, Hassanamisco, Hassanamesit.

Section/Village Names:
Centerville, Farnumsville, Fisherville, Grafton Center, New England, North Grafton, Saundersville, South Grafton.

Granby, Hampshire County.
Incorporated as a town by St 1768, c 2.

1768.	June	11.	Incorporated as a town, from part of South Hadley (Prov. Laws, Vol. IV, p. 1011.)
1781.	June	28.	Bounds between Granby and South Hadley established.
1792.	Mar.	9.	Part of South Hadley annexed.
1824.	June	12.	Bounds between Granby and South Hadley established.
1826.	June	20.	Bounds between Granby and South Hadley established.
1827.	June	16.	Bounds between Granby and South Hadley established.

Section/Village Names:
Cold Hill, Cole Hill, Five Corners, Forge Pond District, Granby Center, Granby Hollow (also know as Aldrich Lake), Ludlow City, Moody Corner, Rock Rimmon, West Parish.

Granville, Hampden County.
Made a town by St 1775-1776, c 3.

1754.	Jan.	25.	Established as the district of Granville from a tract of land called "Bedford". (Prov. Laws, Vol. III, p. 712.)
1775.	Aug.	23.	Made a town, by general act under which districts became towns.
1810.	June	14.	Part established as Tolland.

Archaic Names of the Municipality:
Bedford Plantation, Mathertown.

Section/Village Names:
Beech Hill, Granville Center, East Granville (extinct), North Lane, South Lane, West Granville.

Great Barrington, Berkshire County.
Established as a town by St 1761-1762, c 9.

1761.	June	30.	Established as a town, from part of Sheffield. (Prov. Laws, Vol. IV, p. 465.)
1773.	Feb.	16.	Part included in the new district of Alford.
1773.	Feb.	16.	Lands adjoining annexed.
1777.	Oct.	21.	Part included in the new town of Lee.
1779.	Feb.	11.	Part annexed to Alford.
1819.	Feb.	18.	Part annexed to Alford.
1958.	Apr.	21.	Bounds between Great Barrington and Stockbridge reestablished and part of Stockbridge annexed.

Archaic Names of the Municipality:
Hoplands, Upper Housatonic.

Section/Village Names:
Beartown, Berkshire Heights, Brookside, Egremont Plain, Housatonic, Lake Buel, Monument Valley, Risingdale, Seekonk, Van Deusenville.

Greenfield, Franklin County.
Made a town by St 1775-1776, c 3.

1753.	June	9.	Established as the district of Greenfield from part of Deerfield. (Prov. Laws, Vol. III, p. 671.)
1775.	Aug.	23.	Made a town, by general act under which districts became towns.
1793.	Sept.	28.	Part established as Gill.
1838.	Apr.	14.	Part annexed to Bernardston.
1896.	May	2.	Part of Deerfield known as Cheapside annexed.
1983.	Apr.	4.	Town charter adopted.

Archaic Names of the Municipality:
Deerfield District, Green River, Piconegan.

Section/Village Names:
Cheapside, Country Farms, Factory Hollow, Factory Village, Irish Plains, Log Plain, Lower Meadows, Nash's Mill, Greenfield North Parish, Petty's Plain, Trap Plain, Upper Meadows.

Greenwich, (A Drowned Town) see Hardwick, New Salem, Petersham, and Ware.
Established as a town by St 1753-1754, c 37.

1754.	Apr.	20.	Established as a town, formerly a plantation called Quabin. (Prov. Laws, Vol. III, p. 730.)
1756.	June	9.	Bounds between Greenwich and Hardwick established.
1765.	Feb.	5.	Part of Hardwick annexed.
1765.	Feb.	27.	Part of Belchertown annexed.

1771.	June	22.	Part of Belchertown annexed.
1787.	June	21.	Part of Belchertown annexed.
1801.	Feb.	18.	Part included in the new town of Dana.
1811.	June	19.	Bounds between Greenwich and Dana established.
1816.	Feb.	15.	Part included in the new town of Enfield.
1818.	June	12.	Bounds between Greenwich and Enfield established and part of each town annexed to the other town.
1910.	May	26.	Bounds between Greenwich and Enfield established.
1911.	May	4.	Bounds between Greenwich and Dana established.
1927.	Apr.	26.	All of Greenwich annexed in parts to Hardwick, New Salem, Petersham and Ware.
1938.	Apr.	26.	Act of Apr. 26, 1927, amended.
1938.	Apr.	28.	Act of Apr. 26, 1927, as amended, took effect.

Archaic Names of the Municipality:
Narragansett Number Four, Quabin Plantation, Quobbin.
Section/Village Names:
Greenwich Plains (extinct), Greenwich Village (extinct).

Groton, Middlesex County.

1655.	May	23.*	The Court granted a plantation to be "...called Groaten, ... formerly knowne by the name of Petapawoge...appoynted the select men for the sd towne,...." (Mass. Bay Rec., Vol. III, p. 388.)
1714.	Nov.	2.*	Order that bounds be established between Groton and Nashoba.
1715.	June	14.*	Bounds between Groton and Nashoba established.
1730.	Sept.	10.*	Part annexed to Westford.
1732.	June	29.*	Part included in the new town of Harvard.
1739.	Jan.	4.*	Part annexed to Littleton.
1743.	Feb.	27.*	Bounds between Groton and Littleton established.
1747.	June	8.*	Part annexed to Dunstable.
1752.	Jan.	6.*	Part of Dunstable annexed.
1753.	Jan.	5.	Part established as the district of Shirley.
1753.	Apr.	12.	Part established as the district of Pepperell.
1753.	June	7.	Part annexed to Dunstable.
1793.	Feb.	25.	Part annexed to Dunstable.
1796.	Jan.	26.	Part annexed to Dunstable.
1798.	Feb.	6.	Part annexed to Shirley.
1803.	Feb.	3.	Part of Pepperell annexed.
1803.	June	18.	Part annexed to Dunstable.
1820.	Feb.	15.	Bounds between Groton and Dunstable established.
1857.	May	18.	Part annexed to Pepperell.
1871.	Feb.	14.	Part included in the new town of Ayer.

Archaic Names of the Municipality:
Groaten, Petpauket, Petapawoge, Squnnicook, Wabansconsett.

Section/Village Names:
East Groton, Hollingsworth, Newell, Paper Mill Village, Squannacook Junction, Vose (former R.R. station), West Groton.

Groveland, Essex County.
Incorporated as a town by St 1850, c 62.

1850.	Mar.	8.	Incorporated as a town, from part of Bradford.
1856.	Mar.	21.	Part of Boxford annexed.
1904.	Apr.	22.	Bounds between Groveland and West Newbury established.

Section/Village Names:
Groveland East Parish, Klondike, Norman Hollow, North Groveland, Savaryville, South Groveland.

Hadley, Hampshire County.

1661.	May	22.*	Established as a town. "...ordered by this Court, that the sd toune shall be called Hadley...." formerly the new plantation near Northampton. (Mass. Bay Rec., Vol. IV, Part 2, p. 11.)
1663.	Oct.	21.*	Bounds established.
1664.	May	18.*	One thousand acres of land granted to Hadley.
1670.	May	31.*	Part established as Hatfield.
1673.	May	7.*	Certain lands granted for a new plantation.
1683.	May	16.*	Certain lands granted to Hadley.
1715.	Nov.	25.*	Grant of May 16*, 1683, confirmed.
1740.	Jan.	2.*	Bounds between Hadley and Sunderland established.
1753.	Apr.	12.	Part established as the district of South Hadley.
1759.	Feb.	13.	Part established as the district of Amherst.
1789.	Jan.	15.	Part annexed to Amherst.
1811.	Feb.	28.	Part annexed to Amherst.
1812.	Feb.	18.	Part annexed to Amherst.
1814.	Feb.	17.	Part annexed to Amherst.
1815.	Mar.	1.	Bounds between Hadley and Amherst established and part of each town annexed to the other town.
1850.	Apr.	15.	Part annexed to Northampton.

Archaic Names of the Municipality:
Hockanum, Norwottuck.

Section/Village Names:
East Hadley, Fort River, Hart's Brook, Hockanum, Lawrence Plains, North Hadley, Plainville, Russellville.

Halifax, Plymouth County.
Established as a town by St 1734-1735, c 9.

1734.	July	4.*	Established as a town, from parts of Middleborough, Pembroke and Plympton. (Prov. Laws, Vol. II, p. 717.)
1824.	Feb.	20.	Part of Bridgewater annexed.
1831.	Mar.	16.	Part of Plympton annexed.
1857.	Apr.	11.	Part annexed to East Bridgewater and bounds established.
1863.	Feb.	6.	Bounds between Halifax and Plympton established and part of each town annexed to the other town.

Archaic Names of the Municipality:
Monponsett.

Section/Village Names:
Halifax Station, Monponsett, South Halifax.

Hamilton, Essex County.
Incorporated as a town by St 1793, c 10.

1793.	June	21.	Incorporated as a town, from that part of Ipswich known as "Ipswich Hamlet".
1896.	June	5.	Bounds between Hamilton and Ipswich established and part of each town annexed to the other town.
1904.	Mar.	12.	Bounds between Hamilton and Ipswich established.
1904.	Mar.	12.	Bounds between Hamilton and Essex established.
1905.	May	1.	Bounds between Hamilton and Wenham established.

Archaic Names of the Municipality:
Ipswich Hamlet.

Section/Village Names:
Asbury Grove, Idlewood Lake, Miles River, Mosquito Village, South Hamilton, Willowdale, Woodbury.

Hampden, Hampden County.
Incorporated as a town by St 1878, c 88.
    1878.   Mar.   28.   Incorporated as a town, from part of Wilbraham.

Section/Village Names:
Hampden Center, Scantic.

Hancock, Berkshire County.
Established as a town by St 1776-1777, c 3.
    1776.   July   2.   Established as a town, formerly the plantation called
        "Jericho". (Prov. Laws, Vol. V, p. 550.)
    1798.   June   25.   Part of Hancock annexed to the district of New Ashford.
    1851.   May   20.   Bounds between Hancock and New Ashford established.

Archaic Names of the Municipality:
Jericho Plantation.

Section/Village Names:
Goodrich Hollow, Hancock Village, Lebanon Springs, North Hancock, Shaker
Village.

Hanover, Plymouth County.
Established as a town by St 1727, c 14.
    1727.   June   14.*   Established as a town, from parts of Abington and Scituate.
        (Prov. Laws, Vol. II, p. 429.)
    1835.   Mar.   6.   Bounds between Hanover and Pembroke established.
    1857.   May   15.   Bounds between Hanover and South Scituate established.
    1878.   Feb.   11.   Bounds between Hanover and South Scituate established
        and part of each town annexed to the other town.
    1787.   Mar.   23.   Bounds between Hanover and Rockland established and
        part of each town annexed to the other town.
    1885.   Apr.   23.   Bounds between Hanover and Pembroke established.

Section/Village Names:
Assinippi, Curtis Crossing, Drinkwater, Hanover Center, Hanover Four Corners,
Mann's Corner, North Hanover, South Hanover, West Hanover, Winslow's
Crossing.

Hanson, Plymouth County.
Incorporated as a town by St 1870, c 272.
    1820.   Feb.   22.   Incorporated as a town, from part of Pembroke.
    1903.   Apr.   3.   Bounds between Hanson and Pembroke established.

Archaic Names of the Municipality:
Pembroke West Parish.

Section/Village Names:
Bryantville, Burrage, Gurney's Corners, Indian Head Pond, Monponsett, New State,
North Hanson, South Hanson, Sodom.

Hardwick, Worcester County.
Established as a town by 1738-1739, c 18.
    1739.   Jan.   10.*   Established as a town, formerly the plantation called
        "Lambstown". (Prov. Laws, Vol. II, p. 971.)
    1751.   Jan.   31.*   Part of Hardwick included in the district of New Braintree.
    1756.   June   9.   Bounds between Hardwick and Greenwich established.
    1765.   Feb.   5.   Part annexed to Greenwich.
    1801.   Feb.   18.   Part included in the new town of Dana.
    1814.   June   10.   Part of New Braintree annexed.
    1831.   Feb.   7.   Gore of unincorporated land annexed.
    1833.   Feb.   6.   Land called "Hardwick Gore" annexed.
    1842.   Feb.   4.   Part annexed to Dana.
    1927.   Apr.   26.   Part of Greenwich annexed.
    1938.   Apr.   26.   Act of Apr. 26, 1927, amended.

1938.   Apr.   28.   Act of Apr. 26, 1927, as amended, took effect.

Archaic Names of the Municipality:
Hardwick Gore, Lambstown Plantation.

Section/Village Names:
Creamery, Furnace, Gilbertville, Hardwick Village, Old Furnace, Smith Crossing
Station, Wheelwright (former R.R. station also called Hardwick Depot).

Harvard, Worcester County.
Established as a town by St 1732-1733, c 4.

1732.	June	29.*	Established as a town, from parts of Groton, Lancaster and Stow. (Prov. Laws, Vol. II, p. 644.)
1783.	Feb.	25.	Part included in the new district of Boxborough.
1906.	June	14.	Bounds between Harvard and Littleton established.
1906.	June	14.	Bounds between Harvard and Boxborough established.

Section/Village Names:
Bare Hill, Harvard Center, North Still River, Oak Hill, Old Mill, Pleasant Lake,
Shaboken, Shaker Village, Single Tax, Still River.

Harwich, Barnstable County.
Established as a town by St 1694-1695, c 13.

1694.	Sept.	14.*	Established as a town, formerly a tract of land called "Satuckett". (Prov. Laws, Vol. I, p. 181.)
1772.	July	14.	Part annexed to Eastham.
1803.	Feb.	9.	Part established as Brewster, with a proviso that certain estates of remonstrants be allowed to remain in Harwich.
1811.	June	21.	The Daniel Rogers estate in Harwich annexed to Brewster.
1848.	Apr.	25.	Part of Brewster annexed.
1862.	Apr.	4.	Bounds between Harwich and Orleans established.
1862.	Apr.	14.	Bounds between Harwich and Chatham established.
1945.	July	12.	Bounds between Harwich and Dennis established.
1947.	May	8.	Act of July 12, 1945, amended and bounds between Harwich and Dennis established.

Archaic Names of the Municipality:
Satuckett.

Section/Village Names:
East Harwich, Harwich Center, Harwichport, North Harwich, Pleasant Lake, South
Harwich, West Harwich.

Hatfield, Hampshire County.

1670.	May	31.*	Established as a town, "...and that this toune be called Hattfeilds", from part of Hadley. (Mass. Bay Rec., Vol. IV, Part 2, p. 460.)
1672.	Oct.	9.*	Bounds established.
1695.	Nov.	16.*	Certain tract of land annexed.
1720.	Nov.	12.*	Bounds between Hatfield and Northampton established.
1771.	Apr.	24.	Part established as Whately.
1771.	Apr.	24.	Part included in the new district of Williamsburg.
1845.	Mar.	14.	Bounds between Hatfield and Williamsburg established and part of each town annexed to the other town.
1846.	Mar.	19.	Bounds between Hatfield and Williamsburg established and part of each town annexed to the other town.

Archaic Names of the Municipality:
Hattfeilds, Norwottuck.

Section/Village Names:
Bradstreet, North Hatfield, Riverside, West Brook, West Hatfield.

HAVERHILL, Essex County.
Incorporated as a city by St 1869, c 61.

1641.	June	2.*	Certain men appointed "... to set out the bounds between Salsberry & Pantucket ali: Haverell. They are to determine the bounds" to be enjoyed as " a towne or village." (Mass. Bay Rec., Vol. I, p. 319.)
1643.	May	10.*	"The whole plantation...is divided into four sheires....." The name of Haverhill appears in one of the shires. (Mass. Bay Rec., Vol. II, p. 38.)
1650.	May	23.*	An island in the Merrimack River granted to Haverhill unless anyone proves a clear title to it within three years.
1651.	Oct.	30.*	Haverhill bounds established.
1654.	Nov.	1.*	Bounds between Haverhill and Salisbury established.
1664.	May	18.*	Bounds between Haverhill and "lands of Maj Gen'l Dennison established". (Mass. Bay Rec., Vol. IV, Part 2, p. 105.)
1667.	May	15.*	Bounds between Haverhill and Salisbury-new-town established.
1675.	May	12.*	Haverhill bounds established.
1675.	Oct.	13.*	Bradford is mentioned in the Tax Act. (Mass. Bay Rec., Vol. V, p. 56.)
1701.	Feb.	24.*	The boundary line "...agreed to by the Town of Rowley upon their setting off and alloting out of Merrimack Land (so called) being originally part of their Township, now Bradford." confirmed. (Prov. Laws, Vol. XXI, p. 715.)
1725.	Dec.	8.*	Part of Haverhill included in the new town of Methuen.
1850.	Mar.	8.	Part of Bradford established as Groveland.
1869.	Mar.	10.	Haverhill incorporated as a city.
1869.	May	15.	Act of Mar. 10, 1869, accepted by the town.
1896.	May	4.	Bradford annexed to Haverhill if the act is accepted by both places.
1896.	Nov.	3.	Act of May 4, 1896, accepted by Haverhill and Bradford.
1897.	Jan.	4.	Act of May 4, 1896, took effect.

Archaic Names of the Municipality:
Bradford, Haverall, Merrimack Land (early name for Bradford), Pentucket, Rowley Village on the Merrimack (early name for Bradford).

Section/Village Names:
Ayers Village, Bradford, Brickett Hill, Dustin Square, East Haverhill, Haverhill East Parish, Frye's Corner, Highlands, Island Park, Millvale, Mount Washington, Haverhill North Parish, Paper Mills (former R.R. station), Riverside, Rocks Village (also known as Ricka Village), Rosemont, Sanders Hill, Tilton's Corner, Walnut Square, Ward Hill, Haverhill West Parish, Winnikenni Park.

Hawley, Franklin County.
Incorporated as a town by St 1791, c 25.

1792.	Feb.	6.	Incorporated as a town, formerly the plantation called "Number Seven".
1793.	Mar.	9.	Portion of Plantation Number Seven inadvertenly omitted in the description of the bounds in the act of Feb. 6, 1792, now annexed.
1803.	June	21.	Part annexed to the district of Plainfield.

Archaic Names of the Municipality:
Plantation Number Seven (1762 Townships).

Section/Village Names:
Bozrah, Doane, Dodge Corner, East Hawley, Fullerville, Hallockville, King Corner, Pudding Hollow, South Hawley, West Hawley, West Hill.

Heath, Franklin County.
Incorporated as a town by St 1784, c 39.

1785.	Feb.	14.	Incorporated as a town, from a certain tract of land called "Green and Walker's land" and part of Charlemont.

Archaic Names of the Municipality:
Fort Shirley, Green and Walkers's Land.

Section/Village Names:
Burnt Hill, Cyrus, Dell, Heath Center, North Heath.

Hingham, Plymouth County.

1634.	Sept.	25.*	**Barecove** mentioned in the tax act.

(Mass. Bay Rec, Vol. I, p. 129.)

1635.	July	8.*	Bounds between Barecove and Wessaguscus to be set out.
1635.	Sept.	2.*	"The name of Barecove is changed & hereafter to be called **Hingham.**" (Mass. Bay Rec., Vol. I, p. 156.)
1635.	Sept.	3.*	Bounds between Hingham and Weymouth established.
1640.	May	13.*	Land at "Conihasset" granted to Hingham.
1770.	Apr.	26.	Part established as the district of Cohasset.
1861.	Mar.	21.	Bounds between Hingham and Abington established.
1897.	Apr.	30.	Bounds between Hingham and Cohasset established.
1897.	Apr.	30.	Bounds between Hingham and Scituate established.
1897.	Apr.	30.	Bounds between Hingham and Norwell established.
1928.	Mar.	23.	Bounds between Hingham and Cohasset re-established.

Archaic Names of the Municipality:
Barecove, Conihassett.

Section/Village Names:
Broad Cove, Crow Point, East Hingham, Fort Hill, Hingham Center, Liberty Plain, Lower Plain, Mount Blue, Nantasket Junction, Naval Magazine, Old Colony Hill, Power Station, Prospect Hill, Queen Anne's Corner, Rocky Nook, South Hingham, U.S. Naval Air Station, Upper Plains, Weir River, West Hingham, World's End.

Hinsdale, Berkshire County.
Incorporated as a town by St 1804, c 7.

1804.	June	21.	Incorporated as a town, from parts of Partridgefield and Dalton.
1912.	Feb.	28.	Bounds between Hinsdale and Peru established.

Holbrook, Norfolk County.
Incorporated as a town by St 1872, c 61.

1872.	Feb.	29.	Incorporated as a town, from part of Randolph.
1889.	Apr.	16.	Part annexed to Avon.
1903.	Mar.	11.	Bounds between Holbrook and Braintree established.

Section/Village Names:
Brookville, Holbrook Center, Holbrook Gardens, Turkey Hill.

Holden, Worcester County.
Established as a town by St 1740-1741, c 16.

1741.	Jan.	9.*	Established as a town, from part of Worcester called "North Worcester". (Prov. Laws, Vol. II, p. 1043.)
1793.	Mar.	27.	Bounds between Holden and Paxton established.
1804.	Feb.	13.	Part annexed to Paxton.
1808.	Jan.	30.	Part included in the new town of West Boylston.
1831.	Mar.	19.	Part of Paxton annexed.

1838.   Apr.   9.   Part annexed to Paxton.
1906.   Mar.   13.   Bounds between Holden and Paxton established.
Section/Village Names:
Chaffinville (also called Chaffin or Chaffins), Dawson, Eagleville (also known as
Brick City), Holden Center, Jefferson (also called Jeffersonville formerly
Drydensville), Lovellville, North Woods (also known as Ruralville), Quinapoxet,
Springdale, Uniondale, Unionville, Winter Hill.

Holland, Hampden County.
Made a town by Revised Statutes c 15, Sect. 9.
1783.   July   5.   Incorporated as the district of Holland from part of South
                       Brimfield.
1796.   Feb.   8.   Bounds between district of Holland and South Brimfield
                       established.
1835.   Nov.   4.   Made a town, formerly the district of Holland. (Revised
                       Statutes.)
1836.   May   1.   Act of Nov. 4, 1835, took effect.

Holliston, Middlesex County.
Established as a town by St 1724-1725, c 13.
1724.   Dec.   3.*   Established as a town, from part of "Sherburn". (Prov. Laws,
                       Vol. II, p. 340.)
1744.   Dec.   22.* Bounds between Holliston and Hopkinton established.
1781.   Apr.   28.   Part of Hopkinton annexed.
1829.   Mar.   3.   Bounds between Holliston and Medway established and
                       part of each town annexed to the other town.
1833.   Feb.   11.   Part annexed to Framingham.
1835.   Mar.   27.   Part annexed to Milford and bounds between Holliston,
                       Hopkinton and Milford established.
1846.   Mar.   16.   Part included in the new town of Ashland.
1859.   Apr.   1.   Bounds between Holliston and Milford established.
Section/Village Names:
Braggville, East Holliston, Holliston Center, Metcalf.

HOLYOKE, Hampden County.
Incorporated as a town by St 1850, c 71.
Incorporated as a city by St 1873, c 154.
1850.   Mar.   14.   Incorporated as a town, from part of West Springfield.
1873.   Apr.   7.   Incorporated as a city.
1873.   May   29.   Act of Apr. 7, 1873, accepted by the town.
1909.   June   9.   Part of Northampton annexed.
Section/Village Names:
Brightside, Churchill, Depot Hill (extinct), Elmwood, Ewingville (extinct),
Goodyear Park, Hasting's Heights (extinct), Highland Park, Highlands, Ingleside,
Ireland Parish (extinct), Maple Terrace (extinct), Money Hole Hill (extinct), Oakdale,
Riverside (extinct), Rock Valley, Smith's Ferry, Springdale, The Flats, West Holyoke,
Wyckoff Park.

Hopedale, Worcester County.
Incorporated as a town by St 1886, c 126.
1886.   Apr.   7.   Incorporated as a town, from part of Milford.
Section/Village Names:
South Hopedale, Spindleville.

Hopkinton, Middlesex County.
Incorporated as a town by St 1715-1716, c 136.

1715.	Dec.	13.*	Incorporated as a town, from "a tract of land call'd Moguncoy" and "a Quantity of Country Land adjoining...." (Prov. Laws, Vol. IX, p. 440.)
1735.	June	14.*	Part included in the new town of Upton.
1744.	Dec.	22.*	Bounds between Hopkinton and Holliston established.
1781.	Apr.	28.	Part annexed to Holliston.
1808.	Mar.	8.	Part annexed to Upton.
1835.	Mar.	27.	Part annexed to Milford, part of Milford annexed and bounds between Hopkinton, Holliston, and Milford established.
1846.	Mar.	16.	Part included in the new town of Ashland.
1853.	Apr.	28.	Part of Ashland to be annexed upon payment of a certain sum of money by Hopkinton.
1853.	May	2.	Act of Apr. 28, 1853, took effect.
1907.	May	16.	Bounds between Hopkinton and Milford established.
1907.	May	16.	Bounds between Hopkinton and Upton established.
1962.	July	25.	Bounds between Hopkinton, Milford and Upton established.

Archaic Names of the Municipality:
A "Praying Indian" (Christian) town, Moguncoy, Maguncook.

Section/Village Names:
Claflinville, Hayden Row, Woodville.

Hubbardston, Worcester County.
Made a town by St 1775-1776, c 3.

1767.	June	13.	Incorporated into a district by the name of Hubbardston, from part of Rutland. (Prov. Laws, Vol. IV, p. 953.)
1775.	Aug.	23.	Made a town, by general act under which districts became towns.
1810.	Feb.	16.	Part annexed to Princeton.

Section/Village Names:
Catville, East Hubbardston, Hubbardston Station, Hygienic Blanket Mills, Nicholsville, Pitcherville, Pontville, Williamsville.

Hudson, Middlesex County.
Incorporated as a town by St 1866, c 82.

1866.	Mar.	19.	Incorporated as a town, from parts of Marlborough and Stow.
1868.	Mar.	20.	Part of Bolton annexed.
1905.	May	1.	Bounds between Hudson and Berlin established.
1905.	May	24.	Bounds between Hudson and Stow established.
1971.	Mar.	29.	Town charter adopted.
1979.	July	23.	Bounds between Hudson and Stow revised.

Archaic Names of the Municipality:
Mills, Feltonville.

Section/Village Names:
Coolidgeville, Cove Landing, Gleason Junction Station, Gospel Hill, Gravesville, Lincoln Park, Mirror Lake, Ordway, Wilkinsville.

Hull, Plymouth County.

| 1644. | May | 29.* | "It is ordered, that Nantascot shall be called Hull." (Mass. Bay Rec., Vol. II. p. 74.) |
| 1647. | May | 26.* | Certain qualified men authorized to "...carry on ye affaires of ye town...." (Mass. Bay Rec., Vol. II, p. 189.) |

1662.   May   7.*   "...Bruisters Islands...adjudged by this Court to belong to the
                        toune of Hull...." (Mass. Bay Rec.,Vol. IV, Part 2, p. 56.)
1663.   June   12.* "...Breusters Islands...knoune by the name of Brewsters
                        Islands, doe of right belong unto the inhabitants of Hull."
                        (Mass. Bay Rec., Vol. IV, Part 2, p.81.)

Archaic Names of the Municipality:
Nantascot.

Section/Village Names:
Allerton, Atlantic Hill, Bayside, Bumkin Island, Calf Island, Centre Hill, Great
Brewster, Green Hill, Green Island, Gun Rock, Hampton Hill, Hull Beach, Hull
Village, Jerry's Island, Kenberma, Little Brewster Middle Brewster, Nantasket,
Nantasket Beach, Narrows Light, Outer Brewster, Park Island, Peddock's Island,
Pemberton, Rockland Hill, Sagamore Hill, Stoney Beach, Strawberry Hill, Sunset
Point, Surfside, The Graves, Waveland, Whitehead, Willow Ledge, Windemere.

Huntington, Hampshire County.
Norwich made a town by St 1775-1776, c 3.
1773.   June   29.   Norwich established as a district from part of Murrayfield.
1775.   Aug.   23.   **Norwich** made a town, by general act under which districts
                        became towns.
1780.   Nov.   28.   Part of Norwich included in the new town of Montgomery.
1781.   Nov.   28.   Part of Murrayfield annexed to Norwich.
1792.   Mar.   6.   Part of Norwich annexed to Montgomery.
1794.   Feb.   22.   Part of Norwich annexed to Chesterfield.
1853.   May   25.   Part of Blandford and Chester annexed to Norwich.
1855.   Mar.   9.   The name of the town of Norwich changed to **Huntington.**

Archaic Names of the Municipality:
Norwich, Murrayfield.

Section/Village Names:
Birchville, Goss Hill, Huntsville, Indian Hollow, Knightville, Laurel Hill, North
Bridge, Norwich Bridge, Norwich Hill.

Huntstown - see Ashfield.

Hutchinson - see Barre.

Hyde Park - see Boston.
Incorporated as a town by St 1868, c 139.
1868.   Apr.   22.   Incorporated as a town, from parts of Dedham, Dorchester
                        and Milton.
1868.   May   1.   Act of Apr. 22, 1868, amended and bounds established.
1898.   Apr.   1.   Bounds between Hyde Park and Boston established.
1911.   May   24.   Hyde Park annexed to Boston.
1911.   June   22.   Act of May 24, 1911, amended.
1911.   Nov.   7.   Act of May 24, 1911, as amended, accepted by Hyde Park
                        and Boston.
1912.   Jan.   1.   Act of May 24, 1911, as amended, took effect.

Ipswich, Essex County.
1634.   Aug.   5.*   "It is ordered, that Aggawam shalbe called Ipswitch." (Mass.
                        Bay Rec., Vol. I, p. 123.)
1642.   May   3.*   Bounds between Ipswich, Cape Ann, and Jeffries Creeke
                        established.
1648.   Oct.   18.* Part of Ipswich called"the village at the newe medowes"
                        named "Toppesfield."
1649.   May   4.*   Two-fifths of Plum Island granted to Ipswich.

1694.	Feb.	28.*	Bounds between Ipswich and Topsfield established.
1774.	Feb.	16.	Part annexed to Topsfield.
1785.	Nov.	29.	Part annexed to Rowley.
1793.	June	21.	Part established as Hamilton.
1819.	Feb.	15.	Part established as Essex.
1846.	Mar.	7.	Part annexed to Boxford.
1892.	Apr.	19.	Boundary lines in tide-water between Ipswich and Essex, and Ipswich and Gloucester established.
1896.	June	5.	Bounds between Ipswich and Hamilton established and part of each town annexed to the other town.
1904.	Mar.	12.	Bounds between Ipswich and Hamilton established.
1904.	Mar.	19.	Bounds between Ipswich and Rowley established.

Archaic Names of the Municipality:
Aggawam.

Section/Village Names:
Appletons, Argilla, Candlewood, Ipswich Village, Line Brook Village, Little Neck, Plum Island, The Bluffs, Willowdale.

Jeffryes Creeke - see Manchester and Salem.

Kingston, Plymouth County.
Established as a town by St 1726-1727, c 8.

1726.	June	16.*	Established as a town, from the "North Precinct" of Plymouth, (which also included parts of Duxbury, Pembroke and Plympton.) (Prov. Laws, Vol. II, p. 387.)
1857.	Apr.	14.	Part of Duxbury annexed.

Archaic Names of the Municipality:
Jones River Parish, Plymouth North Precinct.

Section/Village Names:
Blackwater, Crossman Pond, Holmes Mill Pond, Indian Pond Village, Kingston Center, Plympton Depot, Reed's Pond, Rocky Nook, Seaside, Silver Lake, Smith's Lane, Stony Brook, The Hill, Wapping.

Lakeville, Plymouth County.
Incorporated as a town by St 1853, c 338.

1853.	May	13.	Incorporated as a town, from part of Middleborough.
1867.	June	1.	Bounds between Lakeville and Taunton established.

Archaic Names of the Municipality:
Assawampsit.

Section/Village Names:
Beechwoods, Howlands, Lakeside, North Lakeville, Precinct, Turnpike, Upper Four Corners.

Lancaster, Worcester County.
The record is confusing in regard to Nashaway, which appears to have been made Prescott, West Towne and Lancaster all under date of May 18,* 1653.

1653.	May	18.*	Established as a town, on petition "...of the inhabitants of Nashaway... Court doth graunt them the libertje of a touneship...." (Mass. Bay Rec., Vol. IV, Part I, p. 139.)
1653.	May	18.*	"...this Court doth order the plantation at Nashaway... about the name of the towne, that the name of it be henceforth called Lancaster...." (Mass. Bay Rec., Vol. III, p. 302.)
1653.	May	18.*	"Considinge that there is already at Nashaway about 9 familyes ... this court doth hereby giue & grant them Libertyes of a townshipp ...to be called Prescott." (Mass. Bay Rec., Vol. III, p. 302.)

1653.	May	18.*	"This Court, taking the condition of Nashaway into further consideration, doe order, that it shallbe called henceforth West Towne...." (Mass. Bay Rec., Vol. III, p. 303.)
1654.	May	14.*	"...itt is ordered, that the inhabitants of Lancaster haue those libertjes of a touneship that the laws allow...." and the bounds be laid out. (Mass. Bay Rec., Vol. IV, Part I, p. 189.)
1672.	Oct.	11.*	Bounds established.
1713.	June	5.*	Additional lands granted to Lancaster.
1720.	Dec.	2.*	Certain bounds established.
1721.	June	17.	Certain bounds established.
1732.	June	29.*	Part included in the new town of Harvard.
1738.	June	24.*	Part established as Bolton.
1740.	June	23.*	Part established as Leominster.
1762.	Sept.	17.	Part annexed to Shrewsbury.
1768.	Feb.	27.	Part of Shrewsbury annexed.
1781.	Feb.	26.	Part annexed to Shrewsbury.
1781.	Apr.	25.	Part established as Sterling.
1791.	Feb.	8.	Part annexed to Berlin.
1793.	Mar.	12.	Bounds between Lancaster and Sterling established.
1837.	Mar.	7.	Part annexed to Sterling and bounds between Lancaster and Sterling established.
1850.	Mar.	14.	Part established as Clinton.
1906.	May	7.	Bounds between Lancaster and Leominster established.
1908.	Apr.	21.	Bounds between Lancaster and Sterling established.

Archaic Names of the Municipality:
Chockett, Nashaway, Nashwash, Prescott, Weshakim, West Towne.

Section/Village Names:
Ballard Hill, Deershorn, Four Corners, Four Ponds, George Hill, Lancaster Center, North Village, Old Common, Poniken, South Lancaster, Thayer.

Lanesborough, Berkshire County.
Established as a town by St 1765-1766, c 14.

1765.	June	21.	Established as a town, formerly the plantation called "New Framingham". (Prov. Laws, Vol. IV, p. 815.)
1793.	Mar.	14.	Part included in the new town of Cheshire.

Archaic Names of the Municipality:
New Framingham Plantation, Richfield.

Section/Village Names:
Balance Rock, Berkshire Village, Brennon's Hill, Constitution Hill, Gunn's Grove, Lanesborough Village, Pontoosuc Lake, Prospect Hill.

LAWRENCE, Essex County.
Incorporated as a town by St 1847, c 190.
Incorporated as a city by St 1853, c 70.

1847.	Apr.	17.	Incorporated as a town, from parts of Andover and Methuen.
1853.	Mar.	21.	Incorporated as a city.
1853.	Mar.	29.	Act of Mar. 21, 1853, accepted by the town.
1854.	Apr.	4.	Part of Methuen annexed.
1879.	Feb.	4.	Part of Andover and North Andover annexed.
1930.	Apr.	30.	Part of Methuen annexed.
1930.	May	12.	Act of Apr. 30, 1930, accepted by Methuen.
1930.	June	2.	Act of Apr. 30, 1930, accepted by the city.
1946.	May	18.	Part annexed to Methuen.

1947. Mar. 19. Act of May 18, 1946, accepted by Methuen.
1947. June 20. Act of May 18, 1946, accepted by the city.
1972. June 29. Bounds between Lawrence and North Andover changed and established.
1983. Oct. 17. City charter adopted.

Section/Village Names:
Arlington District, Carltonville, Chapinsville, Hallsville, North Lawrence, South Lawrence, Tower Hill.

Lee, Berkshire County.
Incorporated as a town by St 1777-1778, c 11.
1777. Oct. 21. Incorporated as a town, from part of Great Barrington known as "Hoplands", the "Glassworks Grant", and part of Washington and part of "Williams Grant". (Prov. Laws, Vol. V, p. 739.)
1806. Mar. 7. Bounds between Lee and Lenox established.
1806. Mar. 7. Part of Washington annexed and boundary line between Lee and Washington established.
1820. Feb. 7. Bounds between Lee and Lenox established.

Archaic Names of the Municipality:
Glassworks Grant, Hoplands, Larabee, Willams Grant.

Section/Village Names:
Bear Town, Dodgetown (extinct), East Lee, Larabee, North Lee (extinct), South Lee, The Huddle (extinct), Watson (later called Hartwood).

Leicester, Worcester County.
Established as a town by St 1713-1714, c 137.
1714. Feb. 15.* Established as a town in an order confirming to several persons a certain tract of land called "Towtaid". (Prov. Laws, Vol. XXI, p. 836.)
1714. Feb. 16.* Order to lay out the Township of Leicester. (Prov. Laws, Vol. XXI, p. 837.)
1714. June 19.* Order of Feb. 16,* 1714 accepted and confirmed. (Prov. Laws, Vol. XXI, p. 850.)
1722. June 14.* Order confirming the powers of a town. (Prov. Laws, Vol. X, p. 167.)
1730. Sept. 11.* Bounds between Leicester and Brookfield established.
1753. Apr. 12. Part made the district of Spencer.
1758. June 2. Part annexed to Worcester.
1765. Feb. 12. Part included in the new district of Paxton.
1778. Apr. 10. The parish lately set off from Leicester and other towns established as Ward.

Archaic Names of the Municipality:
Strawberry Hill, Towtaid.

Section/Village Names:
Brick City, Cherry Valley, Greenville, Manville, Rochdale, Rock, Woodville.

Lenox, Berkshire County.
Made a town by St 1775-1776, c 3.
1767. Feb. 26. Incorporated as a separate district by the name of Lenox, from part of Richmont.
1770. Nov. 20. Lands adjoining annexed.
1772. Apr. 25. Certain estates set off from the district of Lenox and annexed to Richmont.

1775.	Aug.	23.	Made a town, by general act under which districts became towns.
1795.	Jan.	31.	Part of Washington annexed.
1802.	Feb.	18.	Part of Washington annexed.
1806.	Mar.	7.	Bounds between Lenox and Lee established.
1820.	Feb.	7.	Bounds between Lenox and Lee established.

Archaic Names of the Municipality:
Yokum.

Section/Village Names:
Lenox Dale, Lenox Furnace (extinct), New Lenox.

LEOMINSTER, Worcester County.
Established as a town by St 1740-1741, c 7.
Incorporated as a city by St 1915, c 338.

1740.	June	23.*	Established as a town, from part of Lancaster. (Prov. Laws, Vol. II, p. 1023.)
1838.	Apr.	13.	Part of unincorporated lands called "No Town" annexed.
1906.	May	7.	Bounds between Leominster and Lancaster established.
1915.	May	13.	Incorporated as a city.
1915.	Nov.	2.	Act of May 13, 1915, accepted by the town.
1925.	Feb.	24.	Bounds between Leominster and Fitchburg established and part of each place annexed to the other place.
1941.	Feb.	27.	Bounds between Leominster and Fitchburg established and part of each place annexed to the other place.
1941.	Oct.	27.	Act of Feb. 27, 1941, amended.
1941.	Dec.	27.	Act of Feb. 27, 1941, as amended, took effect.
1943.	June	3.	Bounds established by act of Feb. 27, 1941, struck out, and bounds established between Leominster and Fitchburg, and part of each place annexed to the other place.
1943.	June	16.	Act of June 3, 1943, took effect.
1969.	Nov.	4.	City charter adopted.

Archaic Names of the Municipality:
Lancaster New Grant, No Town.

Section/Village Names:
Gates Crossing, Leominister Center, Morse Hollow, North Leominister, South End, West Leominister, Whalom Park.

Leverett, Franklin County.
Incorporated as a town by St 1773-1774, c 19.

| 1774. | Mar. | 5. | Incorporated as a town, from part of Sunderland. (Prov. Laws, Vol. V, p. 327.) |

Section/Village Names:
Dudleyville, East Leverett, Long Plain, Moores Corner, North Leverett, Slab City, South Leverett.

Lexington, Middlesex County.
Established as a town by St 1712-1713, c 143.

1713.	Mar.	20.*	Established as a town, from part of Cambridge known by the name of the "Northern Precinct". (Prov. Laws, Vol. XXI, p. 813.)
1754.	Apr.	19.	Part included in the new town of Lincoln.
1768.	June	9.	Part annexed to Bedford.
1800.	Jan.	20.	Part of Burlington annexed.
1853.	Feb.	28.	Bounds between Lexington and Lincoln established.

1895.	Apr.	4.	Bounds between Lexington and Waltham located and defined.
1954.	Feb.	16.	Bounds between Lexington and Winchester established.
1964.	Mar.	24.	Bounds between Lexington and Winchester established.

Archaic Names of the Municipality:
Cambridge Farms, Cambridge Northern Precinct.

Section/Village Names:
East Lexington, Munroe, North Lexington, Pierce's Bridge.

Leyden, Franklin County.
Incorporated as a town by St 1809, c 135.

1784.	Mar.	12.	Established as a district by the name of Leyden, from part of Bernardston.
1809.	Feb.	22.	Incorporated as a town, formerly the district of Leyden.
1886.	May	7.	Part annexed to Bernardston upon acceptance of the act by Bernardston.
1886.	June	7.	Act of May 7, 1886, accepted by Bernardston.
1911.	Apr.	24.	Bounds between Leyden and Colrain established.

Section/Village Names:
Beaver Meadow, East Hill, Leyden Center, South Leyden, West Leyden.

Lincoln, Middlesex County.
Established as a town by St 1753-1754, c 35.

| 1754. | Apr. | 19. | Established as a town, from parts of Concord, Lexington and Weston. (Prov. Laws, Vol. III, p. 728.) |
| 1853. | Feb. | 28. | Bounds between Lincoln and Lexington established. |

Section/Village Names:
Lincoln Center, North Lincoln, South Lincoln.

Litchfield - see Dunstable.

Little Compton - see Dartmouth. (Ceded to Rhode Island in 1747.)

Littleton, Middlesex County.
Established as a town by St 1715-1716, c 126.

1698.	Nov.	29.*	Nashoba mentioned as a tract of land for a township. (Prov. Laws, Vol. XXI, p. 689.)
1714.	Nov.	2.*	Order making **Nashoba** and adjoining lands a township and that bounds be established between Nashoba and Groton.
1715.	June	14.*	Bounds between Nashoba and Groton established.
1715.	Dec.	3.*	Established as a town. "Ordered that the name of the Township be henceforth called **Littleton**." (Prov. Laws, Vol. IX, p. 435.)
1725.	Nov.	23.*	Parts of Chelmsford and Concord annexed.
1739.	Jan.	4.*	Part of Groton annexed.
1743.	Feb.	27.*	Bounds between Littleton and Groton established.
1783.	Feb.	25.	Part included in the new district of Boxborough.
1794.	Feb.	20.	Bounds between Littleton and Boxborough established.
1890.	Apr.	30.	Bounds between Littleton and Boxborough established.
1906.	June	14.	Bounds between Littleton and Harvard established.
1906.	June	15.	Bounds between Littleton and Boxborough established.

Archaic Names of the Municipality:
Nashoba, A "Praying Indian" (Christian) town.

Section/Village Names:
East Littleton, Kimball's Corner, Littleton Center, Littleton Common, Nashoba, New Town, North Littleton, Pingreyville, South End.

Longmeadow, Hampden County.
Incorporated as a town by St 1783, c 16.

1783.	Oct.	13.	Incorporated as a town, from part of Springfield called Longmeadow.
1787.	Nov.	16.	A gore of land annexed.
1890.	June	2.	Part annexed to Springfield.
1894.	May	19.	Part established as East Longmeadow.
1894.	July	1.	Act of May 19, 1894, took effect.

Archaic Names of the Municipality:
Masacksick.

Loudon - see Otis.

LOWELL, Middlesex County.
Incorporated as a town by St 1826, c 112.
Incorporated as a city by St 1836, c 128.

1826.	Mar.	1.	Incorporated as a town, from part of Chelmsford.
1834.	Mar.	29.	Part of Tewksbury annexed.
1836.	Apr.	1.	Incorporated as a city.
1836.	Apr.	11.	Act of Apr. 1, 1836, accepted by the town.
1851.	Feb.	28.	Part of Dracut annexed.
1874.	May	18.	Part of Chelmsford and Dracut annexed.
1874.	June	5.	Part of Tewksbury annexed.
1874.	June	23.	Act of May 18, 1874, accepted by Lowell.
1874.	Aug.	1.	Act of May 18, 1874, took effect.
1879.	Apr.	1.	Part of Dracut annexed.
1888.	May	17.	Part of Tewksbury annexed.
1906.	Apr.	30.	Part of Tewksbury annexed.
1955.	Mar.	14.	Bounds between Lowell and Chelmsford established and part of Chelmsford annexed.
1955.	Aug.	4.	Bounds as established by act of Mar. 14, 1955, struck out and bounds between Lowell and Chelmsford established, and part of Chelmsford annexed.

Archaic Names of the Municipality:
Patucket.

Section/Village Names:
Ayers City, Belvidere, Bleachery, Centralville, Highlands, Little Canada, Middlesex Junction, Middlesex Village, Oaklands, Pawtucketville, South Lowell, Wigginville (former R.R. station).

Ludlow, Hampden County.
Made a town by St 1775-1776, c 3.

1774.	Feb.	28.	Established as a district by the name of Ludlow from part of Springfield called "Stony Hill". (Prov. Laws, Vol. V, p. 337.)
1775.	Aug.	23.	Made a town, by general act under which districts became towns.
1830.	June	5.	Bounds between Ludlow and Springfield established.

Archaic Names of the Municipality:
Stony Hill.

Section/Village Names:
Collins, Ludlow Center, Ludlow City, Red Bridge (former R.R. station), Reservoir (formerly Cherry Valley).

Lunenburg, Worcester County.
Established as a town by St 1728-1729, c 20.

1728.	Aug.	1.*	Established as a town, from part of "Turkey Hills" and the land belonging to Woburn and Dorchester and "Boardman's Farm". (Prov. Laws, Vol. II, p. 520.)
1732.	June	30.*	Certain land granted to Lunenburg.
1733.	Apr.	7.*	Certain land granted to Lunenburg.
1764.	Feb.	3.	Part established as Fitchburg.
1846.	Mar.	3.	Bounds between Lunenburg and Shirley established.
1848.	Apr.	25.	Bounds between Lunenburg and Shirley established.

Archaic Names of the Municipality:
Boardman's Farm, Turkey Hills, South Town, Watatick.

Section/Village Names:
Flathill, Goodrichville, Lunenburg Center, Lunenburg Station, Mulpus, North End, South End, West End, Whalom Park.

LYNN, Essex County.
Incorporated as a city by St 1850, c 184.

1631.	July	5.*	Saugus mentioned as a plantation in the tax list. (Mass. Bay Rec., Vol. I, p. 89.)
1635.	Mar.	4.*	**Saugus** called a town in this act. (Mass. Bay Rec., Vol. I, p. 136.)
1635.	Mar.	4.*	Bounds between Saugus and Salem and between Saugus and Marble Harbor to be established.
1635.	July	8.*	Bounds to be set out between Saugus and Boston about Rumney Marsh.
1637.	Nov.	20.*	Bounds between "Saugust" and Salem to be certified.
1637.	Nov.	20.*	The name of Saugus changed to **Lynn** - "Saugus is called Lin." (Mass. Bay Rec., Vol. I, p. 211.)
1639.	Mar.	13.*	Bounds between "Linn" and Salem established.
1639.	Mar.	13.*	"Linn granted 6 miles into the countrey...."
1639.	June	6.*	Bounds to be settled between Lynn, Charlestown and Boston.
1639.	Sept.	9.*	Inland plantation granted to Lynn.
1644.	May	29.*	Part called "Linn-village" established as Reading.
1782.	July	3.	Part established as the district of Lynnfield.
1815.	Feb.	17.	Part established as Saugus.
1850.	Apr.	10.	Incorporated as a city.
1850.	Apr.	19.	Act of Apr. 10, 1850, accepted by the town.
1852.	May	21.	Part established as Swampscott.
1853.	Mar.	29.	Part established as Nahant.
1979.			City charter adopted.

Archaic Names of the Municipality:
Lin, Saugus.

Section/Village Names:
Bachellor's Plain, Blackmarsh, Breed's End, Brickyard, Central District, Diamond District, Dyehouse Village, East Central District, East Lynn, Fay Estate, Glenmere, Glenwood Park, Gravesend, Highlands, High Rock, Lakeshore Park, Linwood, Lynmere, Lynn Common, Lynnhurst, Lynn Woods, Pine Hill, Pine Grove, Pudding Hill, Raddin, Sagamore Hill, West Lynn, Woodend, Wyoma.

Lynnfield, Essex County.
Incorporated as a town by St 1813, c 191.

1782.	July	3.	Established as a district by the name of Lynnfield from part of Lynn.
1814.	Feb.	28.	Incorporated as a town, formerly the district of Lynnfield.
1854.	Apr.	10.	Bounds between Lynnfield and Reading established. ·
1857.	May	27.	Bounds between Lynnfield and North Reading established and part of each town annexed to the other.
1857.	Nov.	3.	Act of May 27, 1857, accepted by Lynnfield.
1858.	Jan.	7.	Act of May 27, 1857, accepted by North Reading and took effect.
1870.	Apr.	2.	Bounds between Lynnfield and Wakefield established.
1901.	May	17.	Bounds between Lynnfield and Saugus established.
1905.	May	2.	Bounds between Lynnfield and Reading established.
1947.	Apr.	10.	Bounds between Lynnfield and Reading established.
1971.	Mar.	8.	Town charter adopted.

Section/Village Names:
Coburnville (extinct), Lynnfield Center, South Lynnfield, Suntaug.

MALDEN, Middlesex County.
Incorporated as a city by St 1881, c 169.

1649.	May	2.*	Established as a town - "Upon the petition of Mistck side men, they are granted to be a distinct towne,...called Mauldon." (Mass. Bay Rec., Vol. II, p. 274.)
1726.	June	7.*	Part of Charlestown annexed.
1727.	June	3.*	Part annexed to Reading.
1734.	Dec.	21.*	Part annexed to Stoneham.
1753.	Dec.	18.	Bounds between Malden and Reading established.
1817.	June	10.	Part annexed to Medford.
1850.	May	3.	Part established as Melrose.
1870.	Mar.	9.	Part established as Everett.
1877.	Apr.	20.	Part of Medford annexed.
1878.	Feb.	20.	Bounds between Malden and Medford established.
1881.	Mar.	31.	Incorporated as a city.
1881.	June	9.	Act of Mar. 31, 1881, accepted by the town.
1910.	June	10.	Bounds between Malden and Medford established and part of Medford annexed.
1917.	Mar.	22.	Bounds between Malden and Medford changed and established.
1969.	Aug.	9.	Bounds between Malden and Medford changed and established.

Archaic Names of the Municipality:
Mauldon, Mystic Side.

Section/Village Names:
Belmont Hill, Bell Rock, Belmont, Edgeworth, Faulkner, Forestdale, Linden, Linden Highlands, Maplewood, Maplewood Highlands, Island Hill, Oak Grove, West End.

Manchester - by - the - Sea, Essex County.

1640.	May	13.*	Grant to inhabitants of Salem for a village at Jeffryes Creeke and the bounds of said village referred to certain men to settle. (Mass. Bay Rec., Vol. I, p. 288.)
1642.	May	3.*	Bounds between Jeffryes Creeke, Cape Ann and Ipswich, established

1645.	May	14.*	Established from part of Salem - "It is ordered, yt Jeffryes Creeke shalbe called **Manchester**." (Mass. Bay Rec., Vol. II, p. 109.)
1672.	May	15.*	Bounds between Manchester and Gloucester established.
1902.	May	6.	Bounds between Manchester and Gloucester to be established.
1903.	Aug.	25.	Bounds as established under act of May 6, 1902, confirmed by the Supreme Judicial Court.
1990.	July	1.	The name of the town of Manchester changed to **Manchester - by - the - Sea**.

Archaic Names of the Municipality:
Jeffryes Creeke.

Section/Village Names:
Crescent Beach, Kettle Cove Village, Magnolia Station, Manchester Cove, North Yarmouth, Old Neck, Smith's Point, West Manchester.

Mansfield, Bristol County.
Made a town by St 1775-1776, c 3.

1770.	Apr.	26.	Incorporated into a district by the name of Mansfield, from part of Norton. (Prov. Laws, Vol. V, p. 48.)
1775.	Aug.	23.	Made a town, by general act under which districts became towns.
1973.	Mar.	1.	Town charter adopted.

Archaic Names of the Municipality:
Taunton North Purchase.

Section/Village Names:
East Mansfield, Robinsonville, West Mansfield, Whiteville.

Marble Harbor - see Marblehead.

Marblehead, Essex County.

1631.	Oct.	18*	"Marble Harbr" mentioned. (Mass. Bay Rec., Vol. I, p. 92.)
1632.	Feb.	3.*	Marble Harbor called a plantation in this act. (Mass. Bay Rec., Vol. I, p. 93.)
1633.	July	2.*	Marblehead mentioned. (Mass. Bay Rec., Vol. I, p. 106.)
1634.	Mar.	4.*	Bounds to be established between "Marble Harbr" and Salem, and "Marble Harbr" and Saugus.
1635.	Mar.	4.*	Bounds between Salem and Saugus and Salem and Marble Harbor to be established.
1635.	May	6.*	"It is ordered, that there shalbe a plantacon att Marble Head...." (Mass Bay Rec., Vol. I, p. 147.)
1649.	May	2.*	Established as a town - "...Salem haveing granted them to be a towne of themselues, & appointed them the bounds of their towne, wch the Corte doth graunt." (Mass. Bay Rec., Vol. II, p. 266.)

Archaic Names of the Municipality:
Marble Harbor, Plantation at Marble Head.

Section/Village Names:
Barnegat, Clifton, Clifton Heights, Devereaux, Goodwin's Landing, Marblehead Neck, Nanepashemet, Peaches Point, Reed's Hill.

Marion, Plymouth County.
Incorporated as a town by St 1852, c 225.

1852.	May	14.	Incorporated as a town, from part of Rochester.
1853.	Apr.	8.	Bounds between Marion and Rochester established.
1859.	Feb.	18.	Bounds between Marion and Wareham established.
1866.	Feb.	13.	Bounds between Marion and Wareham established.
1897.	Apr.	23.	Bounds between Marion and Wareham established.
1909.	Mar.	1.	Bounds between Marion and Wareham established.
1939.	June	12.	Bounds between Marion and Wareham established.

Section/Village Names:
Bird Island, East Marion, Gifford's Corner, Great Hill, Great Neck, Hamlin's Corner, North Marion, Old Landing, Silver Shell, Sippican, Sprague's Cove.

MARLBOROUGH, Middlesex County.
Incorporated as a city by St 1890, c 320.

1660.	May	31.*	The grant to the "Whipsufferage planters" confirmed. "And it is ordered, that the name of the sajd plantation shall be called Marlborow...." (Mass. Bay Rec., Vol. IV, Part 1, p. 424.)
1667.	May	15.*	Bounds as laid out approved and confirmed.
1700.	July	2.*	Land reserved for Indian plantation annexed.
1716.	Nov.	16.*	Tract of land called "Agaganquamasset" purchased from the Indians confirmed.
1717.	Oct.	25.*	Tract of land called "Alcocks Farm" annexed.
1717.	Nov.	18.*	Part called "Chauncey" established as Westborough.
1727.	July	6.*	Part established as Southborough.
1783.	July	11.	Bounds between Marlborough and Stow established.
1784.	Mar.	16.	Part included in the new district of Berlin.
1791.	Feb.	23.	Part of Framingham annexed.
1807.	June	20.	Part annexed to Northborough and bounds established.
1829.	Feb.	11.	Part annexed to Bolton.
1838.	Mar.	16.	Bounds between Marlborough and Bolton established.
1843.	Mar.	24.	Part of Southborough annexed.
1866.	Mar.	19.	Part included in the new town of Hudson.
1890.	May	23.	Incorporated as a city.
1890.	July	14.	Act of May 23, 1890, accepted by the town.
1901.	May	16.	Bounds between Marlborough and Southborough established.
1905.	May	1.	Bounds between Marlborough and Berlin established.

Archaic Names of the Municipality:
Agaganquamasset, Alcocks Farm, A "Praying Indian" (Christian) town
Egogankamesit, Marlborow Plantation, Okommakemesit, Whipsufferage.

Section/Village Names:
French Hill, Marlborough Junction.

Marshfield, Plymouth County.

1640.	Mar.	2.*	"It is enacted by the Court that Greens Harbour shalbe a Towneship... and that it shalbe called by the name of **Rexhame**, but now Marshfeild." (Ply. Col. Rec., Vol. XI, p. 37.)
1641.	Mar.	2.*	Rexham is mentioned in the list of places for which constables are chosen. (Ply. Col. Rec., Vol. II, p. 9.)
1641.	June	1.*	Rexhame is mentioned under "Comitees of seuall Tounes". (Ply. Col. Rec., Vol. II, p. 16.)
1641.	Sept.	7.*	In a list of rates of the towns appears "Rexhame / Marshfield" with a line drawn through Rexhame. (Ply. Col. Rec., Vol. II, p. 9.)

1643.	Mar.	7.*	**Marshfield** bounds established.
1661.	Mar.	5.*	A certain tract of land granted to Marshfield and Duxbury.
1683.	Feb.	23.*	Bounds between Marshfield and Duxbury established.
1712.	Mar.	21.*	Part included in the new town of Pembroke.
1782.	Nov.	8.	Bounds between Marshfield and Scituate established.
1788.	Mar.	10.	Part of Scituate annexed.
1813.	June	14.	Bounds between Marshfield and Duxbury established.
1887.	May	11.	Bounds between Marshfield and Scituate established.
1928.	Mar.	23.	Bounds between Marshfield and Scituate established.
1975.	May	3.	Town charter adopted.

Archaic Names of the Municipality:
Greens Harbour, Rexham, Wrexham.

Section/Village Names:
Brant Rock, Center Marshfield, Duxbury Beach, Ferry Hill, Fieldston, Green Harbor, Marshfield Hills (formerly East Marshfield), North Marshfield, Ocean Bluff, Rexhame, Sea View, Standish.

Mashpee, Barnstable County.
Incorporated as a town by St 1870, c 293.

1763.	June	14.	"Lands belonging to the Indians...in Mashpee be and hereby are erected into a district by the name of Mashpee...." for three years. (Prov. Laws, Vol. IV, p. 639.)
1767.	Mar.	20.	Act of June 14, 1763, revived, to be in force until July 1, 1770.
1770.	Nov.	15.	Act of June 14, 1763, revived, to be in force until the end of the session of the General Court next after Nov. 1, 1775.
1776.	Feb.	9.	Act of June 14, 1763, revived, to be in force until the end of the session of the General Court next after Nov. 1, 1779.
1779.	Nov.	25.	Act of June 14, 1763, revived, to be in force until Nov. 1, 1785.
1788.	June	12.	Act of June 14, 1763, repealed; in this act the spelling is "Marshpee". The act provides that three persons be appointed as Guardians at Marshpee, for ten years.
1789.	Jan.	30.	All former laws respecting Marshpee Indians repealed and a board of overseers established.
1795.	Jan.	22.	Bounds between "Marshpee" and Barnstable established.
1797.	Mar.	7.	Act of June 12, 1788, made perpetual until repealed by the Legislature.
1811.	Feb.	26.	Part of the "plantation of Marshpee" annexed to Sandwich.
1834.	Mar.	31.	The plantation of Marshpee established as the District of Marshpee.
1841.	Mar.	17.	A tract of land formerly in the plantation of Marshpee annexed to Falmouth.
1859.	Apr.	1.	Part of the district of Marshpee annexed to Sandwich.
1860.	Mar.	13.	Part of the district of Marshpee annexed to Sandwich.
1870.	May	28.	Incorporated as a town, by the name of Mashpee, formerly the district of Marshpee.
1872.	Mar.	19.	Part of Sandwich re-annexed.
1885.	June	18.	Bounds between Mashpee and Falmouth established.
1887.	May	27.	Bounds between Mashpee and Sandwich established and part of Sandwich annexed.
1894.	Mar.	28.	Bounds between Mashpee and Barnstable established.
1905.	Apr.	20.	Bounds between Mashpee and Sandwich established and part of Sandwich annexed.
1916.	Apr.	24.	Bounds between Mashpee and Barnstable established.

Archaic Names of the Municipality:
Marshpee, Popponesset, South Sea, Waquoit.

Section/Village Names:
Aquashenet, Chimquist, East Mashpee, Indian Meeting House, Maushop Village, Poponesset, Seconnet, Segreganset, South Mashpee, Succonesset, Wakeby.

74HISTORICAL DATA RELATING TO COUNTIES,

Mattapoisett, Plymouth County.
Incorporated as a town by St 1857, c 202.
1857.　May　　20.　Incorporated as a town, from part of Rochester.

Section/Village Names:
Antassawomock, Antassawomock Neck (extinct), Aucoote, Brant Island,
Cannonville, Crescent Beach, East Mattapoisett, Hammondstown, Hollywood,
Mattapoisett Neck, Ned's Point, Pico Beach, Pine Island, Ram Island, Randall Town
(extinct), Tinkham Town.

Maynard, Middlesex County.
Incorporated as a town by St 1871, c 198.
1871.　Apr.　　19.　Incorporated as a town, from parts of Stow and Sudbury.
1991.　May　　6.　Town charter adopted.

Archaic Names of the Municipality:
Assabet Village.

Section/Village Names:
Assabet Park.

Medfield, Norfolk County.
1650.　May　　22.*　Established from part of Dedham - "Att the request of the
inhabitants of Dedham, the village there is by this Courte
named Meadfeild." (Mass. Bay Rec., Vol. IV, Part 1, p. 7.)
1651.　May　　23.*　Established as a town. "Itt is ordered, that Meadefeild, ...
shall and hereby hath graunted vnto them all the power and
priviledges which other tounes doe enjoy...."(Mass. Bay Rec.,
Vol. IV, Part 1, p. 46.)
1659.　May　　28.*　Certain land granted to Medfield.
1713.　Oct.　　24.*　Part established as Medway.
1903.　May　　27.　Bounds between the town of Medfield and towns of Dover,
Walpole and Norfolk established.
1972.　Mar.　　6.　Town charter adopted.

Archaic Names of the Municipality:
Dedham Village.

Section/Village Names:
Harding, Medfield Junction.

MEDFORD, Middlesex County.
Incorporated as a city by St 1892, c 324.
1630.　Sept.　　28.*　"Meadford" is mentioned in a Tax Act as a plantation. (Mass.
Bay Rec., Vol. I, p. 77.)
1754.　Apr.　　18.　Part of Charlestown annexed.
1754.　Apr.　　20.　Part of Charlestown annexed.
1811.　June　　21.　Part annexed to Charlestown.
1817.　June　　10.　Part of Malden annexed.
1850.　Apr.　　30.　Part included in the new town of Winchester.
1875.　Apr.　　20.　Part of Everett annexed.
1877.　Apr.　　20.　Part annexed to Malden.
1878.　Feb.　　20.　Bounds between Medford and Malden established.
1892.　May　　31.　Incorporated as a city.
1892.　Oct.　　6.　Act of May 31, 1892, accepted by the town.
1910.　June　　10.　Bounds between Medford and Malden established and part
annexed to Malden.
1917.　Mar.　　22.　Bounds between Medford and Malden changed and
established.

| 1956. | Aug. | 10. | Bounds between Medford and Winchester established and part annexed to Winchester. |
| 1969. | Aug. | 29. | Bounds between Medford and Malden changed and established. |

Archaic Names of the Municipality:
Meadford Plantation, Mystic Plantation.

Section/Village Names:
Boulevard Heights, College Hill, Glenwood, Medford Hillside, South Medfield, Tufts College, Wellington, West Medford.

Medway, Norfolk County.
Established as a town by St 1713-1714, c 9.

1713.	Oct.	24.*	Established as a town, from part of Medfield. (Prov. Laws, Vol. I, p. 722.)
1749.	Nov.	28.*	Part of Wrentham annexed.
1792.	Mar.	3.	Bounds between Medway and "Sherburn", established.
1792.	June	25.	Part annexed to Franklin.
1792.	Nov.	13.	Bounds between Medway and Franklin established.
1829.	Mar.	3.	Bounds between Medway and Holliston established and part of each town annexed to the other town.
1832.	Feb.	23.	Bounds between Medway and Franklin established.
1839.	Mar.	13.	Part of Franklin annexed and bounds established.
1870.	Feb.	23.	Part included in the new town of Norfolk.
1885.	Feb.	24.	Part established as Millis.

Section/Village Names:
Braggville, Factory Village, Medway Village, Rockville, West Medway.

MELROSE, Middlesex County.
Incorporated as a town by St 1850, c 309.
Incorporated as a city by St 1899, c 162.

1850.	May	3.	Incorporated as a town, from part of Malden.
1853.	Mar.	15.	Part of Stoneham annexed.
1895.	Mar.	27.	Bounds between Melrose and Stoneham located and defined.
1899.	Mar.	18.	Incorporated as a city.
1899.	May	8.	Act of Mar. 18, 1899, accepted by the town.
1906.	May	9.	Bounds between Melrose and Wakefield changed and established.

Archaic Names of the Municipality:
North Malden.

Section/Village Names:
East Section, Fells, Melrose Highlands, Mount Hood, Wyoming.

Mendon, Worcester County.

1667.	May	15.*	Established as a town, "being the touneship of Qunshapage as lajd out...name thereof be Mendon...." (Mass. Bay Rec., Vol. IV, Part 2, p. 341.)
1669.	May	20.*	Certain lands granted to Mendon.
1710.	June	29.*	Certain land annexed.
1714.	June	1.*	The purchase of land from the Indians in 1691 confirmed by the Court, and annexed to Mendon.
1719.	Nov.	27.*	Part included in the new town of Bellingham.
1727.	June	27.*	Part established as Uxbridge.
1735.	June	14.*	Part included in the new town of Upton.

1754. Apr.   10.   Bounds between Mendon and Uxbridge established.
1770. Apr.   24.   Part of Uxbridge annexed.
1780. Apr.   11.   Part established as Milford.
1845. Mar.   25.   Part established as Blackstone.
1872. Mar.   7.   Bounds between Mendon and Bellingham established.

Archaic Names of the Municipality:
Qunshapauge, Squnshopog.

Section/Village Names:
Albeeville, Brick Alley, Lake Mendon Park, Wigwam Hill.

Merrimac, Essex County.
Incorporated as a town by St 1876, c 131.
1876. Apr.   11.   Incorporated as a town, from part of Amesbury.

Section/Village Names:
Bear Hill, Birch Meadow, Hadley, Highlands, Lake Attitash, Lower Corner,
Merrimac Center, Merrimacport, River Village.

Methuen, Essex County.
Established as a town by St 1725-1726, c 12.
1725. Dec.   8.* Established as a town, from the west part of Haverhill and
                    lands adjoining. (Prov. Laws, Vol. II, p. 367.)
1847. Apr.   17.   Part included in the new town of Lawrence.
1854. Apr.   4.   Part annexed to Lawrence.
1917. Apr.   17.   Incorporated as a city.
1917. Nov.   6.   Act of Apr. 17, 1917, accepted by the town.
1921. Jan.   4.   Act of Apr. 17, 1917, declared unconstitutuional by Mass.
                    Supreme Judicial Court (Mass. Reports, Vol. 236, p. 564.)
1921. May   25.   Act of Apr. 17, 1917, repealed.
1930. Apr.   30.   Part annexed to Lawrence.
1930. May   12.   Act of Apr. 30, 1930, accepted by the town.
1930. June   2.   Act of Apr. 30, 1930, accepted by Lawrence.
1946. May   18.   Part of Lawrence annexed.
1947. Mar.   19.   Act of May 18, 1946, accepted by the town.
1947. June   20.   Act of May 18, 1946, accepted by Lawrence.
1972. Mar.   6.   Town charter adopted which established city form of
                    government.

Section/Village Names:
Arlington District, Bradley Farms, Canobieola Heights, Hawks Brook, Inglewood,
Pleasant Valley.

Middleborough, Plymouth County.
1669. June   1.* Established as a town. "...Namassakett shalbe a township,
                    and to be called by the name of Middleberry...." (Ply. Col.
                    Rec., Vol. V, p. 19.)
1675. June   1.* Boundary line established. Court ordered certain men "...to
                    Run the line between Bridgewater and Middlebery." (Ply.
                    Col. Rec., Vol. XI, p. 241.)
1680. Sept. 28.* Certain lands called "Assowamsett Neck" and places
                    adjacent granted to Middleborough.
1734. July   4.* Part included in the new town of Halifax.
1734. Dec.   11.* Part annexed to Plympton.
1849. Mar.   24.   Bounds between Middleborough and Carver established.
1853. May   13.   Part established as Lakeville.
1921. Mar.   7.   Bounds between Middleborough and Carver established.

Archaic Names of the Municipality:
Assowamsett Neck, Cotuckticut, Ketiticut, Middleberry, Namaskett, Quittaub, Quittaquas, Titicut.

Section/Village Names:
Barden Hills, Bull's Eye Crossing, Court End, East Middleborough, Eddyville, Fall Brook, Four Corners, Highlands, Mount Carmel, Muttock, North Middleborough, Namasket, Neck, Peaseville, Puddingshire, Purchade, Putnams Rock, Rocky Meadow, South Middleborough, Star Mill Village, Tack Factory, The Green, Thomastown, Titicut, Walnut Plains, Wappanucket, Waterville, West End.

Middlefield, Hampshire County.
Incorporated as a town by St 1782, c 52.

| 1783. | Mar. | 12. | Incorporated as a town, from parts of Becket, Chester, Partridgefield, Washington, Worthington and the lands called "Prescott's Grant." |

Archaic Names of the Municipality:
Prescott's Grant.

Section/Village Names:
Bancroft, Factory Village, Glendale, Middlefield Center, Smith Hollow, West Hill.

Middleton, Essex County.
Established as a town by St 1728-1729, c 12.

1728.	June	20.*	Established as a town, from parts of Andover, Boxford, Salem and Topsfield. (Prov. Laws, Vol. II, p. 502.)
1904.	Apr.	22.	Bounds between Middleton and North Andover established.
1904.	Apr.	22.	Bounds between Middleton and Boxford established.
1936.	Feb.	28.	Bounds between Middleton and Topsfield established.
1974.	May	20.	Town charter adopted.

Archaic Names of the Municipality:
Wills Hill.

Section/Village Names:
Box Factory, Bush Corner, East Middleton, Haswell Park, Highland Park, Howe's Station, North Middleton, Paper Mills, South Middleton.

Milford, Worcester County.
Incorporated as a town by St 1779-1780, c 35.

1780.	Apr.	11.	Incorporated as a town, from part of Mendon. (Prov. Laws, Vol. V, p. 1172.)
1835.	Mar.	27.	Bounds between Milford, Holliston and Hopkinton established and parts of Holliston and Hopkinton annexed to Milford and part of Milford annexed to Hopkinton.
1859.	Apr.	1.	Bounds between Milford and Holliston established.
1886.	Apr.	7.	Part established as Hopedale.
1907.	May	16.	Bounds between Milford and Upton established.
1907.	May	16.	Bounds between Milford and Hopkinton established.
1962.	July	25.	Bounds between Milford, Hopkinton and Upton established.

Archaic Names of the Municipality:
Mill River, North Purchase.

Section/Village Names:
Farm Bridge, Braggville, Darlings, North Milford, Rocky Hill, Silver Hill, South Milford.

Millbury, Worcester County.
Incorporated as a town by St 1813, c 12.

1813.	June	11.	Incorporated as a town, from part of Sutton.
1851.	May	24.	Part of Auburn annexed.
1907.	Feb.	11.	Bounds between Millbury and Oxford established.
1907.	May	16.	Bounds between Millbury and Sutton established.

Section/Village Names:
Aldrichville, Armory Village, Bramanville, Buck's Village, Burling Mills, Cordis
Mills, Fort Laverty, Greenwood Section, Millbury Center, Millbury Junction, Old
Common, Park Hill, Power Station, Simpsonville, Tainter Hill, West Millbury,
Wheelersville.

Millis, Norfolk County.
Incorporated as a town by St 1885, c 37.

1885.	Feb.	24.	Incorporated as a town, from part of Medway.

Section/Village Names:
Clicquot, East Millis, Rockville.

Millville, Worcester County.
Incorporated as a town by Special Acts 1916, c 282.

1916.	May	1.	Incorporated as a town, from part of Blackstone.
1933.	July	22.	Millville Municipal Finance Commission established.
1944.	Apr.	20.	Municipal Finance Commission terminated and town government resumed.

Milton, Norfolk County.

1662.	May	7.*	Established as a town, from part of Dorchester called "Uncataquissett." (Mass. Bay Rec., Vol. IV, Part 2, p. 50.)
1712.	May	30.*	"Blue Hill lands" divided between Milton and Braintree.
1868.	Apr.	22.	Part included in the new town of Hyde Park.
1868.	May	1.	Act of Apr. 22, 1868, amended and bounds established.
1885.	Apr.	16.	Bounds between Milton and Quincy established and part of each town annexed to the other town.

Archaic Names of the Municipality:
Blue Hill Lands, Uncataquissett, Unquety.

Section/Village Names:
Adamsville, Blue Hills, Blue Hill Terrace, Brush Hill, East Milton, Mattapan, Milton
Center, Milton Hill, Milton Lower Falls, New State, Pine Tree Brook, Scott's Woods.

Monroe, Franklin County.
Incorporated as a town by St 1821, c 93.

1822.	Feb.	21.	Incorporated as a town, from part of Rowe and land called "the Gore."

Archaic Names of the Municipality:
Gore.

Section/Village Names:
Monroe Bridge.

Monson, Hampden County.
Made a town by St 1775-1776, c 3.

1760.	Apr.	28.	Established as a district by the name of Monson from part of Brimfield. (Prov. Laws, Vol. IV, p. 334.)
1763.	Feb.	7.	Bounds definitely established.
1775.	Aug.	23.	Made a town, by general act under which districts became towns.

1828.   Feb.   8.   Bounds between Monson and Palmer established.

Section/Village Names:
East Hill, Ellis Mills, Granite Quarry, Lyons Village, North Monson, South Monson, State Line.

Montague, Franklin County.
Made a town by St 1775-1776, c 3.
1754.   Jan.   25.   Established as a district by the name of Montague, from part of Sunderland. (Prov. Laws, Vol. III, p. 713.)
1775.   Aug.   23.   Made a town, by general act under which districts became towns.
1803.   Feb.   28.   Part annexed to Wendell.

Archaic Names of the Municipality:
Hunting Hills.

Section/Village Names:
Lake Pleasant, Miller's Falls, Montague Center, Montague City, Turner's Falls.

Monterey, Berkshire County.
Incorporated as a town by St 1847, c 172.
1847.   Apr.   12.   Incorporated as a town, from part of Tyringham.
1851.   May   24.   Part of New Marlborough annexed.
1875.   Apr.   24.   Part of Sandisfield annexed.
1875.   May   19.   Act of Apr. 24, 1875, accepted by the town.
1875.   June   1.   Act of Apr. 24, 1875, took effect.

Montgomery, Hampden County.
Incorporated as a town by St 1780, c 1.
1780.   Nov.   28.   Incorporated as a town from parts of that part of Westfield called the "New Addition" and from parts of Norwich and Southampton.
1792.   Feb.   25.   Part included in the new town of Russell.
1792.   Mar.   6.   Parts of Norwich and Southampton annexed.
1914.   June   3.   Bounds between Montgomery and Russell established.

Archaic Names of the Municipality:
New Addition, Plantation Number Five, East Part (1762 Townships).

Mount Hope - see Bristol.

Mount Washington, Berkshire County.
Established as a town by St 1779-1780, c 3.
1779.   June   21.   Established as a town, formerly the plantation called "Tauconnuck Mountain." (Prov. Laws, Vol. V, p. 1069.)
1817.   June   17.   Bounds between Mount Washington and Egremont established and part of each town annexed to the other town.
1847.   Mar.   12.   Bounds between Mount Washington and the district of Boston Corner established.

Archaic Names of the Municipality:
Tauconnuck (Taconic) Mountain Plantation.

Section/Village Names:
Alandar (extinct).

Murrayfield - see Chester.

Nahant, Essex County.
Incorporated as a town by St 1853, c 114.
    1853.   Mar.   29.   Incorporated as a town, from part of Lynn.

Section/Village Names:
Bass Point, Little Nahant.

Nantucket, Nantucket County.
    1687.   June   27.*   **(Sherburn)**"Sharborn" is mentioned. (New York Original
                               Books of Letters Patent, Vol. VI, p. 254.)
    1692.   ——   The island of Nantucket granted to the Province of Massa-
                               chusetts Bay by the Province Charter (Prov. Laws, Vol. I, p.
                               9.)
    1713.   June   8.*   The island of Tuckannock granted to the inhabitants of
                               Nantucket and shall be under the jurisdiction of the
                               government there established.
    1795.   June   8.   The name of the town of Sherburn changed to **Nantucket**.

Archaic Names of the Municipality:
Nauticon, Sharborn, Sherburn.

Section/Village Names:
Brant Point, Cato District, Coatue, Eel Point, Great Point, Low Beach, Madaket,
Monomoy, Muskeget Island, Nantucket Village, Plainfield, Pocomo, Polpis, Poverty
Point, Quaise, Quidnet, Sankaty Head, Shimmo, Siasconset, Surfside, Tuckernuck
Island, Wauwinet.

Nashaway - see Lancaster.

Nashoba - see Littleton.

Natick, Middlesex County.
Established as a town by St 1780, c13.
    1650.   May   23.*   "Naticke" is mentioned as one of the bounds. (Mass. Bay
                               Rec., Vol. III, p. 189.)
    1651.   Oct.   14.*   Indian plantation at "Naticke" granted 2000 acres of land
                               within Dedham.
    1660.   May   31.*   Bounds of Indian plantation at "Naticke" established.
    1679.   Apr.   16.*   Exchange of land made between the two towns of "Naticke"
                               and "Sherborne."
    1679.   May   30.*   Return of the exchange of land of April 16, 1679, confirmed.
    1701.   Oct.   18.*   Bounds between Natick and Dedham established.
    1744.   Feb.   25.*   Part of Needham annexed.
    1762.   Feb.   23.   Established as the district of Natick.
    1775.   Aug.   23.   Grave doubt existed as to the district of Natick becoming a
                               town under this general act , as the act establishing the
                               district had an exception other than the one expressed in the
                               general act.
    1781.   Feb.   19.   Established as a town, formerly the district of Natick.
    1797.   June   22.   Bounds between Natick and Needham established and part
                               of each town annexed to the other town.
    1820.   Feb.   7.   Part of "Sherburne" annexed.
    1850.   Apr.   26.   Bounds between Natick and Wayland established.
    1871.   Apr.   22.   Part annexed to Framingham.
    1951.   Apr.   2.   Bounds between Natick and Weston established.
    1980.   Mar.   17.   Town charter adopted.

Archaic Names of the Municipality:
Indian Plantation at Naticke, A "Praying Indian" (Christian) town.

Section/Village Names:
Felchville, Lake Crossing, Little South, Morseville, Navy Yard, Nebraska Plain,
North Natick, South Natick, Walkerville, Wellesley Oaks, Wellesley Park, West
Natick.

Nawsett - see Eastham.

Needham, Norfolk County.
Established as a town by St 1711, c 109.

1711.	Nov.	6.*	Established as a town, from a part of Dedham. (Prov. Laws, Vol. XXI, p. 796.)
1712.	Aug.	22.*	Bounds between Needham and Dedham established.
1714.	Nov.	3.*	Bounds between Needham and Dedham established.
1744.	Feb.	25.*	Part annexed to Natick.
1797.	June	22.	Bounds between Needham and Natick established and part of each town annexed to the other town.
1881.	Apr.	6.	Part established as Wellesley.

Section/Village Names:
Birds Hill, Charles River Village, Dog Corner, Greendale, Highlandville, Hurds Corner, Needham Heights, Needham Junction, Needham Upper Falls.

New Ashford, Berkshire County.
Made a town by Revised Statutes, c 15, Sec. 9.

1781.	Feb.	26.	Established as a district by the name of New Ashford, formerly a tract of land called New Ashford lying between Adams, Hancock, Lanesborough and Williamstown.
1793.	Mar.	14.	Part of the district included in the new town of Cheshire.
1798.	Feb.	6.	Part of the district annexed to Cheshire.
1798.	June	25.	Part of Hancock annexed to the district of New Ashford.
1835.	Nov.	4.	Made a town. (Revised Statutes)
1836.	May	1.	Act of Nov. 4, 1835, took effect.
1851.	May	20.	Bounds between New Ashford and Hancock established.
1912.	May	28.	Bounds between New Ashford and Cheshire established.

NEW BEDFORD, Bristol County.
Incorporated as a town by St 1786, c 60.
Incorporated as a city by St 1847, c 60.

1787.	Feb.	23.	Incorporated as a town, from part of Dartmouth.
1812.	Feb.	22.	Part established as Fairhaven.
1831.	Feb.	19.	Bounds between New Bedford and Dartmouth established.
1845.	Mar.	20.	Part of Dartmouth annexed.
1847.	Mar.	9.	Incorporated as a city.
1875.	Apr.	9.	Part of Acushnet annexed.
1888.	May	3.	Part of Dartmouth annexed.

Archaic Names of the Municipality:
Acushena, Acushnet.

Section/Village Names:
Acushnet Station, Belleville, Cannonville, Clark's Point, Clifford, Germantown, Howland Village, Jesserville, Kenersonville, Mount Pleasant Station, North End, Plainville, Rockdale, Shawmut, South End, Winterville.

New Braintree, Worcester County.
Made a town by St 1775-1776, c 3.

1751.	Jan.	31.*	Established as a district from lands called New Braintree and parts of Hardwick and Brookfield. (Prov. Laws, Vol. XIV, p. 518.)
1751.	Apr.	16.*	District established Jan. 31,* 1751 named "New Braintry." (Prov. Laws, Vol., XIV, p. 518.)
1775.	Aug.	23.	Made a town, by general act under which districts became towns.
1791.	June	10.	Bounds between New Braintree and Brookfield established and part of each town annexed to the other town.

1792.	Mar.	8.	Bounds between New Braintree and Brookfield established and part of each town annexed to the other town.
1814.	June	10.	Part annexed to Hardwick.
1911.	Apr.	24.	Bounds between New Braintree and North Brookfield established.
1911.	Apr.	24.	Bounds between New Braintree and West Brookfield established.

Archaic Names of the Municipality:
Braintree Farms, Wenimesset.

New Marlborough, Berkshire County.
Made a town by St 1775-1776, c 3.

1759.	June	15.	Established as a district by the name of New Marlborough, formerly the plantation called New Marlborough. (Prov. Laws, Vol. IV, p. 263.)
1775.	Aug.	23.	Made a town, by general act under which districts became towns.
1795.	June	19.	Part of Sheffield annexed.
1798.	Feb.	7.	Part of Sheffield annexed.
1811.	Feb.	27.	Part of Tyringham annexed.
1812.	Feb.	11.	Part annexed to Tyringham.
1851.	May	24.	Part annexed to Monterey.
1871.	Apr.	19.	Part of Sheffield annexed and bounds established.

Archaic Names of the Municipality:
Housatonic Township Number Two.

Section/Village Names:
Clayton, Hartsville, Mill River, New Marlborough Village, Southfield.

New Salem, Franklin County.
Made a town by St 1775-1776, c 3.

1753.	June	15.	Established as a district by the name of New Salem, formerly the township of New Salem with the additonal grant made to said township. (Prov. Laws, Vol. III, p. 670.)
1775.	Aug.	23.	Made a town, by general act under which districts became towns.
1822.	Jan.	28.	Part included in the new town of Prescott.
1824.	Feb.	20.	Part of Shutesbury annexed.
1830.	Feb.	5.	Part annexed to Athol.
1837.	Mar.	16.	Part annexed to Orange and part to Athol.
1911.	Apr.	27.	Bounds between New Salem and Prescott established.
1927.	Apr.	26.	Part of Enfield, Greenwich and Prescott annexed.
1938.	Apr.	26.	Act of Apr. 26, 1927, amended.
1938.	Apr.	28.	Act of Apr. 26, 1927, as amended, took effect.

Section/Village Names:
Cooleyville, Hagarville, Herrick, Marcedonia, Millington, Morse Village, New Salem Center, New Salem Station, North New Salem, South New Salem.

Newbury, Essex County.

1635.	May	6.*	"Wessacucuon is allowed by the Court to be a plantacon ... & hereafter to be called Newberry." (Mass. Bay Rec., Vol. I, p. 146.)
1649.	May	4.*	Two-fifths of Plum Island granted to Newbury.
1656.	May	14.*	Bounds between Newbury and Rowley established.
1764.	Jan.	28.	Part established as Newburyport.
1819.	Feb.	18.	Part established as Parsons.

1851.	Apr.	17.	Part annexed to Newburyport.
1905.	Mar.	27.	Bounds between Newbury and Rowley established.
1931.	June	9.	Bounds between Newbury and Rowley established.

Archaic Names of the Municipality:
Quascacunquen, Wessacucus.

Section/Village Names:
Byfield, Knight's Crossing, Newbury Lower Green, Newbury Upper Green, Old Town, South Byfield.

NEWBURYPORT, Essex County.
Established as a town by St 1763-1764, c 20.
Incorporated as a city by St 1851, c 296.

1764.	Jan.	28.	Established as a town, from part of Newbury. (Prov. Laws, Vol. IV, p. 676.)
1851.	Apr.	17.	Part of Newbury annexed.
1851.	May	24.	Incorporated as a city.
1851.	June	3.	Act of May 24, 1851, accepted by the town.

Section/Village Names:
Artichoke, Back Bay, Belleville, Curson's Mills, Flat Iron Point, Joppa, Moultonville, Grasshopper Plains, Guinea, Plum Island, Three Roads.

NEWTON, Middlesex County.
Incorporated as a city by St 1873, c 326.

1691.	Dec.	15.*	Established as a town - "Cambridge Village sometimes called New Cambridge...ordered that it be henceforth called Newton...." (Mass. Archives, Vol. CXII, p. 421B.)
1803.	June	21.	An island in the Charles River annexed.
1838.	Apr.	23.	Part annexed to Roxbury.
1849.	Apr.	16.	Part annexed to Waltham.
1873.	June	2.	Incorporated as a city.
1873.	Oct.	13.	Act of June 2, 1873, accepted by the town.
1874.	May	29.	Bounds between Newton and Boston established.
1875.	May	5.	Part of Boston annexed.
1875.	June	23.	Act of May 5, 1875, accepted.
1875.	July	1.	Act of May 5, 1875, took effect.
1898.	Mar.	29.	Bounds between Newton and Boston established.
1898.	May	13.	Bounds between Newton and Boston established.
1907.	Mar.	28.	Bounds between Newton and Brookline established.
1971.	Nov.	2.	City charter adopted.

Archaic Names of the Municipality:
Cambridge Village, New Cambridge, Nonantum.

Section/Village Names:
Auburndale, Chestnut Hill, Eliot, Fairview, Johnsonville, Newton Center, Newton Corner (previously called Angier's Corner), Newton Highlands, Newton Lower Falls, Newton Upper Falls, Newtonville, Nonantum, Norumbega, Oak Hill, Pine Grove, Riverside, Thompsonville, Waban, West Newton, Newton West Parish, Woodland Station.

New Sherburn - see Douglas.

Newe Towne - see Cambridge.

Norfolk, Norfolk County.
Incorporated as a town by St 1870, c 35.

1870.	Feb.	23.	Incorporated as a town, from parts of Franklin, Medway, Walpole and Wrentham.
1871.	Apr.	19.	Bounds between Norfolk and Wrentham established.
1903.	May	23.	Bounds between Norfolk and Foxborough established.
1903.	May	27.	Bounds between the town of Medfield and the towns of Dover, Walpole and Norfolk established.
1927.	Mar.	28.	Bounds between Norfolk and Walpole re-established.

Section/Village Names:
Bush Factory, City Mills, Deanville, Highlands, Highland Lake, Honeypot, Norfolk Center, Pondville, River End, Stony Brook.

NORTH ADAMS, Berkshire County.
Incorporated as a town by St 1878, c 143.
Incorporated as a city by St 1895, c 148.

1878.	Apr.	16.	Incorporated as a town, from part of Adams.
1895.	Mar.	22.	Incorporated as a city.
1895.	Apr.	8.	Act of Mar. 22, 1895, accepted by the town.
1900.	Apr.	25.	Bounds between North Adams and Williamstown established and part of Williamstown annexed.

Archaic Names of the Municipality:
East Hoosuck Plantation.

Section/Village Names:
Blackinton, Beaver, Braytonville, Burdickville, Greylock, Houghtonville, Kempville, Loraine, Notch, The Union, Tunnel Road.

North Andover, Essex County.
Incorporated as a town by St 1855, c 150.

1855.	Apr.	7.	Incorporated as a town, from part of Andover.
1879.	Feb.	4.	Part annexed to Lawrence.
1904.	Mar.	12.	Bounds between North Andover and Boxford established.
1904.	Mar.	12.	Bounds between North Andover and North Reading established.
1904.	Apr.	22.	Bounds between North Andover and Middleton established.
1972.	June	29.	Bounds between North Andover and Lawrence changed and established.

Section/Village Names:
Ingall's Station, Machine Shop Station, Marble Ridge Station, North Andover Center, North Andover Depot, Stevens Village, Waverly Park.

North Attleborough, Bristol County.
Incorporated as a town by St 1887, c 412.

1887.	June	14.	Incorporated as a town, from part of Attleborough.
1887.	July	30.	Act of June 14, 1887, accepted by Attleborough.
1888.	Mar.	6.	Acceptance of the act of June 14, 1887, ratified and confirmed.

Section/Village Names:
Adamsdale (also known as Lanesville), Attleborough Falls, Blaneyville, Hillside (former R.R. station), Holmes Neighborhood, Lymanville, New Boston, Old Town, Robinsonville, Sloweyville.

North Bridgewater - see Brockton.

North Brookfield, Worcester County.
Incorporated as a town by St 1811, c 147.

1812.	Feb.	28.	Incorporated as a town, from part of Brookfield.
1854.	Apr.	15.	Part annexed to Brookfield.
1910.	Mar.	18.	Bounds between North Brookfield and Brookfield established.
1911.	Apr.	24.	Bounds between North Brookfield and West Brookfield established.
1911.	Apr.	24.	Bounds between North Brookfield and New Braintree established.

Archaic Names of the Municipality:
Quabaug Territory.

Section/Village Names:
Bigelow Hollow, Little Canada, Quaboag Village.

North Chelsea - see Revere.

North Reading, Middlesex County.
Incorporated as a town by St 1853, c 71.

1853.	Mar.	22.	Incorporated as a town, from part of Reading.
1857.	May	27.	Bounds between North Reading and Lynnfield established.
1857.	Nov.	3.	Act of May 27, 1857, accepted by Lynnfield.
1858.	Jan.	7.	Act of May 27, 1857, accepted by North Reading and took effect.
1904.	Mar.	12.	Bounds between North Reading and North Andover established.
1904.	Apr.	22.	Bounds between North Reading and Andover established.
1970.	Mar.	7.	Town charter adopted.

Section/Village Names:
Abottville, Back Row (extinct), Bear Meadow, Martin's Pond, Meadow View, Upton Corner, Walnut Corner, West Village.

NORTHAMPTON, Hampshire County.
Incorporated as a city by St 1883, c 250.

1656.	May	14.*	"Forasmuch as the tounes of Springfeild and North Hampton...." (Mass. Bay Rec., Vol. IV, Part 1, p. 259.)
1685.	June	4.*	Bounds between Northampton and Springfield established.
1701.	June	4.*	Certain land granted to Northampton and bounds established between Northampton and Westfield.
1720.	Nov.	12.*	Bounds between Northampton and Hatfield established.
1753.	Jan.	5.	Part established as the district of Southampton.
1778.	Sept.	29.	Part established as Westhampton.
1778.	Sept.	29.	Part annexed to Southampton.
1785.	June	17.	Part included in the new district of Easthampton.
1850.	Apr.	15.	Part of Hadley annexed.
1872.	Mar.	12.	Bounds between Northampton and Westhampton established.
1883.	June	23.	Incorporated as a city.
1883.	Sept.	5.	Act of June 23, 1883, accepted by the town.
1909.	June	9.	Part annexed to Holyoke.
1914.	Apr.	21.	Bounds between Northampton and Easthampton established.

Archaic Names of the Municipality:
Nonotuck.

Section/Village Names:
Bay State Village, Cowles Meadow, Florence, Hospital Hill, Laurel Park, Leeds, Loudville, Mount Tom, North Farms, Park Hill, Pine Grove, Robert's Meadow, West Farms.

Northborough, Worcester County.
Made a town by St 1775-1776, c 3.

1766.	Jan.	24.	Established as a district by the name of Northborough from part of Westborough. (Prov. Laws, Vol. IV, p. 839.)
1775.	Aug.	23.	Made a town, by general act under which districts became towns.
1806.	Feb.	15.	Bounds between Northborough and Berlin established and part of each place annexed to the other place.
1807.	June	20.	Part of Marlborough annexed and bounds established.
1970.	Mar.	2.	Town charter adopted.

Section/Village Names:
Chapinville, Talbot, Woodside Mills.

Northbridge, Worcester County.
Made a town by St 1775-1776, c 3.

1772.	July	14.	Established as a district by the name of Northbridge from part of Uxbridge. (Prov. Laws, Vol. V, p. 198.)
1775.	Aug.	23.	Made a town, by general act under which districts became towns.
1780.	Apr.	20.	Part of Sutton annexed.
1801.	Feb.	17.	Part of Sutton annexed.
1831.	June	15.	Part annexed to Sutton.
1837.	Mar.	7.	Bounds between Northbridge and Sutton established.
1844.	Mar.	16.	Part of Sutton annexed.
1856.	Apr.	30.	Bounds between Northbridge and Uxbridge established and part of each town annexed to the other town.
1908.	Apr.	17.	Bounds between Northbridge and Uxbridge established.

Section/Village Names:
Adam's Corners, Linwood, Northbridge Center, Plummers, Prentice Corner, Quaker District, Riverdale, Rockdale, Whitinsville.

Northfield, Franklin County.
Established as a town by Resolves 1723-1724, c 25.

1714.	Feb.	22.*	The grant for a plantation at "Squakeag" revived and "...the Town to be named Northfield...." (Prov. Laws, Vol. XXI, p. 840.)
1715.	June	10.*	Act of Feb. 22, 1714, continued for three years.
1720.	Dec.	6.*	Committee appointed to manage the affairs of Northfield continued for two years.
1723.	June	15.*	To enjoy all privileges of a town.
1773.	June	29.	Two tracts of land annexed.
1795.	Feb.	28.	Part annexed to Gill.
1860.	Feb.	10.	Part called "Hack's Grant" annexed to Erving.

Archaic Names of the Municipality:
Hack's Grant, Squakeage Plantation.

Section/Village Names:
East Northfield, Gill Station, Mount Hermon, Northfield Farms, Northfield Mountain, Pine Meadow, Plains, South Vernon, West Northfield.

Norton, Bristol County.
Established as a town by St 1711-1712, c 4.

1710.	Mar.	17.*	"The North Precinct of Taunton" granted to be a town by the name of Norton, a bill to perfect the grant to be brought into the next session of the General Court. (Prov. Laws, Vol. XXI, p. 791.)
1711.	June	12.*	Established as a town, from part of Taunton called "North Purchase." (Prov. Laws, Vol. I, p. 676.)

1725.   Dec.   21.*   Part established as Easton.
1753.   Dec.   22.   Part of Stoughton annexed.
1770.   Apr.   26.   Part established as the district of Mansfield.

Archaic Names of the Municipality:
Taunton North Precinct, Taunton North Purchase.

Section/Village Names:
Barrowsville, Chartley, Copper Works, Crane's, East Norton, Meadowbrook,
Norton Center, Norton Furnace, Winneconnet.

Norwell, Plymouth County.
South Scituate incorporated as a town by St 1849, c 13.
1849.   Feb.   14.   **South Scituate** incorporated as a town, from part of Scituate.
1857.   May   15.   Bounds between South Scituate and Hanover established.
1878.   Feb.   11.   Bounds between South Scituate and Hanover established
                     and part of each town annexed to the other town.
1888.   Feb.   27.   Name of South Scituate may be changed to Norwell,
                     Standish, Deane, Cushing or Hatherly upon submission to
                     the voters of South Scituate.
1888.   Mar.   5.   The name of **Norwell** was adopted by the town.
1897.   Apr.   30.   Bounds between Norwell and Hingham established.
1973.   Mar.   17.   Town charter adopted.

Archaic Names of the Municipality:
South Scituate.

Section/Village Names:
Accord, Assinippi, Church Hill, Mount Blue, Norwell Center, Queen Anne's Corner,
Ridge Hill, West Scituate.

Norwich - see Huntington.

Norwood, Norfolk County.
Incorporated as a town by St 1872, c 32.
1872.   Feb.   23.   Incorporated as a town, from parts of Dedham and Walpole.

Section/Village Names:
Ellis, Morrills, Norwood Central, Winslow.

Nottingham - see Dunstable.

Oak Bluffs, Dukes County.
Cottage City incorporated as a town by St. 1880, c 18.
1880.   Feb.   17.   **Cottage City** incorporated as a town, from part of
                     Edgartown.
1907.   Jan.   25.   Corporate name of the town of Cottage City changed to **Oak
                     Bluffs.**
1935.   Apr.   8.   Bounds between Oak Bluffs and Tisbury re-established.
1937.   May   5.   Bounds between Oak Bluffs and Edgartown re-established.
1955.   June   7.   Bounds between Oak Bluffs and Tisbury re-established.

Archaic Names of the Municipality:
Cottage City, Easternmost Chop of Holmes' Hole.

Section/Village Names:
Bellevue Heights, Camp Ground, Central Place, Chicken Alley, Copeland District,
East Chop, Eastville, Ellinwood Heights, Elysian Heights, Farm Neck, Fayal, Forest
Hill, Harthaven, Haven Gates, Head of Pond, Hethern Heights, Lagoon Heights,
Longwood, Major's Cove, Meshaket Grove, North Bluff, Nunnepog, Oak Grove,
Oakland, Prospect Heights, Seaglen, Sengekontacket, Sunset Heights, Vineyard
Highlands, Wesleyan Grove, Windemere.

Oakham, Worcester County.
Made a town by St 1775-1776, c 3.

1762.	June	7.	Incorporated as a district by the name of Oakham from part of Rutland. (Prov. Laws, Vol. IV, p. 571.)
1775.	Aug.	23.	Made a town, by general act under which districts became towns.

Archaic Names of the Municipality:
Rutland West Wing.

Section/Village Names:
Coldbrook, Coldbrook Springs, Lincolnville, Parkers Mills.

Orange, Franklin County.
Incorporated as a town by St 1809, c 59.

1783.	Oct.	15.	Established as a district by the name of Orange from parts of Athol, Royalston, Warwick, and a track of land called "Ervingshire."
1810.	Feb.	24.	Incorporated as a town, formerly the district of Orange.
1816.	Feb.	7.	Part annexed to Athol.
1837.	Mar.	16.	Part of "Erving's Grant" annexed.
1837.	Mar.	16.	Part of New Salem annexed.
1841.	Feb.	27.	Bounds between Orange and Erving established.

Archaic Names of the Municipality:
Erving's Grant, Ervingshire.

Section/Village Names:
Blissville, Chestnut Hill, Eagleville, Fryville, Furnace Village, Holtshire, Lake Mattewa, North Orange, North Pond, Plains, Tully, Walnut Hill, West Orange, Wheeler.

Orleans, Barnstable County.
Incorporated as a town by St 1796, c 64.

1797.	Mar.	3.	Incorporated as a town, from part of Eastham.
1839.	Mar.	9.	Part of Eastham annexed.
1861.	Feb.	20.	Bounds between Orleans and Brewster established.
1862.	Apr.	4.	Bounds between Orleans and Harwich established.
1862.	Apr.	14.	Bounds between Orleans and Chatham established.
1867.	Mar.	23.	Bounds between Orleans and Eastham established and part of each town annexed to the other town.
1935.	June	20.	Bounds between Orleans and Brewster re-established.

Archaic Names of the Municipality:
Namskaket, Pochet.

Section/Village Names:
Barleyneck, East Orleans, Namskaket, Nemequoit, North Orleans, Orleans Center, Pochet, Portnomequot, Rock Harbor, South Orleans, Tonset, West Orleans.

Otis, Berkshire County.
Loudon established as a town by St 1772-1773, c 37.

1773.	Feb.	27.	**Loudon** established as a town by St 1772-1773, c 37, from a tract of land called Tyringham Equivalent. (Prov. Laws, Vol. V, p. 237.)
1789.	June	24.	The District of Bethleham incorporated as a district, formerly the North Eleven Thousand Acres, so called.
1809.	June	19.	The District of Bethleham and the town of Loudon unite as the town of Loudon
1810.	Mar.	1.	The act of June 19, 1809 took effect.

1810.	Mar.	1.	Part of Louden annexed to Becket.
1810.	June	13.	The name of the town of Loudon changed to **Otis**.
1838.	Apr.	9.	A tract of unincorporated land called "East Eleven Thousand Acres" annexed.

Archaic Names of the Municipality:
Bethlehem District, East Eleven Thousand Acres, Loudon, North Eleven Thousand Acres, Tyringham Equivalent.

Section/Village Names:
Algerie, Cold Spring, East Otis, North Otis, West Center, West Otis.

Oxford, Worcester County.

1693.	May	31.*	"Mr Dan Allen" is listed in the records as a representative from Oxford. (Court Rec., Vol. VI, p. 278.)
1731.	Dec.	8.*	Certain lands annexed.
1732.	Feb.	2.*	Part included in new town of Dudley.
1734.	Nov.	22.*	Certain lands annexed.
1754.	Nov.	21.	Part established as the district of Charlton.
1778.	Apr.	10.	The parish lately set off from Oxford and other towns established as Ward.
1789.	Jan.	5.	Part of Charlton annexed.
1793.	Feb.	18.	Part of Sutton annexed.
1807.	Feb.	6.	The "Oxford South Gore" annexed.
1809.	Feb.	23.	Part of Charlton annexed.
1832.	Mar.	6.	Part included in the new town of Webster.
1838.	Mar.	22.	The "Oxford North Gore" annexed.
1907.	Feb.	11.	Bounds between Oxford and Charlton established.
1907.	Feb.	11.	Bounds between Oxford and Millbury established.
1908.	Mar.	27.	Bounds between Oxford and Auburn established.
1972.	Mar.	6.	Town charter adopted.

Archaic Names of the Municipality:
A "Praying Indian" (Christian) town, Manchaug, New Oxford, Nipmuc Country, Oxford North Gore, Oxford South Gore.

Section/Village Names:
Bartlett's Village (extinct), Chase's Village (extinct), Buffumville, Chaffee, Comminsville, Federal Hill, Fort Hill, George's Crossing, Gore, Hawes, Hodges Village, Howarth's Village, Lancaster, Larnedville, Merriam District, North Oxford, North Oxford Mills, North Oxford Station, Oxford Heights, Plains, Sacarrappa, Taft's Mills (extinct), South Oxford, Texas Village, West Oxford.

Palmer, Hampden County.
Made a town by St 1775-1776, c 3.

1752.	Jan.	30.*	Established as a district by the name of Palmer formerly the plantation called "The Elbows". (Prov. Laws, Vol. III, p. 599.)
1760.	Apr.	23.	Part of Brimfield annexed.
1761.	Nov.	25.	Tract of land in Palmer included in the District of Ware.
1763.	Feb.	7.	Bounds definitely established.
1775.	Aug.	23.	Made a town, by general act under which districts became towns.
1828.	Feb.	8.	Bounds between Palmer and Monson established.
1831.	Feb.	7.	Part of Western annexed.
1910.	Apr.	29.	Bounds between Palmer and Ware established.
1974.	Mar.	4.	Town charter adopted.

Archaic Names of the Municipality:
District of Palmer, Kings Field, Kings Town, New Marlborough, The Elbows, The
Elbow Tract,

Section/Village Names:
Baptist Hill, Bondsville, Cooley's Bridge, Depot Village, Forest Lake, Four Corners,
Mount Dumplin, Thorndike, Three Rivers.

Extinct Section Names:
Blanchardville, Bond's Village, Burleigh (school), Carpet Mill, Duckville Hatchery,
Hog Hill, Mason District, Palmer Center, Palmer Depot, Pottersville, Shorley
District, Shaw District, Tenneyville, Whipples Crossing.

Parsons - see West Newbury.

Partridgefield - see Peru.

Paxton, Worcester County.
Made a town by St 1775-1776, c 3.

1765.	Feb.	12.	Incorporated as a district by the name of Paxton from parts of Leicester and Rutland. (Prov. Laws, Vol. IV, p. 734.)
1772.	July	14.	Part of Rutland adjudged to belong to the district of Paxton.
1775.	Aug.	23.	Made a town, by general act under which districts became towns.
1793.	Mar.	27.	Bounds between Paxton and Holden established.
1804.	Feb.	13.	Part of Holden annexed.
1829.	Feb.	20.	Bounds between Paxton and Rutland established.
1831.	Mar.	19.	Part annexed to Holden.
1838.	Apr.	9.	Part of Holden annexed.
1851.	May	24.	Part of Rutland annexed.
1906.	Mar.	13.	Bounds between Paxton and Holden established.

Section/Village Names:
Paxton Navy Yard.

PEABODY, Essex County.
South Danvers incorporated as a town by St 1855, c 358.
Incorporated as a city by Special Acts 1916, c 300.

1855.	May	18.	**South Danvers** incorporated as a town, from part of Danvers.
1856.	Apr.	30.	Bounds between South Danvers and Salem established and part of each place annexed to the other place.
1856.	May	31.	Bounds between South Danvers and Danvers established.
1868.	Apr.	13.	Name of South Danvers changed to **Peabody** upon acceptance by the voters of South Danvers.
1868.	Apr.	30.	Act of Apr. 13, 1868, accepted.
1882.	Mar.	27.	Part of Peabody annexed to Salem.
1916.	May	8.	Peabody incorporated as a city.
1916.	Nov.	7.	Act of May 8, 1916, accepted by the town.

Archaic Names of the Municipality:
South Danvers.

Section/Village Names:
Bleachery, Crow Village, Dublin (extinct), East End, Frog Island, Gardner Park, Glue
Hill, Kingdom, Kingscroft, Mount Pleasant, Needham's Corner, North Peabody,
Paper Mills, Phelps' Mills, Proctor's Crossing, South Peabody, The Rocks, West
Peabody.

Pelham, Hampshire County.
Established as a town by St 1742-1743, c 30.

1743.	Jan.	15.*	Established as a town, formerly a tract of land called "New Lisburn". (Prov. Laws, Vol. III, p. 49.)
1788.	June	16.	Part of Belchertown annexed.
1822.	Jan.	28.	Part included in the new town of Prescott.
1927.	Apr.	26.	Part of Enfield annexed.
1938.	Apr.	26.	Act of Apr. 26, 1927, amended.
1938.	Apr.	28.	Act of Apr. 26, 1927, as amended, took effect.

Archaic Names of the Municipality:
Lisborn, New Lisburne, Stoddards Town.

Section/Village Names:
Bartlett's, Bobbin Hollow, Bobbinsville, East Hollow, East Pelham, New Pelham, Packardsville, Pelham Center, Pelham City, Pelham Hill, Pelham Hollow, West Pelham.

Pembroke, Plymouth County.
Established as a town by St 1711-1712, c 10.

1712.	Mar.	21.*	Established as a town, from part of Duxbury called "Mattakeeset", a tract of land known as "Major's Purchase", and the land called "Marshfield Upper-Lands at Mattakeeset". (Prov. Laws, Vol. I, p. 684.)
1726.	June	16.*	Part included in the new town of Kingston.
1734.	July	4.*	Part included in the new town of Halifax.
1820.	Feb.	22.	Part established as Hanson.
1835.	Mar.	6.	Bounds between Pembroke and Hanover established.
1885.	Apr.	23.	Bounds between Pembroke and Hanover established.
1903.	Apr.	3.	Bounds between Pembroke and Hanson established.

Archaic Names of the Municipality:
Major's Purchase, Marshfield Upper Lands, Mattakeeset.

Section/Village Names:
Bryantville, Crookertown, East Pembroke, Fosterville, North Pembroke, Pembroke Center, Schooset, Standish.

Pepperell, Middlesex County.
Made a town by St 1775-1776, c 3.

1753.	Apr.	12.	Established as a district by the name of "Pepperell" formerly the second precinct of the town of Groton. (Prov. Laws, Vol. III, p. 652.)
1775.	Aug.	23.	Made a town, by general act under which districts became towns.
1803.	Feb.	3.	Part annexed to Groton.
1857.	May	18.	Part of Groton annexed.
1991.	Dec.	20.	Part of Groton annexed.

Archaic Names of the Municipality:
Nissitisset, Groton Second Precinct.

Section/Village Names:
Babatasset, Burkinshaw, East Pepperell, Hollingsworth (former R.R. station), Hovey Corner, Huff's Mills, Keys Hill, Nissitissett, North Pepperell, North Village, Oak Hill, Paugus, Pepperell Station, Primus.

Peru, Berkshire County.
Partridgefield established as a town by St 1771-1772, c 7.

1771.	July	4.	**Partridgefield** established as a town, formerly the plantation Number Two. (Prov. Laws, Vol. V, p. 164.)
1783.	Mar.	12.	Part of Partridgefield included in the new town of Middlefield.
1804.	June	21.	Part of Partridgefield included in the new town of Hinsdale.
1806.	June	19.	Name changed from Partridgefield to **Peru**.
1912.	Feb.	28.	Bounds between Peru and Hinsdale established.

Archaic Names of the Municipality:
Partridgefield, Plantation Number Two (Western Townships of 1762).

Petersham, Worcester County.
Established as a town by St 1753-1754, c 38.

1754.	Apr.	20.	Petersham established as a town, formerly the plantation of "Nichewoag". (Prov. Laws, Vol. III, p. 731.)
1756.	Aug.	23.	Certain lands annexed to Petersham.
1801.	Feb.	18.	Part included in the new town of Dana.
1803.	Feb.	12.	Bounds between Petersham and Dana established.
1842.	Feb.	4.	Parts of Petersham annexed to Dana.
1882.	Apr.	10.	Bounds between Petersham and Dana established.
1927.	Apr.	26.	All of the town of Dana and certain parts of the towns of Greenwich and Prescott annexed.
1938.	Apr.	26.	Act of Apr. 26, 1927, amended.
1938.	Apr.	28.	Act of Apr. 26, 1927, as amended, took effect.

Archaic Names of the Municipality:
Capt. Whites Town, Nichewoag Plantation, Volunteers Town.

Section/Village Names:
Ledgeville, New Salem Station, Nichewaug, Sacket's Harbor.

Phillipston, Worcester County.
Gerry incorporated as a town by St 1786, c 34.

1786.	Oct.	20.	**Gerry** incorporated as a town, from parts of Athol and Templeton.
1789.	Feb.	2.	Bound between Gerry and Templeton established.
1799.	Feb.	26.	Part of Gerry annexed to Royalston.
1806.	Feb.	28.	Part of Gerry annexed to Athol.
1814.	Feb.	5.	Corporate name of the town of Gerry, changed to **Phillipston**.
1837.	Mar.	29.	Bounds between Phillipston and Royalston established.
1892.	Apr.	5.	Part annexed to Templeton.
1908.	Apr.	17.	Bounds between Phillipston and Templeton established.

Archaic Names of the Municipality:
Gerry.

Section/Village Names:
Cummings Corner, East Phillipston, Goulding Village, Lamb City, Phillipston Center, Phillipston Corner, Powers Mills, Ward Hill.

PITTSFIELD, Berkshire County.
Established as a town by St 1760-1761, c 34.
Incorporated as a city by St 1889, c 411.

1761.	Apr.	21.	Established as a town, formerly the plantation called "Poontoosuck". (Prov. Laws, Vol. IV, p. 434.)
1889.	June	5.	Incorporated as a city.

| 1890. | Feb. | 11. | Act of June 5, 1889, accepted by the town. |
| 1972. | June | 8. | Bounds between Pittsfield and Dalton altered, revised, and relocated. |

Archaic Names of the Municipality:
Boston Township Number Three, Fort Anson, Pontoosuck Plantation, Wendellstown, Windal's Town.

Section/Village Names:
Allendale, Arrowhead, Balance Rock (former R.R. station), Barkerville, Beech Grove, Bel Air, Bobtown, Coltsville, Eveningside, Franklin Square, Lower Barkerville, Morningside, North Adams Junction, Park Annex, Peck's, Pomeroy, Pontoosuc, Pittsfield Junction, Russell's, Springside, Stearnsville, Taconic, Tillotson's, The Bars, Upper Barkerville, West Pittsfield.

Plainfield, Hampshire County.
Incorporated as a town by St 1807, c 119.

1785.	Mar.	16.	Incorporated as a district by the name of Plainfield from part of Cummington.
1794.	Feb.	4.	Part of Province land annexed to the district of Plainfield.
1803.	June	21.	Part of Hawley annexed to the district of Plainfield.
1807.	June	15.	Incorporated as a town, formerly the district of Plainfield.

Section/Village Names:
Hallockville, Plainfield Center.

Plainville, Norfolk County.
Incorporated as a town by St 1905, c 255.

| 1905. | Apr. | 4. | Incorporated as a town, from part of Wrentham. |

Section/Village Names:
Blake's Hill, Franklin Hill, Guinea, Rabbit Hill, Shepardville, West Side.

Plymouth, Plymouth County.
The first entry appearing in "Plimouths great Book of Deeds of Lands Enrolled" is dated 1620.

1670.	June	7.*	Bounds between Plymouth and Sandwich as established Jan. 19,* 1663, ordered to be recorded.
1707.	June	4.*	Part established as Plympton.
1726.	June	16.*	The "North Precinct" (including parts of Duxbury, Pembroke and Plympton) established as Kingston.
1739.	July	10.*	Part called the plantation of "Agawam" included in the new town of Wareham.
1827.	Jan.	20.	Part annexed to Wareham.
1973.	Mar.	15.	Town charter adopted.

Archaic Names of the Municipality:
Accomack, Agawam Plantation, Apaum, Kamesit, Kitaumet, New Plymouth, Patuxet, Plimouth, Sauquish, Tionet, Umpame.

Section/Village Names:
Barkers, Billington Sea, Cedarville, Chiltonville, Clark's Island, Collingwood, Cordage (formerly Seaside), Darby, Eagle Hill, Ellis Four Corners, Ellisville, Four Corners, Gurnet, Hobs Hole, Holmes Dam, Jabez Corner, Jackson's Brook, Little Long Pond, Long Pond, Manomet, Manter's Point, North Plymouth, Oak Ridge, Plymouth Woods, Poverty Point, Priscilla Beach, Pumping Station, Raymond Red Brook, Rocky Hill, Saquish, South Plymouth, South Pond Village, Stoney Beach, Vallerville, Wares, Wellingsley, West Plymouth, White Horse Beach.

Plympton, Plymouth County.
Established as a town by St 1707, c 5.

1707.	June	4.*	Established as a town, from part of Plymouth. (Prov. Laws, Vol. XXI, p. 747.)
1726.	June	16.*	Part included in the new town of Kingston.
1734.	July	4.*	Part included in the new town of Halifax.
1734.	Dec.	11.*	Part of Middleborough annexed.
1790.	June	9.	Part established as Carver.
1793.	Feb.	8.	Bounds between Plympton and Carver established.
1831.	Mar.	16.	Part annexed to Halifax.
1863.	Feb.	6.	Bounds between Plympton and Halifax established and part of each town annexed to the other town.

Archaic Names of the Municipality:
Wenatukset.

Section/Village Names:
Neck, North Plympton, Prospect Hill, Silver Lake, Winnetuxet.

Prescott (A Drowned Town) - see New Salem and Petersham.
Incorporated as a town by St 1821, c 34.

1822.	Jan.	28.	Incorporated as a town, from parts of Pelham and New Salem.
1911.	Apr.	27.	Bounds between Prescott and New Salem established.
1927.	Apr.	26.	Annexed to the towns of Petersham and New Salem.
1938.	Apr.	26.	Act of Apr. 26, 1927, amended.
1938.	Apr.	28.	Act of Apr. 26, 1927, as amended, took effect.

Section/Village Names: (Extinct)
Mellon Hollow, North Prescott, Prescott Hill, Prescott Hollow, Soapstone.

Princeton, Worcester County.
Incorporated as a town by St 1770-1771, c 23.

1759.	Oct.	20.	Established as a district by the name of Princeton from part of Rutland and certain lands adjacent. (Prov. Laws, Vol. IV, p. 266.)
1771.	Apr.	24.	Incorporated as a town, formerly the district of Princeton and all lands adjoining not included in any other town or district. (Prov. Laws ,Vol. V, p. 124.)
1773.	Mar.	6.	All lands adjoining the district of Princeton included in the act of Apr. 24, 1771, set off and the same lands to remain as they were before the passage of the said act. (Prov. Laws, Vol. V, p. 238.)
1810.	Feb.	16.	Part of Hubbardston annexed.
1838.	Apr.	4.	Part of unincorporated lands of "No Town" annexed.
1870.	Apr.	22.	Part of Westminster annexed.

Archaic Names of the Municipality:
No Town, Potash Farm, Rutland East Wing, Wachuset.

Section/Village Names:
Brook's Station, East Princeton, Everettville, Mount Wachusett, Princeton Depot, West Sterling.

Provincetown, Barnstable County.
Established as a town by St 1727, c 11.

1727.	June	14.*	Established as a town, formerly the Precinct of Cape Cod. (Prov. Laws, Vol. II, p. 426.)
1813.	June	12.	Part of Truro annexed and bounds established.

1829.	Mar.	2.	Part of Truro annexed and bounds established.
1836.	Mar.	30.	Part of Truro annexed.
1973.	July	1.	Town charter adopted.

Archaic Names of the Municipality:
Cape Cod Precinct.

Section/Village Names:
Long Point, Mayflower Heights, Peaked Hill, Pilgrim Heights, Puritan Heights (former R.R. station), Race Point, Wood End.

QUINCY, Norfolk County.
Incorporated as a town by St 1791, c 36.
Incorporated as a city by St 1889, c 347.

1792.	Feb.	22.	Incorporated as a town, from part of Braintree. In the same act part of that part of Dorchester called "Squantum and the farms" was annexed.
1814.	Feb.	10.	Part of that part of Dorchester called "Squantum and the farms" annexed.
1819.	Feb.	12.	Part of Dorchester annexed.
1820.	Feb.	21.	Bounds between Quincy and Dorchester established, and part of that part of Dorchester called "Squantum" annexed.
1855.	May	2.	Part of that part of Dorchester called "Squantum" annexed.
1856.	Apr.	24.	Part of Braintree annexed.
1885.	Apr.	16.	Bounds between Quincy and Milton established, and part of each town annexed to the other town.
1888.	May	17.	Incorporated as a city.
1888.	June	11.	Act of May 17, 1888, accepted by the town.

Archaic Names of the Municipality:
Merrymount, Mount Wollaston, Braintree North, Precinct.

Section/Village Names:
Adams Shore, Atlantic, Barry's Corner, Bellevue, Brewer's Corner, Germantown, Hough's Neck, Merrymount Park, Montclair, Norfolk Downs, North Quincy, Post Island, Quincy Adams, Quincy Neck, Quincy Point, Rock Island, South Quincy, Squantum, The Farms, West Quincy, Wollaston, Wollaston Heights.

Randolph, Norfolk County.
Incorporated as a town by St 1792, c 49.

1793.	Mar.	9.	Incorporated as a town, from part of Braintree with a proviso that certain estates of remonstrants be allowed to remain in Braintree.
1811.	June	22.	Estates of Samuel Chessman and Levi Thayer, remonstrants, under act of Mar. 9, 1793, re-annexed.
1861.	Mar.	21.	Bounds between Randolph and Abington established.
1872.	Feb.	29.	Part established as Holbrook.
1889.	Apr.	16.	Part annexed to Avon.

Archaic Names of the Municipality:
Cochato.

Section/Village Names:
Beulah Park, Holbrook Gardens, Jones City, New Dublin, North Randolph, Randolph Farms, Spotless Town, Tower Hill, West Corners.

Raynham, Bristol County.
Established as a town by St 1730-1731, c 14.

| 1731. | Apr. | 2.* | Established as a town, from part of Taunton. (Prov. Laws, Vol. II, p. 590.) |

1866.   Feb.   27.   Bounds between Raynham and Taunton established.

Archaic Names of the Municipality:
Taunton East Precinct, Squawbetty.

Section/Village Names:
Judson, North Raynham, Prattville, Raynham Center, South Raynham.

Reading, Middlesex County.
1644.   May   29.*   Established from part of Lynn - "It is ordered, that Linn
                          village, ...shalbe called Redding." (Mass. Bay Rec., Vol. II, p.
                          73.)
1644.   May   29.*   Bounds between Reading and Woburn established.
1644.   June   10.*   House of Deputies concurs with the vote of May 29, 1644.
1651.   Oct.   14.*   Land granted to Reading.
1727.   June   3.*   Part of Malden annexed.
1730.   Sept.   25.*   Part included in the new town of Wilmington.
1734.   Dec.   21.*   Part annexed to Stoneham.
1751.   Apr.   5.*   Bounds between Reading and Stoneham established.
1753.   Dec.   18.   Bounds between Reading and Malden established.
1812.   Feb.   25.   Part of Reading established as South Reading.
1813.   June   16.   Part of South Reading annexed.
1853.   Mar.   22.   Part established as North Reading.
1854.   Apr.   10.   Bounds between Reading and Lynnfield established.
1905.   May   2.   Bounds between Reading and Lynnfield established.
1934.   Apr.   27.   Bounds between Reading and Woburn established.
1947.   Apr.   10.   Bounds between Reading and Lynnfield established.
1986.   Mar.   24.   Town charter adopted.
1986.   July   1.   Town charter became effective.

Archaic Names of the Municipality:
Linn Village, Redding.

Section/Village Names:
Dragon Corner, Reading Highlands.

Rehoboth, Bristol County.
Barrington established as a town by St 1717-1718, c 114.
1645.   June   4.*   Established as a town - "That Seacunck be called
                          Rehoboath". (Ply. Col. Rec., Vol. XI, p. 46.)
1649.   June   6.*   Rehoboth bounds to be established.
1667.   Oct.   30.*   Part of Rebohoth included in the new town of
                          Wannamoisett.
1668.   June   3.*   Certain lands annexed to Rehoboth.
1670.   Aug.   11.*   Bounds between Rehoboth and Swansea established.
1671.   July   5.*   The land called "North Purchase" granted to Rehoboth.
1682.   July   7.*   Bounds established.
1694.   Oct.   19.*   Part called the "North Purchase" established as
                          Attleborough.
1697.   Sept.   10.*   Bounds between Rehoboth and Attleborough established.
1710.   June   26.*   Part called "Mile & Half of Land", set off to Attleborough.
1717.   Nov.   18.*   **Barrington** established as a town, from part of Swansea.
                          (Prov. Laws, Vol. IX, p. 563.)
1735.   Dec.   23.*   A gore of land annexed to Rehoboth and Swansea.
1747.   Feb.   5.*   Western part of Barrington which remained in this province
                          after settlement of the Rhode Island boundry annexed to
                          Rehoboth.
1812.   Feb.   26.   Part established as Seekonk.

Archaic Names of the Municipality:
Barrington, North Purchase, Seacunck, Seconet, Sowamsett.

Section/Village Names:
Anawan, Great Rock, Harris, Hornbine, Horton Signal, Long Hill, North Rehoboth, Oak Swamp, Perryville, Rehoboth Center, Rehoboth Village, Rocky Hill, South Rehoboth, West Central.

REVERE, Suffolk County.
North Chelsea incorporated as a town by St 1846, c 127.
Revere incorporated as a city by St 1914, c 687.

1846.	Mar.	19.	**North Chelsea** incorporated as a town, from part of Chelsea.
1752.	Mar.	27.	Part of North Chelsea established as Winthrop.
1871.	Mar.	24.	Name of the town of North Chelsea to be changed to **Revere** if accepted by the town within ninety days.
1871.	Apr.	3.	Act of Mar. 24, 1871, accepted by the town.
1914.	June	19.	Incorporated as a city.
1914.	Nov.	3.	Act of June 19, 1914, accepted by the town.

Archaic Names of the Municipality:
Allotment Number Thirteen, North Chelsea, Rumney Marsh.

Section/Village Names:
Beachmont, Crescent Beach, Fenno's Corner, Franklin Park, North Revere, Oak Island, Point of Pines, Revere Beach, Revere Center, Revere Highlands.

Rexhame - see Marshfield.

Richmond, Berkshire County.
Richmont incorporated as a town by St 1765-1766, c 16.

1765.	June	21.	**Richmont** incorporated as a town, formerly the new plantation called Yokum Town and Mount Ephraim. (Prov. Laws, Vol. IV, p. 817.)
1767.	Feb.	26.	Part of Richmont established as the district of Lenox.
1772.	Apr.	25.	Certain estates set off from the district of Lenox to Richmont.
1785.	Mar.	3.	Name of the town of Richmont changed to **Richmond**.
1834.	Mar.	27.	Bounds between Richmond and West Stockbridge established.

Archaic Names of the Municipality:
Mount Ephraim Plantation, Plantation Number Eight (1762 Townships), Richmont, Yokum Town Plantation.

Section/Village Names:
Richmond Furnace, Rossiter Corners, Stevens Corner.

Richmont - see Richmond.

Rochester, Plymouth County.

1686.	June	4.*	Established as a town - The Court granted the desires of the "...inhabitants of Scippican, alias Rochester to become a township...." (Ply. Col. Rec., Vol. VI, p. 189.)
1714.	June	11.*	Bounds between Rochester and Tiverton established.
1739.	July	10.*	Part of Rochester included in the new town of Wareham.
1836.	Apr.	9.	Part of Rochester annexed to Fairhaven and bounds established.
1852.	May	14.	Part established as Marion.
1853.	Apr.	8.	Bounds between Rochester and Marion established.
1857.	May	20.	Part of Rochester established as Mattapoisett.

1864.	Apr.	20.	Bounds between Rochester and Wareham established.
1866.	Feb.	15.	Bounds between Rochester and Wareham established.
1887.	June	3.	Bounds between Rochester and Wareham established.
1939.	June	12.	Bounds between Rochester and Wareham established.

Archaic Names of the Municipality:
Mattapoisett, Monehansett, Scippican.

Section/Village Names:
Bisbee's Corner, Cowen's Corner, East Rochester, Look's Mills, North Rochester, Pierceville, Rochester Center, Roundsville Mills, Sherman's Corner.

Rockland, Plymouth County.
Incorporated as a town by St 1874, c 44.

1874.	Mar.	9.	Incorporated as a town, from part of Abington.
1878.	Mar.	23.	Bounds between Rockland and Hanover established, and part of each town annexed to the other town.
1969.	Mar.	8.	Town charter adopted.

Section/Village Names:
Hatherly.

Rockport, Essex County.
Incorporated as a town by St 1840, c 8.

| 1840. | Feb. | 27. | Incorporated as a town, from part of Gloucester. |

Archaic Names of the Municipality:
Sandy Bay, Gloucester Fifth Precinct, Loblolley, Tragabigzanda.

Section/Village Names:
Bearskin Neck, Dogtown Commons (extinct), Folly Cove, Land's End, Ocean View, South Rockport, Stonehaven, Thatcher's Island.

Rowe, Franklin County.
Incorporated as a town by St 1784, c 34.

1785.	Feb.	9.	Incorporated as a town, from land called "Myrifield" and lands adjoining.
1822.	Feb.	21.	Part included in the new town of Monroe.
1838.	Apr.	2.	Part of the unincorporated land called "Zoar" annexed.

Archaic Names of the Municipality:
Fort Pelham, Merifield, Myrifield, Plantation Number Ten (1762 Townships), Zoar.

Section/Village Names:
Davis, Heywoods, Hoosac Tunnel Station, Monroe Bridge Station, Rowe Village.

Rowley, Essex County.

1639.	Sept.	4.*	"Mr. Ezechi: Rogers plantation shalbee called Rowley." (Mass. Bay Rec., Vol. I, p. 271.)
1640.	May	13.*	Bounds fixed.
1640.	Oct.	7.*	Additional grant of land to Rowley.
1649.	May	4.*	One-fifth of Plum Island granted to Rowley.
1656.	May	14.*	Bounds between Rowley and Newbury established.
1668.	May	27.*	"...inhabitants of Rouley liuing ouer against Hauerill, the Court,...." granted them the right to establish a village. (Mass. Bay Rec., Vol. IV, Part 2, p. 380.)
1685.	Aug.	12.*	Part established as township of Rowley Village and bounds established.
1701.	Feb.	24.*	Bounds between Rowley and Bradford established.
1785.	Nov.	29.	Part of Ipswich annexed.

1808.	June	10.	Part annexed to Boxford.
1810.	June	13.	Part annexed to Boxford.
1825.	June	18.	Bounds between Rowley and Boxford established.
1838.	Apr.	21.	Part established as Georgetown.
1904.	Mar.	12.	Bounds between Rowley and Boxford established.
1904.	Mar.	19.	Bounds between Rowley and Ipswich established.
1905.	Mar.	27.	Bounds between Rowley and Newbury established.
1931.	June	9.	Bounds between Rowley and Newbury established.

Archaic Names of the Municipality:
Mr. Ezechial Rogers Plantation.

Section/Village Names:
Bean Crossing, Burk's Corner, Chaplinville, Danielsville, Doles' Corner, Glen Mills, Leighton Corner, Millwood, Nelson Island, Rooty Plain, Sodom.

Rowley Village - see Boxford.

ROXBURY - see Boston.
Incorporated as a city by St 1846, c 95.

1630.	Sept.	28.*	Mentioned in the list of plantations to be taxed as "Rocsbury" and on Oct. 19,* as "Rocksbury". (Mass. Bay Rec., Vol. I, p. 77, 79.)
1633.	Mar.	4.*	Bounds between Roxbury and Boston established.
1635.	Apr.	7.*	Bounds between Roxbury and Newe Towne established.
1636.	May	25.*	Certain lands granted to Roxbury.
1638.	May	2.*	Certain lands granted to Roxbury.
1638.	May	16.*	Bounds between Roxbury and Dedham established.
1641.	Oct.	7.*	Bounds between Roxbury and Boston at Muddy River established.
1660.	Oct.	16.*	Certain lands granted to Roxbury.
1675.	May	12.*	Bounds between Roxbury and Dedham established.
1836.	Mar.	16.	Bounds between Roxbury and Boston established.
1837.	Apr.	19.	Bounds between Roxbury and Boston established.
1838.	Apr.	23.	Part of Newton annexed.
1844.	Feb.	24.	Part annexed to Brookline.
1846.	Mar.	12.	Incorporated as a city.
1846.	Mar.	25.	Act of Mar. 12, 1846, accepted by the town.
1850.	May	3.	Part annexed to Boston and bounds between Roxbury and Boston established.
1851.	May	24.	Part established as West Roxbury.
1860.	Apr.	3.	Part annexed to Boston and bounds between Roxbury and Boston established.
1860.	Apr.	16.	Act of Apr. 3, 1860, accepted by Roxbury.
1860.	May	8.	Act of Apr. 3, 1860, accepted by Boston.
1867.	June	1.	Annexed to Boston.
1867.	Sept.	9.	Act of June 1, 1867, accepted by Roxbury and Boston.
1868.	Jan.	5.	Act of June 1, 1867, took effect.

Archaic Names of the Municipality:
Rocsbury, Rocksbury.

Royalston, Worcester County.
Established as a town by St 1764-1765, c 21.

1765.	Feb.	19.	Established as a town, formerly a tract of land known by the name of "Royalshire". (Prov. Laws, Vol. IV, p. 738.)
1780.	June	17.	Part annexed to Winchendon.
1783.	Oct.	15.	Part included in the new district of Orange.

1799.	Feb.	26.	Parts of Athol and Gerry annexed.
1803.	Mar.	7.	Part of Athol annexed.
1837.	Mar.	29.	Bounds between Royalston and Phillipston established.

Archaic Names of the Municipality:
Royalshire.

Section/Village Names:
North East Royalston, North Royalston, Royalston Center, South Royalston, West Royalston.

Russell, Hampden County.
Incorporated as a town by St 1791, c 39.

1792.	Feb.	25.	Incorporated as a town, from part of that part of Westfield called the "New Addition" and from part of Montgomery.
1809.	Feb.	22.	Bounds between Russell and Blandford established.
1914.	June	3.	Bounds between Russell and Montgomery established.

Archaic Names of the Municipality:
New Addition.

Section/Village Names:
Crescent Mills, Fairfield, South Quarter Woods, Woronoco.

Rutland, Worcester County.
Established as a town by St 1713-1714, c 169.

1714.	Feb.	23.*	Established as a town, formerly a tract of land purchased from the Indians named "Naquag". (Prov. Laws, Vol. XXI, p. 842.)
1715.	Dec.	1.*	Original grant of land to Rutland confirmed.
1722.	June	18.*	To enjoy all the power and privileges of other towns.
1753.	Apr.	12.	Part established as the Rutland District.
1759.	Oct.	20.	Part included in the district of Princeton.
1762.	June	7.	Part established as the district of Oakham.
1765.	Feb.	12.	Part included in the new town of Paxton.
1767.	June	13.	Part established as the district of Hubbardston.
1772.	July	14.	Part adjudged to belong to the district of Paxton.
1829.	Feb.	20.	Bounds between Rutland and Paxton established.
1851.	May	24.	Part annexed to Paxton.

Archaic Names of the Municipality:
Nagueag, Naquag.

Section/Village Names:
Barrack Hill, Muschopauge, New Boston, North Rutland, Pound Hill, Rutland Center, Rutland Heights (extinct), West Rutland, White Hall.

Rutland, District of - see Barre.

SALEM, Essex County.
Incorporated as a city by St 1836, c 42.

1630.	Aug.	23.*	Mentioned "...Mattapan and Salem only exempted". (Mass. Bay Rec., Vol. I, p. 73.)
1634.	Mar.	4.*	Bounds to be established between "Marble Harbr" and Salem , and "Marble Harbr" and Saugus.
1635.	Mar.	4.*	Bounds between Salem and Saugus and Salem and Marble Harbor to be established.
1637.	Nov.	20.*	Bounds between Salem and "Saugust" to be certified.
1639.	Mar.	13.*	Bounds between Salem and Lynn established.
1639.	Nov.	5.*	Land granted to inhabitants of Salem to establish Salem Village. Marginal note reads: "Land graunted to Salem Village, now Wenham". (Mass. Bay Rec., Vol. I, p. 279.)

1640.	May	13.*	Grant of land to inhabitants of Salem for a village at "Jeffryes Creeke" and the bounds of said village referred to certain men to settle. (Mass. Bay Rec., Vol. I, p. 288.)
1642.	May	3.*	Bounds between Jeffryes Creeke, Cape Ann and Ipswich, established.
1645.	May	14.*	Part called "Jeffryes Creeke" established as Manchester.
1649.	May	2.*	Part established as Marblehead.
1658.	Oct.	19.*	Bounds between Salem and Topsfield established.
1660.	Oct.	16.*	Certain islands known by the name of the "Miserjes & Bakers Island", granted to Salem.
1664.	May	29.*	Bounds between Salem and Topsfield established.
1668.	Nov.	7.*	Part called "Bass River" established as Beverly.
1728.	June	20.*	Part included in the new town of Middleton.
1752.	Jan.	28.*	Part established as the district of Danvers.
1753.	Sept.	11.	Part annexed to Beverly.
1836.	Mar.	23.	Incorporated as a city.
1836.	Apr.	4.	Act of Mar. 23, 1836, accepted by the town.
1840.	Mar.	17.	Bounds between Salem and Danvers established.
1856.	Apr.	30.	Bounds between Salem and South Danvers established and part of each place annexed to the other place.
1867.	Apr.	3.	Part annexed to Swampscott.
1882.	Mar.	27.	Part of Peabody annexed.

Archaic Names of the Municipality:
Fort Mary, Naumkeag, Nehume, Sholom Naumkeag.

Section/Village Names:
Atlantic, Baker's Island (former R.R. station), Blubber Hollow, Buffum's Corner, Carltonville, Castle Hill, Forest River, Gallows Hill, Juniper Point, Misery Island, Navon, North Salem, Salem Neck, Salem Willows, South Salem, The Point, Turnpike, Winter Island.

Salisbury, Essex County.

1639.	Sept.	4.*	"The other plantation beyond Merrimack shallbee called Colechester." (Mass. Bay Rec., Vol. I, p. 271.)
1639.	Nov.	5.*	**Colechester** called a town. (Mass. Bay Rec., Vol. I, p. 277.)
1640.	Oct.	7.*	Name of the town of Colechester changed, "Colechester is henceforward to bee called **Salsbury**". (Mass. Bay Rec., Vol. I, p. 305.)
1641.	June	2.*	Bounds between Salsberry & Pantucket, ali: Haverell" established.
1648.	May	13.*	A certain island granted to Salisbury.
1654.	Nov.	1.*	Bounds between Salisbury and Haverhill established.
1666.	May	23.*	Part established as Salisbury new town.
1844.	Mar.	15.	Part called "Little Salisbury" annexed to Amesbury.
1886.	June	16.	Part annexed to Amesbury.
1886.	July	1.	Act of June 16, 1886, took effect.

Archaic Names of the Municipality:
Colechester, Plantation beyond Merrimack.

Section/Village Names:
Cushing, Ring's Island, Salisbury Beach, Salisbury Center, Salisbury Plains.

Salisbury-new-town - see Amesbury.

Sandisfield, Berkshire County.
Established as a town by St 1761-1762, c 43.

| 1762. | Mar. | 6. | Established as a town, formerly the plantation called "Number Three". (Prov. Laws, Vol. IV, p. 531.) |

1797.	June	19.	District of Southfield incorporated as a district formerly the South Eleven Thousand Acres.
1819.	Feb.	8.	District of Southfield and the town of Sandisfield united as the town of Sandisfield.
1838.	Apr.	9.	Part of unincorporated land called "East Eleven Thousand Acres" annexed.
1853.	May	4.	Bounds between Sandisfield and Tolland established.
1855.	May	15.	Bounds between Sandisfield and Tolland established.
1875.	Apr.	24.	Part annexed to Monterey.
1875.	June	1.	Act of Apr. 24, 1875, took effect.

Archaic Names of the Municipality:
East Eleven Thousand Acres, Housatonic Township Number Three, Southfield District, South Eleven Thousand Acres.

Section/Village Names:
Montville, New Boston, Sandisfield Center, South Sandisfield, West New Boston (previously known as Free Quarter).

Sandwich, Barnstable County.

1638.	Mar.	6.*	Certain persons were ordered to "... goe to Sanditch, and set forth their bounds of the lands graunted to them". (Ply. Col. Rec., Vol. I, p. 80.)
1652.	Mar.	2.*	Bounds between Sandwich and Barnstable to be established.
1662.	June	10.*	Bounds between Sandwich and Barnstable to be established.
1670.	June	7.*	Bounds between Sandwich and Plymouth as established Jan. 19,* 1663, ordered to be recorded.
1672.	Oct.	29.*	Bounds between Sandwich and Barnstable established.
1681.	July	7.*	Bounds between Sandwich and "Suckanesset" established.
1684.	Oct.	28.*	Bounds established.
1735.	Nov.	28.*	Bounds between Sandwich and lands of the proprietors of Mashpee confirmed.
1811.	Feb.	26.	Part of the plantation of "Marshpee" annexed.
1859.	Apr.	1.	Part of the district of "Marshpee" annexed.
1860.	Mar.	13.	Part of the district of "Marshpee" annexed.
1872.	Mar.	19.	Part re-annexed to Mashpee.
1880.	Mar.	19.	Bounds between Sandwich and Falmouth established.
1884.	Apr.	2.	Part established as Bourne.
1887.	May	27.	Bounds between Sandwich and Mashpee established and part annexed to Mashpee.
1905.	Apr.	20.	Bounds between Sandwich and Mashpee established and part annexed to Mashpee.
1916.	Apr.	24.	Part annexed to Barnstable.

Archaic Names of the Municipality:
Pocasset, Pokesset, Sanditch, Scusset, Shaume.

Section/Village Names:
East Sandwich, Farmersville, Forestdale, Greenville (extinct), Jarvesville, Monument Village (current town of Bourne), Plowed Neck, Sagamore Hill, Sand Hill, Scorton, South Sandwich, Spectacle Pond, Spring Hill, Wakeby.

Saugus, Essex County.
Incorporated as a town by St 1814, c 107.

1815.	Feb.	17.	Incorporated as a town, from part of Lynn.
1841.	Feb.	22.	Part of Chelsea annexed.
1901.	May	17.	Bounds between Saugus and Lynnfield established.

1933.	June	27.	Part annexed to Wakefield.
1933.	July	11.	Act of June 27, 1933, accepted by Wakefield.
1933.	Sept.	18.	Act of June 27, 1933, accepted by the town.

Section/Village Names:
Bailey's Hill, Beach View, Bowkerville, Cliftondale, Cobbetts Corners, East Saugus, Grand View, Kenwood, Lawndale, Lincoln Heights, Lynnhurst, North Saugus, Oaklandville, Pleasant Hill, Saugus Center, Seagrit, Twin Springs, Vinegar Hill, Westlands.

Saugus - see Lynn.

Savoy, Berkshire County.
Incorporated as a town by St 1796, c 46.

1797. Feb.		20.	Incorporated as a town. Lands as described in the Act are shown on a Map on file in the Mass. Archives as "Plantation Number Six". (Maps and Plans, Third Series, Vol. 13, p. 19.)

Archaic Names of the Municipality:
Bullocks Grant, New Seekonk, Plantation Number Six (Western Townships of 1762), Guilford.

Section/Village Names:
Brier, Newstate, Savoy Center, Savoy Hollow.

Scituate, Plymouth County.

1633.	July	1.*	Mentioned. "...between the brooke at Scituate,...." (Ply. Col. Rec., Vol. I, p. 13.)
1636.	Oct. 4*, 5.*		The town of Scituate authorized to dispose of lands. (Ply. Col. Rec., Vol. I, p. 44.)
1640.	Nov.	30.*	Land granted to Scituate.
1643.	Mar.	7.*	Bounds established.
1727.	June	14.*	Part included in the new town of Hanover.
1782.	Nov.	8.	Bounds between Scituate and Marshfield established.
1788.	Mar.	10.	Part annexed to Marshfield.
1823.	June	14.	Part annexed to Cohasset.
1840.	Mar.	20.	Bounds between Scituate and Cohasset established and part of each town annexed to the other town.
1849.	Feb.	14.	Part established as South Scituate.
1887.	May	11.	Bounds between Scituate and Marshfield established.
1897.	Apr.	30.	Bounds between Scituate and Cohasset established.
1897.	Apr.	30.	Bounds between Scituate and Hingham established.
1928.	Mar.	23.	Bounds between Scituate and Marshfield established.
1972.	Mar.	25.	Town charter adopted.

Archaic Names of the Municipality:
Assanippi, Satuit.

Section/Village Names:
Beechwood, Belle House Neck, Clapp's Corner, Egypt, First Cliff, Fourth Cliff, Greenbush, Hatherly, Humarock, Jericho, Minot, Mungo's Corner, North Scituate (formerly Gannett Corner), North Scituate Beach, Pincin Hill, Rivermoor, Sand Hills, Scituate Center, Scituate Harbor, Scituate Neck, Scituate Station, Second Cliff, Shanghai, Sherman's Corner, Sodom, The Glades, Third Cliff, Walnut Tree Hill, Webster Village.

Seekonk, Bristol County.
Incorporated as a town by St 1812, c 138.

1812.	Feb.	26.	Incorporated as a town, from part of Rehoboth.

1861.   Apr.   10.   Part of Pawtucket and "so much of the territory over which
                        the inhabitants of Seekonk may have claimed or exercised
                        actual jurisdiction" lying east of the Massachusetts-Rhode
                        Island boundary line to be determined by the U S. Supreme
                        Court "to be taken and deemed the town of Seekonk...." (St
                        1861, c 187)
1862.   Jan.   29.   Territory named in the act of April 10, 1861, established as a
                        municipal district by the name of East Seekonk. Said district
                        of East Seekonk to cease "so soon as the proper town officers
                        of the future town of Seekonk shall have been elected and
                        qualified...." (St 1862, c 2)
1976.   Apr.   5.   Town charter adopted.

Archaic Names of the Municipality:
East Seekonk.

Section/Village Names:
Baker's Corner, Barrington, Central Village, East Junction, Lebanon Mills, Luther's
Corner, North Seekonk, Perrins Crossing, South Seekonk.

Sharon, Norfolk County.
Stoughtonham made a town by St 1775-1776, c 3.
1765.   June   21.   Stoughtonham incorporated as a district from part of
                        Stoughton. (Prov. Laws, Vol. IV, p. 808.)
1775.   Aug.   23.   **Stoughtonham** made a town, by general act under which
                        districts became towns.
1778.   June   10.   Part of Stoughtonham included in the new town of
                        Foxborough.
1783.   Feb.   25.   The town of Stoughtonham name changed to **Sharon**.
1789.   Feb.   16.   Part of Stoughton annexed.
1792.   Feb.   22.   Part of Stoughton annexed.
1793.   Mar.   12.   Bounds between Sharon and Foxborough established and
                        part of Sharon annexed to Foxborough.
1804.   Feb.   28.   Part annexed to Walpole.
1811.   June   21.   Part annexed to Walpole.
1833.   Jan.   30.   Bounds between Sharon and Foxborough established and
                        part of each town annexed to the other town.
1850.   Feb.   28.   Part annexed to Foxborough.
1864.   Mar.   26.   Part of Stoughton annexed.
1874.   May   1.   Part annexed to Walpole.
1899.   Mar.   24.   Bounds between Sharon and Canton established.
1924.   Apr.   28.   Bounds between Sharon and Stoughton established.
1957.   Apr.   11.   Bounds between Sharon and Stoughton established.

Archaic Names of the Municipality:
Mashapoag, Massapoag, Pole Plain, Stoughtonham.

Section/Village Names:
East Sharon, Knife Works, Mann's Hill, Massapoag Lake, Moose Hill, Plains, Sharon
Center, Sharon Heights, South Sharon.

Sheffield, Berskhire County.
Established as a town by St 1733, c 1.
1733.   Jan.   22.*   Established as a town, formerly the lands in the lower
                        plantation called "Houssat [o][a] nn [o]ck". (Prov. Laws, Vol.
                        II, p. 673.)
1753.   June   19.   Certain lands lying west of Sheffield annexed.
1760.   Jan.   21.   Certain estates annexed.
1761.   June   30.   Part established as Great Barrington.
1790.   Feb.   22.   Part annexed to Egremont.

1796.	June	19.	Part annexed to New Marlborough.
1798.	Feb.	7.	Part annexed to New Marlborough.
1824.	Feb.	16.	Part annexed to Egremont.
1869.	June	4.	Bounds between Sheffield and Egremont established.
1871.	Apr.	19.	Part annexed to New Marlborough and bounds established.

Archaic Names of the Municipality:
Houssatannock Lower Plantation, Schaghticoke, Skatecook, Scaticook.

Section/Village Names:
Ashley Falls, East Sheffield (now Clayton in New Marlborough).

Shelburne, Franklin County.
Made a town by St 1775-1776, c 3.

1768.	June	21.	Established as a district by the name of Shelburne, from part of Deerfield. (Prov. Laws, Vol. IV, p. 1013.)
1775.	Aug.	23.	Made a town, by general act under which districts became towns.
1781.	Feb.	19.	Part annexed to Conway.
1793.	Mar.	19.	Certain tract of land between Shelburne and North River annexed.

Archaic Names of the Municipality:
Deerfield Pasture, Deerfield Northwest.

Section/Village Names:
Bardwell, East Shelburne, Foxtown, Frankton, Patten, Pecksville, Shelburne Center, Shelburne Falls, Skinner.

Sherburn - see Nantucket.

Sherborn, Middlesex County.

1674.	Oct.	7.*	Established as a town. Land granted the petitioners and proprietors at or near "Boggestow", "...the name of the place to be called Sherborne". (Mass. Bay Rec., Vol. V, p. 23.)
1679.	Apr.	16.*	Exchange of land made between the two towns of "Sherborne" and "Naticke". (Mass. Bay Rec., Vol. V, p. 227.)
1679.	May	30.*	Return of the exchange of land of Apr. 16,* 1679, confirmed. (Mass. Bay Rec., Vol. V, p. 229.)
1684.	May	17.*	The grant of land made to the inhabitants at or near " Boggestow" confirmed and the name of the town to be Sherborne. (Mass. Bay Rec., Vol. V, p. 443.)
1700.	July	11.*	Part annexed to Framingham.
1710.	June	16.*	Bounds between Sherborn and Framingham established.
1724.	Dec.	3.*	West part of the town of "Sherburn" established as Holliston.
1792.	Mar.	3.	Bounds between "Sherburn" and Medway established.
1820.	Feb.	7.	Part of "Sherburn" annexed to Natick.
1852.	May	3.	The corporate name ot the town of "Sherburn" changed to Sherborn.
1924.	Apr.	12.	Part annexed to Framingham if the act is accepted by the town.
1925.	Jan.	1.	Act of Apr. 12, 1924, took effect.

Archaic Names of the Municipality:
Boggestow, Sherborne, Sherburn, Sherburne.

Section/Village Names:
Dowse's Corner, Edward's Plain, North Sherborn, South Sherborn, West Sherborn, Whitney's.

Shirley, Middlesex County.
Made a town by St 1775-1776, c 3.

1753.	Jan.	5.	Established as a district by the name of Shirley, from part of Groton. (Prov. Laws, Vol. III, p. 637.)
1765.	Jan.	25.	Certain land known as "Stow Leg" annexed.
1775.	Aug.	23.	Made a town, by general act under which districts became towns.
1798.	Feb.	6.	Part of Groton annexed.
1846.	Mar.	3.	Bounds between Shirley and Lunenburg established.
1848.	Apr.	23.	Bounds between Shirley and Lunenburg established.
1871.	Feb.	14.	Part included in the new town of Ayer.

Archaic Names of the Municipality:
Stow Leg.

Section/Village Names:
East Shirley, Lakeville, Mitchellville, Mount Henry, Newell, North Shirley, Shaker Village, Shirley Center, Shirley Village, Tinker Hill, Woodsville.

Shrewsbury, Worcester County.
Established as a town by St 1727-1728, c 44.

1720.	Dec.	6.*	A committee paid for "...Running the Lines of Shrewsbury, ...Wch Service they perform'd In July 1717...." (Prov. Laws, Vol. X, p. 48.)
1722.	Aug.	16.*	Shrewsbury is mentioned in a list of frontier towns.
1727.	Dec.	15.*	Established as a town. (Prov. Laws, Vol. XI, p. 236.)
1742.	Jan.	9.*	Part annexed to Grafton.
1762.	June	3.	Part annexed to Westborough.
1762.	Sept.	17.	Part of Lancaster annexed.
1768.	Feb.	27.	Part annexed to Lancaster.
1781.	Feb.	26.	Part of Lancaster annexed.
1786.	Mar.	1.	Part established as Boylston.
1793.	Mar.	2.	Part annexed to Westborough.
1826.	Mar.	3.	Part annexed to Grafton.
1907.	Feb.	11.	Bounds between Shrewsbury and Westborough established.
1907.	Feb.	11.	Bounds between Shrewsbury and Grafton established.

Section/Village Names:
Edgemere, Grafton Colony, Half Moon Park, Lake Shore, Meeting House Hill,
Quinsigamond, Shrewsbury Center, Shrewsbury Lower Village, South Shrewsbury, White City.

Shutesbury, Franklin County.
Established as a town by St 1761-1762, c 8.

1761.	June	30.	Established as a town, formerly the plantation called "Roadtown". (Prov. Laws, Vol. IV, p. 464.)
1781.	May	8.	Part included in the new town of Wendell.
1824.	Feb.	20.	Part annexed to New Salem.

Archaic Names of the Municipality:
Roadtown Plantation.

Section/Village Names:
Baconsville, Cooleyville, Lock's Pond, Lock's Village, South Shutesbury.

Somerset, Bristol County.
Incorporated as a town by St 1789, c 35.

1790.	Feb.	20.	Incorporated as a town, from part of Swansea known by the name of "Shewamet Purchase".
1854.	Apr.	4.	Part of Dighton annexed.

Archaic Names of the Municipality:
Shewamet purchase.

Section/Village Names:
Brayton Point, Egypt, Pottersville, Sherman Terrace, South Somerset, Wilbur's
Crossing.

SOMERVILLE, Middlesex County.
Incorporated as a town by St 1842, c 76.
Incorporated as a city by St 1871, c 182.

1842.	Mar.	3.	Incorporated as a town, from part of Charlestown.
1856.	Apr.	30.	Bounds between Somerville and Cambridge established and part of each place annexed to the other place.
1862.	Apr.	29.	Bounds between Somerville and Cambridge established and part of each place annexed to the other place.
1871.	Apr.	14.	Incorporated as a city.
1871.	Apr.	27.	Act of Apr. 14, 1871, accepted by the town.
1891.	May	4.	Bounds between Somerville and Boston established.
1910.	Mar.	16.	Bounds between Somerville and Arlington established.

Section/Village Names:
Bleachery, Brick Bottom, Central Hill, Clarendon Hill, Duck Village, East
Somerville, North Somerville, Prospect Hill (former R.R. station), Somerville
Highlands, Somerville Junction, Spring Hill, Tufts College, Union Square, West
Somerville, Willow Bridge, Winter Hill.

South Abington - see Whitman.

South Brimfield - see Wales.

South Danvers - see Peabody.

South Hadley, Hampshire County.
Made a town by St 1775-1776, c 3.

1753.	Apr.	12.	Established as a district by the name of South Hadley from part of Hadley. (Prov. Laws, Vol. III, p. 655.)
1768.	June	11.	Part of the district of South Hadley established as Granby.
1775.	Aug.	23.	Made a town, by general act under which districts became towns.
1781.	June	28.	Bounds between South Hadley and Granby established.
1792.	Mar.	9.	Part annexed to Granby.
1824.	June	12.	Bounds between South Hadley and Granby established.
1826.	June	20.	Bounds between South Hadley and Granby established.
1827.	June	16.	Bounds between South Hadley and Granby established.

Section/Village Names:
Falls, Fall Woods, Hadley Acres, Moody Corner, Pearl City, South Hadley Center,
South Hadley Falls, Thermopylae, Wickfield, Woodlawn.

South Reading - see Wakefield.

South Scituate - see Norwell.

Southampton, Hampshire County.
Made a town by St 1775-1776, c 3.

| 1753. | Jan. | 5. | Established as a district by the name of Southampton, from part of Northampton. (Prov. Laws, Vol. III, p. 638.) |
| 1775. | Aug. | 23. | Made a town, by general act under which districts became towns. |

1778.	Sept.	29.	Part of Northampton annexed.
1780.	Nov.	28.	Part included in the new town of Montgomery.
1785.	June	17.	Part included in the new district of Easthampton.
1792.	Mar.	6.	Part annexed to Montgomery.
1828.	Feb.	1.	Bounds between Southampton and Easthampton established.
1841.	Mar.	13.	Part annexed to Easthampton.
1850.	Apr.	4.	Part annexed to Easthampton.
1862.	Feb.	21.	Bounds between Southampton and Easthampton established.
1872.	Mar.	12.	Bounds between Southampton and Westhampton established.

Archaic Names of the Municipality:
New Hampton, Newtown on the Manham, Northampton Second Precint.

Section/Village Names:
Fomer, Glendale, Russellville.

Southborough, Worcester County.
Established as a town by St 1727, c 13.

1727.	July	6.*	Established as a town, from part of Marlborough. (Prov. Laws, Vol. II, p. 428.)
1786.	Mar.	7.	Part of Framingham annexed.
1835.	Mar.	5.	Bounds between Southborough and Westborough established.
1843.	Mar.	24.	Part annexed to Marlborough.
1901.	May	16.	Bounds between Southborough and Marlborough established.

Archaic Names of the Municipality:
Stony Brook.

Section/Village Names:
Cordaville, Fayville, Southville.

Southbridge, Worcester County.
Incorporated as a town by St 1815, c 126.

1816.	Feb.	15.	Incorporated as a town, from parts of Charlton, Dudley and Sturbridge.
1822.	Feb.	23.	Part of Dudley annexed.
1839.	Apr.	6.	Part of Sturbridge annexed.
1871.	May	4.	Bounds between Southbridge and Sturbridge established.
1907.	Feb.	11.	Bounds between Southbridge and Charlton established.
1907.	Feb.	11.	Bounds between Southbridge and Dudley established.
1973.	Mar.	2.	Town charter adopted which established city form of government.

Archaic Names of the Municipality:
Eye of the Commonwealth, Honest Town, Spec Town.

Section/Village Names:
Ammidown, Brookside, Clemence Hill, Dennison District, Dresser Hill, Fairlawn, Fort Sumpter, Globe Village, Hillside Park, Hooker District, Lawson Villa, Lebanon Hill, Lensdale, Morse District, Sandersdale, Shuttleville, The Flat, Westville.

Southfield, District of - see Sandisfield.

Southwick, Hampden County.
Made a town by St 1775-1776, c 3.

1770.	Nov.	7.	Established as a district by the name of Southwick from part of Westfield. (Prov. Laws, Vol. V, p. 75.)
1775.	Aug.	23.	Made a town, by a general act under which districts became towns.

1779.   Oct.   6.   Part of Westfield annexed.
1837.   Mar.   20.   Bounds between Southwick and Westfield established.

Archaic Names of the Municipality:
Outer Commons.

Section/Village Names:
Congamond, Gilletts Corner, Kellogg Plantations, North Longyard, Point Grove, Rising Corners, Root District, South Longyard, Southwick Center.

Spencer, Worcester County.
Made a town by St 1775-1776, c 3.

1753.   Apr.   12.   Established as a district by the name of Spencer from part of Leicester. (Prov. Laws, Vol. III, p. 653.)
1775.   Aug.   23.   Made a town, by general act under which districts became towns.

Archaic Names of the Municipality:
Leicester West Parish.

Section/Village Names:
Hillsville, North Spencer, Proutyville, Smithville, South Spencer, Westville, Wire Village.

SPRINGFIELD, Hampden County.
Incorporated as a city by St 1852, c 94.

1641.   June   2.*   Mentioned - "The Answer to the Petition...of Springfeild, ...claiming any jurisdiction or interest in Agawam, now Springfeild...." (Mass. Bay Rec., Vol. I, p. 320.)
1647.   Nov.   11.*   "...Woronoko,...shalbe be reputed as a part of ye toune of Springfeild...." (Mass. Bay Rec., Vol II, p. 224.)
1648.   Mar.   —.   Certain lands annexed.
1669.   May   19.*   Part called "Woronoake" established as Westfield.
1670.   May   31.*   Bounds between Springfield and Westfield established.
1684.   May   17.*   Bounds established.
1685.   June   4.*   Bounds between Springfield and Northampton established.
1740.   Jan.   9.*   Bounds between Springfield and Suffield established.
1743.   June   3.*   Bounds between Springfield and Suffield established.
1763.   June   15.   Part established as Wilbraham.
1774.   Feb.   23.   Part established as West Springfield.
1774.   Feb.   28.   Part called "Stony Hill" established as Ludlow.
1783.   Oct.   13.   Part established as Longmeadow.
1799.   June   11.   Part called "The Elbows" annexed to Wilbraham.
1830.   June   5.   Bounds between Springfield and Ludlow established.
1848.   Apr.   29.   Part established as Chicopee.
1852.   Apr.   12.   Incorporated as a city.
1852.   Apr.   21.   Act of Apr. 12, 1852, accepted by the town.
1890.   June   2.   Part of Longmeadow annexed.
1928.   Mar.   1.   Part of East Longmeadow annexed.
1945.   May   7.   Bounds between Springfield and Chicopee established.
1946.   Oct.   15.   Act of May 7, 1945, took effect.

Archaic Names of the Municipality:
Agawam, Agawain, Elbows, Stony Hill, Woronoake, Woronoko.

Section/Village Names:
Armory, Armory Hill, Athol Junction, Brightwood, Camp Ground, Crescent Hill, East Springfield, Fiberloid, Forest Park, Franconia, Glenwood, Highland, Iceville, Indian Orchard, Jenksville, McKnight, Merrick, Oak Knoll, Oaklands, Pine Point, Round Hill, Rushville, Sixteen Acres, Trafton Park, Wachogue, Water Shops.

Sterling, Worcester County.
Established as a town by St 1780, c 27.

1781.	Apr.	25.	Sterling established as a town, from part of Lancaster.
1793.	Mar.	12.	Bounds between Sterling and Lancaster established.
1808.	Jan.	30.	Part included in the new town of West Boylston.
1837.	Mar	7.	Bounds between Sterling and Lancaster established and part of Lancaster annexed.
1908.	Apr.	21.	Bounds between Sterling and Lancaster established.

Archaic Names of the Municipality:
Chockett, Chocksett, Stillwater River, Woonkechoxsett.

Section/Village Names:
Cookshire, Chocksett, Justice Hill, Kendall Hill, Meeting House Hill, North Roe, Pottery Village, Pratt's Junction (former R.R. station), Red Stone Hill, Rowley Hill, Squareshire, Sterling Junction (former R.R. station), The Quag, Washacum (formerly Sterling Center station), West Sterling.

Stockbridge, Berkshire County.
Established as a town by St 1739-1740, c 6.

1739.	June	22.*	Established as a town, formerly the plantation called "the Indian town, on Housatunnock River". (Prov. Laws, Vol. II, p. 991.)
1774.	Mar.	9.	Part established as the district of West Stockbridge.
1774.	June	17.	Bounds established.
1829.	Mar.	2.	Part annexed to West Stockbridge.
1830.	Feb.	6.	Act of Mar. 2, 1829, perfected.
1958.	Apr.	21.	Bounds between Stockbridge and Great Barrington re-established and part annexed to Great Barrington.

Archaic Names of the Municipality:
Housatonic, Indian Town Plantation, Muhikanew, Wnahktucook, Waahtoohook.

Section/Village Names:
Cheever, Furnace District, Glendale, Interlaken (previously called Curtisville), Larrywaug, Lake Mahkeenac, Quarry, Stockbridge Bowl.

Stoneham, Middlesex County.
Established as a town by St 1725-1726, c 14.

1725.	Dec.	17.*	Established as a town, from part of Charlestown. (Prov. Laws, Vol II, p. 368.)
1734.	Dec.	21.*	Part of Malden annexed.
1734.	Dec.	21.*	Part of Reading annexed.
1751.	Apr.	5.*	Bounds between Stoneham and Reading established.
1853.	Mar.	15.	Part annexed to Melrose.
1856.	Apr.	5.	Part annexed to South Reading.
1889.	Mar.	13.	Part annexed to Wakefield.
1895.	Mar.	27.	Bounds between Stoneham and Melrose located and defined.
1895.	Apr.	20.	Part of Woburn annexed.

Section/Village Names:
Farm Hill, Haywardville, Lindonwood, Middlesex Fells.

Stoughton, Norfolk County.
Established as a town by St 1726-1727, c 16.

1726.	Dec.	22.*	Established as a town, from part of Dorchester. (Prov. Laws, Vol. II, p. 408.)
1733.	Apr.	25.*	Part annexed to Dedham.

1737.	Dec.	10.*	Part annexed to Dedham.
1738.	Dec.	11.*	Bounds between Stoughton and Dedham established.
1752.	Nov.	25.	Part annexed to Walpole.
1753.	Mar.	30.	Part annexed to Walpole.
1753.	June	13.	Part annexed to Walpole.
1753.	Dec.	22.	Part annexed to Norton.
1753.	Dec.	28.	Part annexed to Wrentham.
1755.	Oct.	25.	Part annexed to Walpole.
1765.	June	21.	Part established as the district of Stoughtonham.
1770.	Nov.	20.	Part annexed to Bridgewater.
1778.	June	10.	Part included in the new town of Foxborough.
1780.	June	17.	Part annexed to Dedham.
1789.	Feb.	16.	Part annexed to Sharon.
1792.	Feb.	22.	Part annexed to Sharon.
1793.	Mar.	12.	Part annexed to Foxborough.
1797.	Feb.	23.	Part established as Canton.
1798.	Feb.	8.	Part annexed to Bridgewater.
1847.	Mar.	31.	Part of Canton annexed.
1864.	Mar.	26.	Part annexed to Sharon.
1888.	Feb.	21.	Part established as Avon.
1924.	Apr.	28.	Bounds between Stoughton and Sharon established.
1957.	Apr.	11.	Bounds between Stoughton and Sharon established.
1971.	Mar.	15.	Town charter adopted.

Archaic Names of the Municipality:
Dorchester Village, Punkapoag.

Section/Village Names:
Belcher's Corner, Cobb's Tavern, Dry Pond, Gill's Corner, North Stoughton, Red Bridge, South Stoughton, Stoughton Center, Swan's Tavern, Talbot Corner, West Stoughton.

Stoughtonham - see Sharon.

Stow, Middlesex County.

1683.	May	16.*	Established as a town, formerly a plantation between Concord and Lancaster called "Pompositticut". (Mass. Bay Rec., Vol. V, p. 408.)
1717.	Apr.	12.*	Bounds between Stow and Concord established.
1730.	Dec.	29.*	Part of Sudbury annexed.
1732.	June	29.*	Part included in the new town of Harvard.
1783.	Feb.	25.	Part included in the new district of Boxborough.
1783.	July	11.	Bounds between Stow and Marlborough established.
1866.	Mar.	19.	Part included in the new town of Hudson.
1871.	Apr.	19.	Part included in the new town of Maynard.
1905.	May	24.	Bounds between Stow and Hudson established.
1979.	July	23.	Bounds between Stow and Hudson revised.

Archaic Names of the Municipality:
Assabet, Pompositticut Plantation.

Section/Village Names:
Gleasondale, Lake Boon, Lower Village, Rockbottom, Stow Center.

Sturbridge, Worcester County.
Established as a town by St 1738-1739, c 11.

| 1738. | June | 24.* | Established as a town, from a tract of land called "New Medfield". (Prov. Laws, Vol. II, p. 946.) |
| 1754. | Oct. | 25. | Certain lands annexed. |

1792.	June	26.	Part of Charlton annexed.
1794.	June	25.	Part of a gore of land called "Middlesex Gore" annexed.
1816.	Feb.	15.	Part included in the new town of Southbridge.
1839.	Apr.	6.	Part annexed to Southbridge.
1871.	May	4.	Bounds between Sturbridge and Southbridge established.
1973.	Apr.	30.	Town charter adopted.

Archaic Names of the Municipality:
Middlesex Gore, New Medfield, Tanteusque, Black Lead Mines.

Section/Village Names:
Car Barn District (extinct), Fiskdale, Lead Mine Section, Podunk (extinct), Snellville (extinct), Sturbridge Center (known as the Common Area), Sturbridge Village, Westville (extinct).

Suckanesset - (Sacconeesett) see Falmouth.

Sudbury, Middlesex County.

1639.	Sept.	4.*	"It was ordered, that the newe plantation by Concord shalbee called Sudbury." (Mass. Bay Rec., Vol. I, p. 271.)
1640.	May	13.*	Land granted to Sudbury.
1640.	Oct.	7.*	Called a town in this act.
1649.	May	2.*	Land granted to Sudbury.
1651.	May	13.*	Bounds between Sudbury and Watertown established.
1701.	June	13.*	Bounds between Sudbury and Framingham established.
1721.	June	9.*	Certain farms annexed.
1730.	Dec.	29.*	Part annexed to Stow.
1780.	Apr.	10.	Part established as East Sudbury.
1871.	Apr.	19.	Part included in the new town of Maynard.

Archaic Names of the Municipality:
Asabet.

Section/Village Names:
East Sudbury, Mill Village, North Sudbury, South Sudbury, West Sudbury.

Suffield.

1674.	June	3.*	"... that the name of the place be Suffeild...." (Mass. Bay Rec., Vol. V, p. 13.)
1740.	Jan.	9.*	Bounds between Suffield and Springfield established.
1743.	June	3.*	Bounds between Suffield and Springfield established.
1749.	May	—.*	Ceded to Connecticut.

Sunderland, Franklin County.
Swampfield established as a town by St 1713-1714, c 149.

1673.	May	7.*	Inhabitants of Hadley granted land for a plantation. (Mass. Bay Rec., Vol. IV, Part 2, p. 557.)
1714.	Feb.	17.*	Established as a town, reviving the grant of May 1673 for a plantation, and "... The Town to be named **Swampfield**." (Prov. Laws, Vol. XXI, p. 839.)
1718.	Nov.	12.*	The committee managing the affairs of Swampfield discharged "...and that the Name of the said Town be hence forward called **Sunderland**...." (Prov. Laws, Vol. IX, p. 621.)
1729.	Aug.	28.*	Land granted to Sunderland.
1740.	Jan.	2.*	Bounds between Sunderland and Hadley established.
1754.	Jan.	25.	Part established as the district of Montague.
1774.	Mar.	5.	Part established as Leverett.

Archaic Names of the Municipality:
Plumtrees, Swampfield.

Section/Village Names:
Meadows, North Sunderland, Plumtrees.

Sutton, Worcester County.

1714.	Oct.	28.*	"Voted a Concurrence with the Representatives, Approving & Confirming a Survey & Plat of the Laying out the Township of Sutton." (Court Rec., Vol. IX, p. 425.)
1715.	June	21.*	Certain lands granted to the township of Sutton.
1726.	Dec.	6.*	Certain farms annexed.
1728.	June	5.*	Part annexed to Westborough.
1735.	June	14.*	Part included in the new town of Upton.
1737.	June	10.*	Part annexed to Grafton.
1742.	Jan.	9.*	Part annexed to Grafton.
1749.	Feb.	1.*	Certain bounds established.
1757.	Aug.	30.	Certain lands annexed.
1769.	June	29.	Bounds between Sutton and Uxbridge established.
1778.	Apr.	10.	The parish lately set off from Sutton and other towns established as Ward.
1780.	Apr.	20.	Part annexed to Northbridge.
1789.	June	5.	A certain gore of land annexed.
1793.	Feb.	18.	Part annexed to Oxford.
1801.	Feb.	17.	Part annexed to Northbridge.
1813.	June	11.	Part established as Millbury.
1831.	June	15.	Part of Northbridge annexed.
1837.	Mar.	7.	Bounds between Sutton and Northbridge established.
1842.	Mar.	3.	Part annexed to Grafton.
1844.	Mar.	16.	Part annexed to Northbridge.
1907.	May	16.	Bounds between Sutton and Millbury established.
1907.	May	16.	Bounds between Sutton and Douglas established.

Archaic Names of the Municipality:
Nipmuc Country, Manchaug.

Section/Village Names:
Aldrichville, East Sutton, Leland Hill, Manchaug, Marbleville, Old Stone, Pleasantdale, Pleasant Valley, Potter Hill, Putnam Hill, Smithville, South Sutton, Sutton Center, West Sutton, Wilkinsonville, Woodbury Village.

Swampfield - see Sunderland.

Swampscott, Essex County.
Incorporated as a town by St 1852, c 310.

1852.	May	21.	Incorporated as a town, from part of Lynn.
1867.	Apr.	3.	Part of Salem annexed.
1969.	Mar.	3.	Town charter adopted.

Section/Village Names:
Beach Bluff, Edgewood, Mountain Park, Phillips Beach, Upper Swampscott.

Swansea, Bristol County.
Barrington established as a town by St 1717-1718, c 114.

1667.	Oct.	30.*	**Wannamoisett** established as a town, from certain lands within the limits of the town of Rehoboth and certain adjacent lands. (Ply. Col. Rec., Vol. IV, p. 169.)

1668.	Mar.	5.*	Name changed. "...the township...att Wannamoisett and places adjacent, shall hensforth be called and knowne by the name of **Swansey**." (Ply. Col. Rec., Vol. IV, p. 175.)
1669.	July	5.*	A neck of land called "Papasquash Neck", excepting one hundred acres, annexed to Swansea.
1670.	Aug.	11.*	Bounds between Swansea and Rehoboth established.
1679.	July	5.*	Swansea bounds established.
1679.	Nov.	1.*	Bounds between Swansea and Mount Hope to be established.
1717.	Nov.	18.*	Part of Swansea established as the town of Barrington.
1747.	Feb.	5.*	Eastern part of Barrington which remained in this province after settlement of the Rhode Island boundry annexed to Swansea.
1790.	Feb.	20.	Part known as "Shewamet purchase" established as Somerset.
1900.	Mar.	1.	"The name of the town variously spelled Swansea, Swansey and Swanzey shall be Swansea."

Archaic Names of the Municipality:
Barrington, Capasquash Neck, Mattapoisett, Papasquash Neck, Swansey, Wannamoisett.

Section/Village Names:
Barneyville, East Swansea, Gardner's Neck, Hortonville, North Swansea, Ocean Grove, South Swansea, Swansea Center, Swansea Village, Touisset, Two Mile Purchase.

TAUNTON, Bristol County.
Incorporated as a city by St 1864, c 209.

1639.	Mar.	3.*	"That Cohannett shalbe called Taunton". (Ply. Col. Rec., Vol. XI, p. 34.)
1640.	Mar.	3.*	Land at "Assonet" granted to Taunton.
1640.	June	19.*	Bounds established.
1672.	Oct.	29.*	Certain lands granted to Taunton.
1682.	July	—.*	Land called "Assonet Neck" annexed.
1711.	June	12.*	Part established as the town of Norton.
1712.	May	30.*	Part established as the town of Dighton.
1731.	Apr.	2.*	Part established as the town of Raynham.
1735.	Apr.	18.*	Part included in the town of Berkley.
1810.	Feb.	6.	Certain lands belonging to Taunton in Berkley annexed to Berkley.
1842.	Mar.	3.	Certain lands belonging to Taunton in Berkley annexed to Berkley.
1864.	May	11.	Incorporated as a city.
1864.	June	6.	Act of May 11, 1864, accepted by the town.
1866.	Feb.	27.	Bounds between Taunton and Raynham established.
1867.	June	1.	Bounds between Taunton and Lakeville established.
1879.	Apr.	1.	Part annexed to Berkley.
1879.	Apr.	12.	Act of Apr. 1, 1879, accepted by Berkley and took effect.

Archaic Names of the Municipality:
Assonet, Assonet Neck, Cohannett, Titicut.

Section/Village Names:
Bear Hole, Brittaniaville, Chace's (former R.R. station), Cotley, Dean Station, East Taunton, Elliott's Corner, Hart Corners, Hopewell, Lawrence Station, North Dighton Station, North Taunton, Oakland, Richmond, Sabbatia Park, Schooset, Seaddings, Squawbetty, Thatcher's Corner, Wade's Corner, Walker, Weir, Weir Junction, Weir Village (former R.R. station), Westville, Wheeler's Corner, Whittenton, Whittenton Junction, Woodward Springs.

Templeton, Worcester County.
Established as a town by St 1761-1762, c 45.

1762.	Mar.	6.	Established as a town, formerly the plantation called "Narragansett Number Six." (Prov. Laws, Vol. IV, p. 533.)
1785.	June	27.	Part included in the new town of Gardner.
1786.	Oct.	20.	Part included in the new town of Gerry.
1789.	Feb.	2.	Bounds between Templeton and Gerry established.
1892.	Apr.	5.	Part of Phillipston annexed.
1908.	Apr.	17.	Bounds between Templeton and Phillipston established.

Archaic Names of the Municipality:
Narragansett Plantation Number Six.

Section/Village Names:
Baldwinville, East Templeton, Otter River, Templeton Center.

Tewksbury, Middlesex County.
Established as a town by St 1734-1735, c 17.

1734.	Dec.	17.*	Established as a town, from part of Billerica. (Prov. Laws, Vol. II, p. 739.)
1834.	Mar.	29.	Part annexed to Lowell.
1874.	June	5.	Part annexed to Lowell.
1888.	May	17.	Part annexed to Lowell.
1903.	May	21.	Bounds between Tewksbury and Andover established.
1906.	Apr.	30.	Part annexed to Lowell.

Archaic Names of the Municipality:
Wamesit, A "Praying Indian" (Christian) town.

Section/Village Names:
Almont, Atherton (former R.R. station), Baldwin (former R.R. station), Burtt's, East Tewksbury, Fairlawn, Lakeview, Lawrence Station, Mace's Station, North Tewksbury, Oakland Park, Pattenville, Salem Junction, Shawsheen Road Park, Silver Lake Park, South Lowell, South Tewksbury, Tewksbury Center, Tewksbury Junction, Tewksbury Station, Wamesit, West Tewksbury.

Tisbury, Dukes County.

1671.	July	8.*	"Tisbury-Towne", formerly known by the name of "Middletowne", mentioned. (New York Original Books of Letters Patent, Vol. IV, pp. 81 and 82.)
1709.	Nov.	8.*	Bounds established.
1830.	Feb.	5.	Bounds between Tisbury and Edgartown established.
1862.	Apr.	23.	Bounds between Tisbury and Edgartown established.
1882.	Feb.	27.	Bounds between Tisbury and Chilmark established.
1892.	Apr.	28.	Part established as West Tisbury.
1935.	Apr.	8.	Bounds between Tisbury and Oak Bluffs re-established.
1955.	June	7.	Bounds between Tisbury and Oak Bluffs re-established.

Archaic Names of the Municipality:
Takemmy, Chappaquonsett, Middletown, Tockiming.

Section/Village Names:
Chappaquansett, Daggettville, Ingleside, Makonikey, Oaklandale, Red Coat Hill, Vineyard Haven (previously called Holmes Hole Neck), Tashmoo, West Chop.

Tiverton - see Dartmouth and Freetown. (Portions ceded to Rhode Island in 1747.)

Tolland, Hampden County.
Incorporated as a town by St 1810, c 14.

1810.	June	14.	Incorporated as a town from part of Granville.
1853.	May	4.	Bounds between Tolland and Sandisfield established.
1853.	May	15.	Bounds between Tolland and Sandisfield established.

Topsfield, Essex County.

1648.	Oct.	18.*	"The village at the newe medowes at Ipswich is named Toppesfeild." (Mass. Bay Rec., Vol. II, p. 258.)
1650.	Oct.	18.*	Established as a town. (Mass. Bay Rec., Vol. IV, Part 1, p. 33.)
1658.	Oct.	19.*	Bounds between Topsfield and Salem established.
1664.	May	29.*	Bounds between Topsfield and Salem established.
1694.	Feb.	28.*	Bounds between Topsfield and Ipswich established.
1701.	Feb.	25.*	Bounds between Topsfield and Boxford established.
1707.	Nov.	28.*	Bounds between Topsfield and Boxford established.
1728.	June	20.*	Part included in the new town of Middleton.
1774.	Feb.	16.	Part of Ipswich annexed.
1936.	Feb.	28.	Bounds between Topsfield and Middleton established.

Archaic Names of the Municipality:
New Medowes Village.

Section/Village Names:
Lake Village, Springville, Sweeneyville, Town Hill.

Townsend, Middlesex County.
Established as a town by St 1732-1733, c 3.

| 1732. | June | 29.* | Established as a town, from part of "Turkey Hills". (Prov. Laws, Vol. II, p. 643.) |
| 1767. | Mar. | 6. | Part included in the new town of Ashby. |

Archaic Names of the Municipality:
Muspetanapus Hill, Northtown, Turkey Hills.

Section/Village Names:
Barker Hill, Bayberry Hill, Caper Corner, Joslinville, North End, Old City, South Row, Townsend Harbor, Townsend Hill, Wallace Hill, West Townsend.

Troy - see Fall River.

Truro, Barnstable County.
Established as a town by St 1709-1710, c 4.

1709.	July	16.*	Established as a town, formerly a tract of land called "Pawmett", to "...be called by the name of Truroe...." (Prov. Laws, Vol. I. p. 642.)
1714.	Oct.	21.*	Bounds between Truro and Province Lands established.
1813.	June	12.	Part annexed to Provincetown and bounds established.
1829.	Mar.	2.	Part annexed to Provincetown and bounds established.
1836.	Mar.	30.	Part annexed to Provincetown.
1837.	Feb.	22.	Bounds between Truro and Wellfleet established.

Archaic Names of the Municipality:
Dangerfield, Meeshaum, Pawmett, Tashmuit.

Section/Village Names:
Beach Point, Castle Village, Corn Hill, Dyer's Hollow, Harding's Hollow, Head Pamet, Higgins Hollow, High Head Highland, Highland Light, Hogsback, Neck, North Truro, Pond Village, South Truro, The Castle, Truro Center, Truro Station, Whitmanville.

Tyngsborough, Middlesex County.
Established as a town by St 1809, c 148.

1789.	June	22.	Incorporated as a district by the name of Tyngsborough, from part of Dunstable.
1792.	Mar.	3.	Part of Dunstable annexed to the district of Tyngsborough.
1798.	Jan.	29.	Part of Dunstable annexed to the district of Tyngsborough and bounds established.

1809.   Feb.   23.   Established as a town, formerly the district of Tyngsborough.
1814.   June   10.   Bounds between Tyngsborough and Dunstable established.

Section/Village Names:
Lakeview Park.

Tyringham, Berkshire County.
Established as a town by St 1761-1762, c 47.
1762.   Mar.   6.   Established as a town, formerly the plantation called
                      "Number One". (Prov. Laws, Vol. IV, p. 534.)
1811.   Feb.   27.   Part annexed to New Marlborough.
1812.   Feb.   11.   Part of New Marlborough annexed.
1847.   Apr.   12.   Part established as Monterey.

Archaic Names of the Municipality:
Housatonic Township Number One, Twelve Mile Pond.

Section/Village Names:
Goose Pond.

Upton, Worcester County.
Established as a town by St 1735-1736, c 11.
1735.   June   14.* Established as a town, from parts of Hopkinton, Mendon,
                      Sutton and Uxbridge. (Prov. Laws, Vol. II, p. 764.)
1763.   Jan.   24.   Part annexed to Westborough.
1808.   Mar.   8.   Part of Hopkinton annexed.
1907.   May   16.   Bounds between Upton and Milford established.
1907.   May   16.   Bounds between Upton and Hopkinton established.
1962.   July   25.   Bounds between Upton, Milford and Hopkinton established.

Section/Village Names:
Upton Center, West Upton.

Uxbridge, Worcester County.
Established as a town by St 1727, c 12.
1727.   June   27.* Established as a town, from part of Mendon. (Prov. Laws,
                      Vol. II, p. 427.)
1735.   June   14.* Part included in the new town of Upton.
1736.   June   5.*   Certain lands granted to Uxbridge.
1742.   Apr.   16.* Certain lands annexed to Uxbridge.
1746.   June   4.*   Part of the district of New Sherborn annexed.
1754.   Apr.   10.   Bounds between Uxbridge and Mendon established.
1769.   June   29.   Bounds between Uxbridge and Sutton established.
1770.   Apr.   24.   Part annexed to Mendon.
1772.   July   14.   Part established as the district of Northbridge.
1856.   Apr.   30.   Bounds between Uxbridge and Northbridge established, and
                      part of each town annexed to the other town.
1864.   Apr.   25.   Bounds between Uxbridge and Douglas established.
1908.   Apr.   17.   Bounds between Uxbridge and Northbridge established.

Archaic Names of the Municipality:
Wacantuck, Waeuntug, A "Praying Indian" (Christian) town.

Section/Village Names:
Aldrich District, Calumet, Carpenter Hill, Centreville, East Side, Elmdale, Happy
Hollow, Hecla, Ironstone, Linwood, Millville Line, North Uxbridge, Quaker City,
Rice City, Rivulet, Rogersville, Scaden, South Uxbridge, Southwick District,
Uxbridge Center, West Uxbridge, Wheelockville, Williams Hill.

Wakefield, Middlesex County.
South Reading incorporated as a town by St 1811, c 131.

1812.	Feb.	25.	**South Reading** incorporated as a town, from part of Reading.
1813.	June	16.	Part of South Reading annexed to Reading.
1856.	Apr.	5.	Part of Stoneham annexed to South Reading.
1868.	Feb.	25.	The town of South Reading shall take the name of **Wakefield.**
1868.	June	30.	Act of Feb. 25, 1868, took effect.
1870.	Apr.	2.	Bounds between Wakefield and Lynnfield established.
1889.	Mar.	13.	Part of Stoneham annexed.
1906.	May	9.	Bounds between Wakefield and Melrose changed and established.
1933.	June	27.	Part of Saugus annexed.
1933.	July	11.	Act of June 27, 1933, accepted by the town.
1933.	Sept.	18.	Act of June 27, 1933, accepted by Saugus.

Archaic Names of the Municipality:
South Reading.

Section/Village Names:
Greenwood, Montrose, Wakefield Center, Wakefield Junction, Wakefield Park.

Wales, Hampden County.
South Brimfield made a town by St 1775-1776, c 3.

1762.	Sept.	18.	South Brimfield incorporated as a district from part of Brimfield. (Prov. Laws, Vol. IV, p. 601.)
1766.	Feb.	21.	The district of South Brimfield divided into two parishes, the east and west.
1775.	Aug.	23.	**South Brimfield** made a town, by general act under which districts became towns.
1783.	July	5.	The east parish incorporated as the district of Holland.
1796.	Feb.	8.	Bounds between South Brimfield and the district of Holland established.
1828.	Feb.	20.	The town of South Brimfield shall be named **Wales**.

Archaic Names of the Municipality:
South Brimfield.

Section/Village Names:
Shawville.

Walpole, Norfolk County.
Established as a town by St 1724-1725, c 14.

1724.	Dec.	10.*	Established as a town, from part of Dedham. (Prov. Laws, Vol. II, p. 342.)
1752.	Nov.	25.	Part of Stoughton annexed.
1753.	Mar.	30.	Part of Stoughton annexed.
1753.	June	13.	Part of Stoughton annexed.
1755.	Oct.	25.	Part of Stoughton annexed.
1778.	June	10.	Part included in the new town of Foxborough.
1784.	Feb.	12.	Part annexed to Dedham.
1804.	Feb.	28.	Part of Sharon annexed.
1811.	June	21.	Part of Sharon annexed and part of Dedham re-annexed.
1833.	Mar.	27.	Part of Foxborough annexed.
1834.	Mar.	28.	Part of Foxborough annexed.
1852.	Apr.	30.	Part of Dedham annexed.
1870.	Feb.	23.	Part included in the new town of Norfolk.
1872.	Feb.	23.	Part included in the new town of Norwood.
1872.	Feb.	27.	Bounds between Walpole and Dover established.

1874. May   1.   Part of Sharon annexed.
1903. May   23.   Bounds between Walpole and Foxborough established.
1903. May   27.   Bounds between the town of Medfield and the towns of
                   Dover, Walpole and Norfolk established.
1904. Mar. 12.   Bounds between Walpole and Dover established.
1927. Mar. 28.   Bounds between Walpole and Dover established.
1927. Mar. 28.   Bounds between Walpole and Norfolk established.
1937. Mar. 29.   Bounds between Walpole and Foxborough established.
1973. Jan. 15.   Town Charter adopted.

Section/Village Names:
Allen's Corner, Cedar (former R.R. station), East Walpole, Morey Pond, North End,
North Walpole, Sharon Corner, South Walpole, Walpole Center, Walpole Heights,
Walpole Junction, West Walpole.

WALTHAM, Middlesex County.
Established as a town by St 1737-1738, c 21.
Incorporated as a city by St 1884, c 309.
1738. Jan.   4.* Established as a town, from part of Watertown. (Prov. Laws,
                   Vol. II, p. 919.)
1755. June   4.   Part of Cambridge annexed.
1766. June 25.   Bounds between Waltham and Weston established.
1849. Apr. 16.   Part of Newton called the South Side annexed.
1859. Mar. 18.   Part included in the new town of Belmont.
1884. June   2.   Incorporated as a city.
1884. July 16.   Act of June 2, 1884, accepted by the town.
1895. Apr.   4.   Bounds between Waltham and Lexington located and
                   defined.
1939. Mar. 22.   Bounds between Waltham and Belmont established.

Section/Village Names:
Beaver Brook, Bleachery Station, Blue Hill, Candlewood, Cedarwood, Clemetis
Brook, Crescent Park, Ellison Park, Highlands, Lakeview, Lincoln Woods, Piety
Corner, Pigeon Hill, Prospectville, Rangeley Acres, Reed's Corner, Riverview
Station, Rock Alley, Roberts, South Side, South Waltham, The Bleachery District,
The Chemistry District, The Island, Trapelo Road District, Waltham Heights,
Warrendale, Waverley Oaks, West End.

Wannamoisett - see Swansea.

Ward - see Auburn.

Ware, Hampshire County.
Made a town by St 1775-1776, c 3.
1750. June 19.* Ware River Parish bounds established. (Prov. Laws, Vol. XIV,
                   p. 421.)
1761. Nov. 25.   Incorporated as a district by the name of Ware, formerly, the
                   Ware River Parish and a certain tract of land in Palmer.
                   (Prov. Laws, Vol. IV, p. 486.)
1775. Aug. 23.   Made a town, by general act under which districts became
                   towns.
1823. Feb.   8.   Parts of Brookfield and Western annexed.
1910. Apr. 29.   Bounds between Ware and Palmer established.
1927. Apr. 26   Parts of Enfield and Greenwich annexed.
1938. Apr. 26.   Act of Apr. 26, 1927, amended.
1938. Apr. 28.   Act of Apr. 26, 1927, as amended, took effect.

Archaic Names of the Municipality:
Hack's Farm, Ware River Parish.

Section/Village Names:
Brimstone Hill, Gibbs Crossing, Ware Center, West Ware Center.

Ware River Parish - see Ware.

Wareham, Plymouth County.
Established as a town by St 1739-1740, c 7.

1739.	July	10.*	Established as a town, from part of Rochester and a plantation in Plymouth called "Agawam". (Prov. Laws, Vol. II, p. 992.)
1827.	Jan.	20.	Parts of Carver and Plymouth annexed.
1859.	Feb.	18.	Bounds between Wareham and Marion established.
1864.	Apr.	20.	Bounds between Wareham and Rochester established.
1866.	Feb.	13.	Bounds between Wareham and Marion established.
1866.	Feb.	15.	Bounds between Wareham and Rochester established.
1887.	June	3.	Bounds between Wareham and Rochester established.
1897.	Apr.	14.	Bounds between Wareham and Bourne established.
1897.	Apr.	23.	Bounds between Wareham and Marion established.
1901.	May	16.	Bounds between Wareham and Carver established.
1909.	Mar.	1.	Bounds between Wareham and Marion established.
1939.	June	12.	Bounds between Wareham and Rochester established.
1939.	June	12.	Bounds between Wareham and Marion established.

Archaic Names of the Municipality:
Agawam Plantation, Cowesit, Quansit.

Section/Village Names:
Agawam, Center Village, Barney's Point, Cohasset Narrows, East Wareham, Fearing's Hill, Great Neck, Hamilton Beach, Indian Neck, Kenney Mills, Locke Bog, Long Neck, Narrow's Village, Oakdale, Onset, Onset Bay, Onset Junction, Parker Mills, Parkwood Beach, Parlowtown, Pinehurst Beach, Point Independence, South Wareham, Swift's Beach, Tempest Knob Station, Tihonet, Tremont, Wareham Center, Waters Bog, West Wareham, Yellow Town.

Warren, Worcester County.
Western established as a town by St 1741-1742, c 17.

1742.	Jan.	16.*	**Western** established as a town, from parts of the towns of Brimfield and Brookfield and part of Kingsfield, so called. (Prov. Laws, Vol. II, p. 1088.)
1823.	Feb.	8.	Part of Western annexed to Ware.
1831.	Feb.	7.	Part of Western annexed to Palmer.
1834.	Mar.	13.	The name of the town of Western shall be **Warren**.

Archaic Names of the Municipality:
Kingsfield, Kingstown, Western.

Section/Village Names:
Lower Warren, West Warren.

Warwick, Franklin County.
Established as a town by St 1762-1763, c 17.

1763.	Feb.	17.	Established as a town, formerly the plantation "called... Roxbury-Canada... with sundry farms lying therein... belonging to this province...." (Prov. Laws, Vol. IV, p. 604.)
1783.	Oct.	15.	Part included in the new town of Orange.

Archaic Names of the Municipality:
Gardner's Township, Mount Grace, Roxbury Canada.

Section/Village Names:
Barber Hill, Beech Hill, Brush Valley, Chestnut Hill, Flower Hill, Mayo Corner, Warwick Center.

Washington, Berkshire County.
Established as a town by St 1776-1777, c 40.

1777.	Apr.	12.	Established as a town, formerly the plantation called "Hartwood", with several contiguous grants. (Prov. Laws, Vol. V, p. 635.)
1777.	Oct.	21.	Part included in the new town of Lee.
1783.	Mar.	12.	Part included in the new town of Middlefield.
1795.	Jan.	31.	Part annexed to Lenox.
1802.	Feb.	18.	Part annexed to Lenox.
1806.	Mar.	7.	Part annexed to Lee and the line between Washington and Lee established.

Archaic Names of the Municipality:
Plantation Number Eight, Hartwood Plantation.

Section/Village Names:
Washington City, Whitney District.

Watertown, Middlesex County.

1630.	Sept.	7.*	Established as a town - "It is ordered,... & the towne vpon Charles Ryver, Waterton." (Mass. Bay Rec., Vol. I, p. 75.)
1635.	Apr.	7.*	Bounds between Watertown and New Towne established.
1638.	June	8.*	Bounds between Watertown, Concord and Dedham established.
1639.	Mar.	13.*	Bounds between Watertown and Cambridge established.
1639.	May	22.*	Bounds between Watertown and Dedham established.
1651.	May	13.*	Bounds between Watertown and Sudbury established.
1651.	May	13.*	Bounds between Watertown and Concord established.
1713.	Jan.	1.*	Part established as Weston.
1738.	Jan.	4.*	Part established as Waltham.
1754.	Apr.	19.	Part annexed to Cambridge and bounds established.
1855.	Apr.	27.	Part annexed to Cambridge.
1859.	Mar.	18.	Part included in the new town of Belmont.
1885.	Mar.	10.	Part annexed to Cambridge.
1898.	Mar.	9.	Bounds between Watertown and Cambridge established, and part of each place annexed to the other place.
1903.	May	23.	Bounds between Watertown and Belmont established.
1911.	Apr.	29.	Bounds between Watertown and Belmont established.
1922.	Mar.	24.	Bounds between Watertown and Belmont, and Watertown and Cambridge established.
1980.	May	5.	Town charter adopted which established a city form of government.

Archaic Names of the Municipality:
Nonsuch, Peagsgusset, Pequosset, Pegwisset, Pigsgusset, The Town Upon the Charles River, Waterton.

Section/Village Names:
Arsenal, Bemis, East Watertown, Mount Auburn, Union Market, Waverly, West Watertown.

Wayland, Middlesex County.
East Sudbury incorporated as a town by St 1779-1780, c 34.

1780.	Apr.	10.	**East Sudbury** incorporated as a town, from part of Sudbury. (Prov. Laws, Vol. V, p. 1170.)
1835.	Mar.	11.	The name of the town of East Sudbury shall be **Wayland**.
1850.	Apr.	26.	Bounds between Wayland and Natick established.

Archaic Names of the Municipality:
East Sudbury.

Section/Village Names:
Cochituate, Lockerville, Tower Hill.

Webster, Worcester County.
Incorporated as a town by St 1832, c 93.
| 1832. | Mar. | 6. | Incorporated as a town, from parts of Dudley and Oxford and certain territory in the county of Worcester. |
| 1841. | Feb. | 27. | Bounds between Webster and Douglas established. |

Section/Village Names:
Beacon Park, East Village, Fienner Hill, Glenwood, Gore District, Hub Section, Kingsbury District, Lake Section, Merino Village, North Village, Point Pleasant (former R.R. station), Polandville, South Village, Stevensville, Tanner District.

Wellesley, Norfolk County.
Incorporated as a town by St 1881, c 172.
| 1881. | Apr. | 6. | Incorporated as a town, from part of Needham. |

Archaic Names of the Municipality:
Coowate, West Needham.

Section/Village Names:
Bostonville, Lake Crossing, Newton Lower Falls, Overbrook, Rice Crossing, Unionville, Wellesley Farms, Wellesley Fells, Wellesley Hills.

Wellfleet, Barnstable County.
Made a town by St 1775-1776, c 3.
1763.	June	16.	Incorporated as a district by the name of Wellfleet, from part of Eastham. (Prov. Laws, Vol IV, p. 664.)
1775.	Aug.	23.	Made a town, by general act under which districts became towns.
1837.	Feb.	22.	Bounds between Wellfleet and Truro established.
1847.	Apr.	26.	Part of Eastham annexed.
1887.	May	6.	Bounds between the tidewaters of Wellfleet and Eastham established.

Archaic Names of the Municipality:
Punnonakanit.

Section/Village Names:
Big Chief Hill, Billingsgate Island (now gone), Briar Lane, Dog Town, Fresh Brook, Great Beach Hill, Great Island, Griffin Island, Hen House Hill, Indian Neck, John Brown's Crossing, Lieutenant Island, Money Hill, Pamet Point, Physic Point, Pleasant Point, Pucker Town, South Wellfleet, Spring Valley, The Jungle.

Wellington - see Dighton.

Wendell, Franklin County.
Incorporated as a town by St 1780, c 35.
| 1781. | May | 8. | Incorporated as a town, from part of Shutesbury and certain land called "Ervingshire." |
| 1803. | Feb. | 28. | Part of Montague and a gore of land annexed. |

Archaic Names of the Municipality:
Ervingshire.

Section/Village Names:
Bear Mountain, Farley, Liberty Hill, Lock's Village, Mormon Hollow, Stoneville, Wendell Center, Wendell Depot.

Wenham, Essex County.
| 1643. | Sept. | 7.* | Established as a town, "It is ordeed, that Enon shalbee called Wennam. Wennam is granted to bee a towne...." (Mass. Bay Rec., Vol. II, p. 44.) |

| 1679. | May | 28.* | Bounds between Wenham and Beverly and "the village" established. |
| 1905. | May | 1. | Bounds between Wenham and Hamilton established. |

Archaic Names of the Municipality:
Enon, Wennam.

Section/Village Names:
East Wenham, Idlewood Grove, Mapleville, Wenham Depot, Wenham Neck, West Wenham.

Wessaguscus - see Boston and Weymouth.

West Boylston, Worcester County.
Incorporated as a town by St 1807, c 48.

1808.	Jan.	30.	Incorporated as a town, from parts of Boylston, Holden and Sterling.
1820.	Feb.	10.	Part of Boylston annexed.
1820.	June	17.	Part of Boylston annexed.
1905.	May	2.	Bounds between West Boylston and Boylston established.

Section/Village Names:
Boylston Common, Central Village, City Line, Depot Village, Harrisville, Malden Hill, Oakdale, Oakland, Old Common.

West Bridgewater, Plymouth County.
Incorporated as a town by St 1822, c 82.

1822.	Feb.	16.	Incorporated as a town, from part of Bridgewater.
1825.	Jan.	26.	Bounds between West Bridgewater and North Bridgewater established.
1893.	May	8.	Part annexed to Brockton, if the act is accepted by Brockton.
1893.	Nov.	7.	Act of May 8. 1893, accepted by Brockton.
1894.	Mar.	1.	Act of May 8, 1893, took effect.

Section/Village Names:
Cochesett, Eastondale, Elmville, Jerusalem, Matfield, Richard's Corner, Westdale.

West Brookfield, Worcester County.
Incorporated as a town by St 1848, c 36.

1848.	Mar.	3.	Incorporated as a town, from part of Brookfield.
1910.	May	13.	Bounds between West Brookfield and Brookfield established.
1911.	Apr.	24.	Bounds between West Brookfield and New Braintree established.

West Cambridge - see Arlington.

West Newbury, Essex County.
Parsons incorporated as a town by St 1818, c 103.

1819.	Feb.	18.	**Parsons** incorporated as a town, from part of Newbury.
1820.	June	14.	"The name of the town of Parsons shall hereafter be called and known by the name of **West Newbury**."
1904.	Apr.	22.	Bounds between West Newbury and Grovelandestablished.

Archaic Names of the Municipality:
Parsons.

Section/Village Names:
West Newbury First Parish, Long Hill, West Newbury Second Parish, Silloway's Hill.

West Roxbury - see Boston.
Incorporated as a town by St 1851, c 250.

1851.	May	24.	Incorporated as a town, from part of Roxbury.
1852.	Apr.	21.	Part of Dedham annexed.
1852.	Apr.	30.	Act of Apr. 21, 1852, accepted by West Roxbury.
1853.	July	4.	Act of Apr. 21, 1852, took effect.
1870.	Apr.	2.	Bounds between West Roxbury and Boston established.
1872.	Apr.	12.	Part of West Roxbury known as Mount Hope Cemetery annexed to Boston.
1873.	May	29.	West Roxbury annexed to Boston.
1873.	Oct.	7.	Act of May 29, 1873, accepted by West Roxbury and Boston.
1874.	Jan.	5.	Act of May 29, 1873, took effect.

West Springfield, Hampden County.
Established as a town by St 1773-1774, c 26.

1774.	Feb.	23.	Established as a town, from part of Springfield. (Prov. Laws, Vol. V, p. 335.)
1802.	Mar.	3.	Part of Westfield annexed.
1850.	Mar.	14.	Part established as Holyoke.
1855.	May	17.	Part established as Agawam.
1960.	May	2.	Bounds between West Springfield and Agawam re-established.

Archaic Names of the Municipality:
Aries Little, Mittineague.

Section/Village Names:
Amostown, Ashleyville, Cayenne, Country Club, Mittineague, Paucatuck, Prospect Hill, Riverdale, Tatham, Westside.

West Stockbridge, Berkshire County.
Made a town by St 1775-1776, c 3.

1774.	Mar.	9.	Established as a district by the name of West Stockbridge from part of Stockbridge. (Prov. Laws, Vol. V, p. 325.)
1774.	June	17.	Bounds established.
1775.	Aug.	23.	Made a town by general act, under which districts became towns.
1793.	Mar.	2.	Gore of land annexed.
1829.	Mar.	2.	Part of Stockbridge annexed.
1830.	Feb.	6.	Act of Mar. 2, 1829, perfected.
1834.	Mar.	27.	Bounds between West Stockbridge and Richmond established.
1847.	Mar.	17.	Part annexed to Alford.

Archaic Names of the Municipality:
Indian Town, Queensborough.

Section/Village Names:
Freedleyville, Leet Ore Bed, Maple Hill, Moscow, Pixley Hill, Rockdale, State Line, West Center, Williamsville.

West Tisbury, Dukes County.
Incorporated as a town by St 1892, c 216.

| 1892. | Apr. | 28. | Incorporated as a town from part of Tisbury. |

Section/Village Names:
Davistown, Lambert's Cove, Makonikey, North Tisbury.

Westborough, Worcester County.
Established as a town by St 1717-1718, c 110.

1717.	Nov.	18.*	Established as a town from part of Marlborough called "Chauncey". (Prov. Laws, Vol. IX, p. 561.)
1728.	June	5.*	Part of Sutton annexed.
1762.	June	3.	Part of Shrewsbury annexed.
1763.	Jan.	24.	Part of Upton annexed.
1766.	Jan.	24.	Part established as the district of Northborough.
1793.	Mar.	2.	Part of Shrewsbury annexed.
1835.	Mar.	5.	Bounds between Westborough and Southborough established.
1907.	Feb.	11.	Bounds between Westborough and Shrewsbury established.
1907.	Feb.	11.	Bounds between Westborough and Grafton established.
1974.	Mar.	4.	Town charter adopted.

Archaic Names of the Municipality:
Chauncey, Jack Straw Hill.

Section/Village Names:
Piccadilly, Rocklawn Mills, Wessonville.

Western - see Warren.

WESTFIELD, Hampden County.
Incorporated as a city by St 1920, c 294.

1669.	May	19.*	Established as a town, from part of Springfield called "Woronoake". (Mass. Bay Rec., Vol. IV, Part 2, p. 432.)
1670.	May	31.*	Bounds between Westfield and Springfield established.
1701.	June	4.*	Certain land granted to Westfield and bounds established between Westfield and Northampton.
1713.	Feb.	23.*	Land granted to Westfield.
1770.	Nov.	7.	Part established as the district of Southwick.
1779.	Oct.	6.	Part annexed to Southwick.
1780.	Nov.	28.	Part of that part called the "New Addition" included in the new town of Montgomery.
1792.	Feb.	25.	Part of that part called the "New Additon" included in the new town of Russell.
1802.	Mar.	3.	Part annexed to West Springfield.
1837.	Mar.	20.	Bounds between Westfield and Southwick established.
1920.	Apr.	9.	Incorporated as a city.
1920.	Nov.	2.	Act of Apr. 9, 1920, accepted by the town.

Archaic Names of the Municipality:
Streamfield, Woronoake, Woronoco.

Section/Village Names:
East Farms, Little River, Middle Farms, Mundale, Pochassie, Springdale, Westfield, Westfield West Parish, Wyben (formerly West Farms).

Westford, Middlesex County.
Established as a town by St 1729-1730, c 2.

1729.	Sept.	23.*	Established as a town, from part of Chelmsford, to be called "...by the name of Wesford...." (Prov. Laws, Vol. II, p. 528.)
1730.	Sept.	10.*	Part of Groton annexed.
1975.	May	19.	Bounds between Westford and Chelmsford altered, revised and relocated.

Section/Village Names:
Brookside, Carlisle Station, Chamberlain's Corner, Cold Spring, Forge Village, Francis Hill, Graniteville, Nabnasset, Nashoba, North End, Oak Hill, Parkerville, Pine Ridge, Snake Meadow Hill, Westford Corner, West Graniteville, Whidden's Corner.

Westhampton, Hampshire County.
Incorporated as a town by St 1778, c 13.

1778.	Sept.	29.	Incorporated as a town, from part of Northampton. (Prov. Laws, Vol. V, p. 900.)
1872.	Mar.	12.	Bounds between Westhampton, and Easthampton, and Northampton and Southampton established.

Section/Village Names:
Loudville.

Westminster, Worcester County.
Incorporated as a town by St 1759, c 5.

1759.	Oct.	20.	Established as a district by the name of Westminster formerly "...called the proprietors of Narragansett township, Number Two...." (Prov. Laws, Vol. IV, p. 265.)
1770.	Apr.	26.	Incorporated as a town, formerly the district of Westminster. (Prov. Laws, Vol. V, p. 50.)
1783.	Feb.	26.	Certain land formerly assessed by Westminster, annexed to Fitchburg.
1785.	June	27.	Part included in the new town of Gardner.
1796.	Feb.	27.	Part of Fitchburg annexed.
1813.	Feb.	16.	Part of Fitchburg annexed.
1824.	Jan.	28.	Part annexed to Ashburnham.
1838.	Apr.	10.	Part of the unincorporated lands called "No Town" annexed.
1870.	Apr.	22.	Part annexed to Princeton.
1908.	Apr.	17.	Bounds between Westminster and Gardner established.

Archaic Names of the Municipality:
Narragansett Township Number Two, No Town.

Section/Village Names:
Academy Hill, Baker's Grove, Ball Hill, Bean Porridge Hill, Beach Hill, Bragg Hill, Church Rock, Crow Hills, Dean Hill, Flag Meadow Pond, Fowler Hill, Greenwood Pond, Holme's Park, Lakewood Park, Leino Park, Many Ranta, Marshall's Corner, Meeting House Pond, Minot District, Mishap Hill, Mud Pond, Narrows, North Westminster, North Common, Notown, Powder House, Prospect Hill, Raymond's Corner, Round Meadow, Scrabble Hollow, Smith Village, South Westminster, State Reservation, Steam Valley, Wachusett Lake, Wachusett Park, Wachusett Village, Westminster Depot, Whitmanville.

Weston, Middlesex County.
Established as a town by St 1712-1713, c 135.

1713.	Jan.	1.*	Established as a town, from part of Watertown commonly called "the Farms". (Prov. Laws, Vol. XXI, p. 812.)
1754.	Apr.	19.	Part included in the new town of Lincoln.
1766.	June	25.	Bounds between Weston and Waltham established.
1951.	Apr.	2.	Bounds between Weston and Natick established.

Archaic Names of the Municipality:
Nonesuch, The Farms, Watertown Farmers Precinct, Watertown West Precinct.

Section/Village Names:
Cherry Brook, Hastings, Kendal Green, Riverside, Silver Hill, Stony Brook.

Westport, Bristol County.
Incorporated as a town by St 1787, c 9.

1787.	July	2.	Incorporated as a town, from part of Dartmouth.
1793.	Feb.	25.	Part of Dartmouth annexed.
1795.	Feb.	28.	Part of Dartmouth annexed.
1805.	Mar.	4.	Part of Dartmouth annexed.
1828.	Feb.	20.	Bounds between Westport and Dartmouth established.

| 1861. | Apr. | 10. | Certain lands lying east and south of described line to become part of Westport after the entry of a decree of the U. S. Supreme Court concering the Rhode Island boundary. |
| 1894. | June | 14. | Bounds between Westport and Fall River located and defined. |

Archaic Names of the Municipality:
Acoakset, Coaksett.

Section/Village Names:
Acoaxet, Akins Corner, Berryman's Four Corners, Beulah, Brownell's Corner, Cadman's Corner, Central Village, Davis Corner, Gifford's Corner, Greenwood Park, Head of Westport, Hemlock, Horse Neck Beach, Indian Town, Kirby's Corner, Lawton's Corner, North Westport, Quansett, Railroad Park, Sanford's Bound, South Westport, State Side, Wardell's Corner, Westport Factory Station, Westport Factory Village, Westport Harbor, Westport Point.

Westwood, Norfolk County.
Incorporated as a town by St 1897, c 226.

| 1897. | Apr. | 2. | Incorporated as a town, from part of Dedham. |
| 1970. | Mar. | 2. | Town charter adopted. |

Archaic Names of the Municipality:
Clapboard Trees, West Parish of Dedham.

Section/Village Names:
Ellis (extinct), Green Lodge (extinct), Islington.

Weymouth, Norfolk County.

1630.	Sept.	28.*	**Wessaguscus** mentioned in the tax act. (Mass. Bay Rec., Vol. I, p. 77.)
1635.	Mar.	4.*	Bounds between Wessaguscus and Mount Wooliston to be determined.
1635.	July	8.*	Bounds between Wessaguscus and Barecove to be established.
1635.	Sept.	2.*	"The name of Wessaguscus is also changed, & hereafter to be called **Waymothe.**" (Mass. Bay Rec., Vol. I, p. 156.)
1635.	Sept.	3.*	Bounds between Weymouth and Hingham established.
1637.	Mar.	9.*	"Round Island" and "Grape Island" granted to Weymouth.
1847.	Mar.	31.	Bounds between Weymouth and Abington established.

Archaic Names of the Municipality:
Waymothe, Wessaguscus, Wessagusson.

Section/Village Names:
Bay View, East Weymouth, Fort Point, Grape Island, Great Hill, Lovell's Corner, Lovell's Grove, Nash, North Weymouth, Old Spain, Pond Plain, Porter, Rose Cliff, Round Island (extinct), South Weymouth, Thomas Corner, Wessagusset, Weymouth Center, Weymouth Heights, Weymouth Landing.

Whately, Franklin County.
Established as a town by St 1770-1771, c 22.

1771.	Apr.	24.	Established as a town, from part of Hatfield. (Prov. Laws, Vol. V, p. 122.)
1810.	Mar.	5.	Part of Deerfield annexed.
1811.	June	21.	Bounds between Whately and Conway established.
1849.	Feb.	2.	Bounds between Whately and Williamsburg established.

Section/Village Names:
Claverack, East Whately, West Whately.

Whitman, Plymouth County.
South Abington incorporated as a town by St 1875, c 36.

1875.	Mar.	4.	**South Abington** incorporated as a town, from parts of Abington and East Bridgewater.
1875.	Apr.	24.	Part of South Abington annexed to Brockton and part of Brockton annexed to South Abington.
1886.	Mar.	5.	The town of South Abington may take the name of Standish, Brainard, Whitman or Grandon.
1886.	May	3.	Name of South Abington changed to **Whitman**.

Archaic Names of the Municipality:
Little Comfort, South Abington.

Section/Village Names:
Auburnville, East Whitman, Northville, South Abington, West Crook, Whitman Line Park.

Wilbraham, Hampden County.
Established as a town by St 1763-1764, c 9.

1763.	June	15.	Established as a town, from part of Springfield. (Prov. Laws, Vol. IV, p. 644.)
1799.	June	11.	Part of Springfield called "The Elbows" annexed.
1878.	Mar.	28.	Part established as Hampden.

Archaic Names of the Municipality:
Elbows, Springfield Fourth Precinct, Outward Commons, Springfield Mountains.

Section/Village Names:
Butlerville, East Wilbraham (previously called Ellis Mills), Glendale, North Wilbraham, Stony Hill.

Williamsburg, Hampshire County.
Made a town by St 1775-1776, c 3.

1771.	Apr.	24.	Incorporated as a district by the name of ""Williamsburgh" from part of Hatfield and certain adjoining lands. (Prov. Laws, Vol. V, p. 125.)
1775.	Aug.	23.	Made a town, by general act under which districts became towns.
1795.	June	24.	Bounds between Williamsburg and Chesterfield and Goshen established.
1797.	Feb.	7.	Bounds between Williamsburg and Chesterfield and Goshen established.
1810.	Feb.	16.	Bounds between Williamsburg and Chesterfield and Goshen established.
1845.	Mar.	14.	Bounds between Williamsburg and Hatfield established and part of each town annexed to the other town.
1846.	Mar.	19.	Bounds between Williamsburg and Hatfield established and part of each town annexed to the other town.
1849.	Feb.	2.	Bounds between Williamsburg and Whately established.

Section/Village Names:
Haydenville, Searsville, Skinnerville, Village Hill.

Williamstown, Berkshire County.
Established as a town by St 1765-1766, c 7.

| 1765. | June | 21. | Established as a town, formerly the plantation called "West Hoosuck". (Prov. Laws, Vol. IV, p. 809.) |
| 1838. | Apr. | 9. | Certain unincorporated lands annexed. |

1900. Apr. 25. Bounds between Williamstown and North Adams established and part annexed to North Adams.

Archaic Names of the Municipality:
West Hoosuck Plantation.

Section/Village Names:
Beechdale, Buxton, Cards Corner, Charityville, Colesville, Goodell Hollow, Hemlock Brook, Northwest Hill, Riverside, Sandsprings, Sherwood, South Williamstown, Sweet's Corner, The Hopper, White Oaks, Williamstown Station.

Wilmington, Middlesex County.
Established as town by St 1730, c 2.

1730.	Sept.	25.*	Established as a town, from parts of Reading and Woburn. (Prov. Laws, Vol. II, p. 556.)
1733.	June	13.*	Part of Billerica annexed.
1737.	Dec.	23.*	Bounds between Wilmington and Billerica established.
1970.	Aug.	14.	Bounds between Wilmington and Burlington changed and established.

Archaic Names of the Municipality:
Land of Nod.

Section/Village Names:
Aldrich, Brown's Crossing, East Wilmington, North Wilmington, Silver Lake, Wilmington Center, Wilmington Junction.

Winchendon, Worcester County.
Established as a town by St 1764-1765, c 5.

1764.	June	14.	Established as a town, formerly the plantation called "Ipswich-Canada". (Prov. Laws, Vol. IV, p. 721.)
1780.	June	17.	Part of Royalston and all the lands to the New Hampshire state line, annexed.
1785.	June	27.	Part included in the new town of Gardner.
1787.	Mar.	2.	Part of Gardner annexed.
1794.	Feb.	22.	Part annexed to Gardner.
1851.	May	24.	Part annexed to Gardner.
1908.	Apr.	17.	Bounds between Winchendon and Gardner established.
1981.	May	4.	Town charter adopted.

Archaic Names of the Municipality:
Ipswich-Canada Plantation.

Section/Village Names:
Bullardville, Centreville, Glenallan, Happy Hollow, Harrisville, Hydeville, New Boston, Red School, Spring Village, Waterville, Winchendon Center, Winchendon Springs.

Winchester, Middlesex County.
Incorporated as a town by 1850, c 255.

1850.	Apr.	30.	Incorporated as a town, from parts of Medford, West Cambridge and Woburn.
1875.	May	12.	Part annexed to Woburn.
1954.	Feb.	16.	Bounds between Winchester and Lexington established.
1956.	Aug.	10.	Bounds between Winchester and Medford established and part of Medford annexed.
1964.	Mar.	24.	Bounds between Winchester and Lexington established.
1975.	Mar.	5.	Town charter adopted.

Archaic Names of the Municipality:
Black Horse Village, South Woburn, Woburn Gates.

Section/Village Names:
Cutter Village, Mystic, Symme's Corner, Wedgemere, Winchester Highlands.

Windsor, Berkshire County.
Gageborough established as a town by St 1771-1772, c 6.

1771.	July	4.	**Gageborough** established as a town, formerly the new plantation called Number Four. (Prov. Laws, Vol. V, p. 162.)
1778.	Oct.	16.	"Part of a tract of land called Plantation Number Five annexed to the Town of Gageborough now to be known as **Windsor."**
1793.	Mar.	14.	Part included in the new town of Cheshire.
1794.	Feb.	26.	Part of Cheshire re-annexed.
1795.	Feb.	28.	Part annexed to Dalton.
1796.	Feb.	23.	Part annexed to Dalton.

Archaic Names of the Municipality:
Gageborough, Plantation Number Four (1762 Townships).

Section/Village Names:
East Windsor, Windsor Bush, Windsor Hill.

Winthrop, Suffolk County.
Incorporated as a town by St 1852, c 53.

1852.	Mar.	27.	Incorporated as a town, from part of North Chelsea.

Archaic Names of the Municipality:
Pullen Point.

Section/Village Names:
Battery, Belle Isle (former R.R. station), Cottage Hill, Cottage Park, Great Head, Ingalls, Ocean Spray, Playstead, Point Shirley, Thornton, Winthrop Beach, Winthrop Center, Winthrop Highlands.

WOBURN, Middlesex County.
Incorporated as a city by St 1888, c 374.

1642.	Sept.	27.*	"Charlestowne village is called Wooborne." (Mass. Bay Rec., Vol. II, p. 28.)
1644.	May	29.*	Bounds between Woburn and Reading established.
1664.	Oct.	19.*	Two thousand acres of land granted to Woburn.
1666	Oct.	10.*	Bounds between Woburn and Billerica established.
1669.	Oct.	12.*	Bounds between Woburn and Billerica established.
1728.	Aug.	1.*	Land belonging to Woburn annexed to Lunenburg.
1730.	Sept.	25.*	Part included in the new town of Wilmington.
1741.	July	28.*	Bounds between Woburn and Billerica established.
1799.	Feb.	28.	Part established as Burlington.
1850.	Apr.	30.	Part included in the new town of Winchester.
1873.	May	12.	Part of Winchester annexed.
1888.	May	18.	Incorporated as a city.
1888.	May	29.	Act of May 18, 1888, accepted by the town.
1895.	Apr.	20.	Part of Woburn annexed to Stoneham.
1934.	Apr.	27.	Bounds between Woburn and Reading established.

Archaic Names of the Municipality:
Charlestowne Village, Waterfield, Woburn Gates.

Section/Village Names:
Allenville Green, Button End, Central Square, Cummingsville, Durensville, East Woburn (previously called Fulton Village), Hammond Square, Horn Pond (former R.R. station), Hungry Plain (extinct), Kelltown, Mishawum, Montvale, New Boston, North Woburn (previously called New Bridge Village), Oakland (no longer used), Richardson Row, Shaker Glen, South End, South Wilmington Station (former R.R. station), The Newlands, Thompsonville, Walnut Hill, West Side, Woburn Four Corners, Woburn Highlands.

WORCESTER, Worcester County.
Incorporated as a city by St 1848, c 32.

1684.	Oct.	15.*	Established as a town, formerly the plantation called "Quansigamond". (Mass. Bay Rec., Vol. V, p. 460.)
1741.	Jan.	9.*	Part called "North Worcester" established as Holden.
1743.	Apr.	5.*	Certain lands annexed.
1758.	June	2.	Part of Leicester annexed.
1778.	Apr.	10.	The parish lately set off from Worcester and other towns established as Ward.
1785.	June	14.	Certain lands annexed.
1838.	Mar.	22.	"Grafton Gore" annexed.
1848.	Feb.	29.	Incorporated as a city.
1848.	Mar.	18.	Act of Feb. 29, 1848, accepted by the town.
1907.	Feb.	11.	Bounds between Worcester and Grafton established.
1985.	Nov.	5.	City charter adopted.

Archaic Names of the Municipality:
Grafton Gore, Lydbury, Quansigamond, Quansigamug, Quinsigamond.

Section/Village Names:
Barber's, Barnardville, Beacon, Brightly, Beaver Brook, Bell Hill, Belmont Hill, Blithewood, Bloomingdale, Bradley (former R.R. station), City Line, College Hill, Columbus Park, Crown Hill, East Worcester, Fairmount, Goldthwaite Park, Grafton Hill, Green Island, Greendale, Green Hill, Highland, Hillcroft, Hopeville, Indian Hill, Island, Jamesville, Lakemont, Lakeside, Lakeview, Lakewood, Leesville, Lincoln Park, Main South, Meadows, Mount Saint James, Neighborly, New Worcester, Newton, Northville, North Worcester, Oak Hill, Piedmont, Quinsigamond, Saint Ann's Hill, Sandy Bar, South Worcester, Summit, Tallawanda, Tatnuck, Trowbridgeville, Tyson's Corner, Union Hill, Valley Falls, Vernon Hill, West Tatnuck, Westwood Hills, West Worcester.

Worthington, Hampshire County.
Established as a town by St 1768, c 16.

1768.	June	30.	Established as a town, from the new plantation called "Number Three". (Prov. Laws, Vol. IV, p. 1028.)
1783.	Mar.	12.	Part included in the new town of Middlefield.
1799.	June	21.	Part of Chester annexed.

Archaic Names of the Municipality:
Plantation Number Three (Western Townships of 1762).

Section/Village Names:
Clark Hill, Four Corners, Ringville, Riverside, Samponville, South Worthington, Stevensville, Sunnyside, West Worthington, Worthington Center, Worthington Corners.

Wrentham, Norfolk County.

1673.	Oct.	15.*	Established as a town, upon petition of the inhabitants of "Wollonopaug", as by agreement with Dedham. (Mass. Bay Rec., Vol. IV, Part 2, p. 569.)
1719.	Nov.	27.*	Part included in the new town of Bellingham.
1735.	Apr.	11.*	Bounds between Wrentham and Bellingham established.
1749.	Nov.	28.*	Part annexed to Medway.
1753.	Dec.	28.	Part of Stoughton annexed.
1778.	Mar.	2.	Part established as Franklin.
1778.	June	10.	Part included in the new town of Foxborough.
1819.	Feb.	3.	Bounds between Wrentham and Foxborough established.
1830.	Feb.	18.	Bounds between Wrentham and Attleborough established and part of Attleborough annexed.

1831.	Feb.	7.	Part annexed to Foxborough.
1870.	Feb.	23.	Part included in the new town of Norfolk.
1871.	Apr.	19.	Bounds between Wrentham and Norfolk established.
1905.	Apr.	4.	Part established as Plainville.

Archaic Names of the Municipality:
Wollomonopaug, Wollonopaug.

Section/Village Names:
Sheldonville, Wampum, West Wrentham.

Yarmouth, Barnstable County.

1639.	Jan.	7.*	"The names of those to whom graunt of the lands at Mattacheeset, now called Yarmouth...." (Ply. Col. Rec., Vol. I, p. 108.)
1641.	June	17.*	Bounds between Yarmouth and Barnstable established.
1658.	Mar.	11.*	Yarmouth and Barnstable agreed upon bounds.
1793.	June	19.	Part established as Dennis.

Archaic Names of the Municipality:
Hokkanom, Mattacheeset, Nobscussett.

Section/Village Names:
Bass River, Camp Station, Hockanum, Middleton, Point Gammon, Pond Village, South Yarmouth, Town House, Weir Village, West Yarmouth, Yarmouth Farms, Yarmouthport, Yarmouth Village.

Index

A

A "Praying Indian" (Christian) town
  20, 52, 61, 67, 80, 89, 115, 117
A "Praying Indian" (Christian) town
  Egogankamesit 72
Abbott Village 13
Abel's Hill 34
Aberdeen 23
Abington 11
Abottville 85
Academy Hill 23, 126
Acapesket 47
Accomack 93
Accord 87
Acoakset 127
Acoaxet 127
Acre 35
Acton 11
Acton Center 11
Acushena 38, 81
Acushnet 11, 81
Acushnet Station 81
Adams 11
Adam's Corners 86
Adams Shore 95
Adamsdale 84
Adamsville 35, 78
Agaganquamasset 72
Agamenticus Heights 51
Agassiz 29
Agawain 109
Agawam 12, 38, 109, 120
Agawam Plantation 93, 120
Aggawam 63
Akins Corner 127
Alandar 79
Albee Corners 31
Albeeville 76
Alcocks Farm 72
Aldenville 34
Aldrich 129
Aldrich District 117
Aldrich Lake 52
Aldrichville 78, 113
Alford 12
Alford Center 12
Algerie 89
Allendale 93
Allen's Corner 12, 119
Allenville Green 130
Allerton 62
Allotment Number Thirteen 97

Allston 23
Allston Heights 23
Almont 115
Alpine Place 49
Amesbury 12
Amesbury Ferry 12
Amherst 13
Amherst City 13
Amherst East Parish 13
Amherst Fields 13
Amherst North Parish 13
Amherst Woods 13
Ammidown 108
Amostown 124
Anawan 97
Andover 13
Andover North Parish 13
Andover South Parish 13
Andover Village 13
Andover West Parish 13
Andrew Square 23
Andrewstown 33
Angier's Corner 83
Annasnappet 29
Annisquam 51
Annisquam Willows 51
Antassawomock 74
Antassawomock Neck 74
Apaum 93
Apple Valley 14
Appletons 63
Apponegansett 38
Aquashenet 73
Argilla 63
Aries Little 124
Arlington 13
Arlington District 65, 76
Arlington Heights 14
Armory 109
Armory Hill 109
Armory Village 78
Arnoldsville Renfrew 11
Arrowhead 93
Arsenal 121
Artichoke 83
Asabet 112
Asbury Grove 55
Ashburnham 14
Ashby 14
Ashby Center 14
Ashdod 43
Ashfield 14
Ashfield Plain 14
Ashland 15

E

142

HISTORICAL DATA RELATING TO COUNTIES,

G

N

Y

Z

BARNSTABLE COUNTY

BERKSHIRE COUNTY

BRISTOL COUNTY

DUKES COUNTY

ESSEX COUNTY

FRANKLIN COUNTY

HAMPDEN COUNTY

HAMPSHIRE COUNTY

174

MIDDLESEX COUNTY

NANTUCKET COUNTY

NORFOLK COUNTY

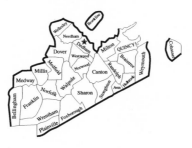

PLYMOUTH COUNTY

SUFFOLK COUNTY

WORCESTER COUNTY